MONKEES ARCHIVES 1

MONKEES
ARCHIVES VOL 2

White Lightning Publishing
Copyright ©2016 White Lightning Publishing

This volume reprints artifacts related to the Monkees. Through research, we believe that all pieces to be in the public domain. If you hold valid and current copyrights aresented, please contact us at WhiteLightningPublishing@gmail.com with proof so that we can remove materials on future printings.

MONKEES ARCHIVES 1

WHEN MICKY WAS IN THE MISSING LINKS

By Ron Fury

Ron Fury has known Micky Dolenz for over two years— ever since they first met when Ron was managing a teen club in Denver, Colorado. Following his work there, Ron and his family moved to Hollywood where he became Production Coordinator for Dick Clark's "Where The Action Is." Most recently Ron has been working in an executive position with KHJ television in Los Angeles.

I met Micky in 1964 when he played at a club I was managing in Denver. I'd just gotten out of the Air Force when I met the man who owned this club. He asked me if I wanted to manage it and I accepted, even though there wasn't a lot of money on it; I hadn't been used to a lot of money in the service, anyway. While I was there this man went to California to audition some groups. When he came back he said that Micky Dolenz and Eddie Hodges were coming up for a couple of weekends.

Micky and Eddie and the rest of the group drove up in three beat-up Volkswagens and they hardly had enough money to put gas in them. None of them stayed in a hotel. Some of them stayed at another club that this man owned and Eddie and Micky stayed at the house.

The club was called the Sugar Shack and the kids really liked the Missing Links. Eddie was kind of the star of the show because he was better known at that time, but all the guys were so good that we booked them for another week— even though Eddie had to leave. They finally played for a month and a half because the kids liked them so much.

The Act

All the guys worked hard trying to be professional. They played a lot of Beatle-type songs and then they played oldies. Micky was always shined up really good on stage — sport jacket, the whole thing. He was trying to get rid of the Circus Boy image because that's what the kids remembered him as. When the kids mentioned it, he sort of shied away, but he tried to be real nice, too. He was trying to become a good performer in every way. They worked until one in the morning, then they would party and after that they would sleep until two or three in the afternoon.

Their Days

There wasn't a whole lot to do around Denver during the day, and, of course, they worked nights. We did drive up to the mountains several times and we saw Buffalo Bill's grave on Lookout Mountain. Since there wasn't much going on during the days, the guys went out at night after the show and stayed out pretty late, then they used the days for sleeping, mostly.

(Continued on page 6)

MONKEES ARCHIVES 1

THIS SHOT OF MICKY was taken in the driveway of Screen Gems Studio where the Monkees' show is filmed. In front of Micky is a piece of his abstract sculpture that he created. Notice the gate guard up behind Micky where the stop sign is. No one can get by this guard to get on to the set, but there are always plenty of girls who try. Micky often surprises the fans by going up to the gate and signing autographs on his lunch hour or breaks. He has boundless energy.

MONKEES ARCHIVES 1

One thing that we did do during the day was talk. Micky was excited about being a good performer and he spent most of his time trying to improve different parts of his performance. He wanted his own group and a couple of times he mentioned that he wanted to be a serious actor, too. He proved to me that he could be a good serious actor, if he wanted to. The first day that I saw him I knew that his talent was just bubbling over, much more than with the other guys. I guess it was just that Micky was brought up to be a professional in everything that he did, and he stood out like a light. He wasn't messing-off, like being late to performances and such, like a lot of guys in show business do. He wanted to entertain, and he was very serious about it.

How He Looked

Like I said, Micky always looked good on stage. Lots of times he changed clothes twice during a performance so he always looked good. His hair was the same color as it is now, but it wasn't as long. He weighed about the same. During the day he wore sweat shirts and levis and cord pants, but during the shows it was always a sport jacket and a nice shirt. He always took care of himself. He wanted to get a new image — to become something more than ex-Circus Boy — but he wasn't quite sure what the next step was. He was kind of between images.

Micky Now

I always believed that Micky would make it big—he just had it in him. He still works just as hard trying to stay on top as he did trying to get on top. He wants to be very good in acting and singing and everything.

The best thing is that Micky really hasn't changed a bit as far as his personality is concerned. He's still very considerate of other people and he really loves his fans. Lots of times when people make it big they forget where they started and they won't open a door for you or say thank you or anything. I'll tell you about something that happened just the other day. We were eating in Norm's—that's a small restaurant right next to the recording studios — and I happened to look back and Micky was holding the door for some stranger walking out. He does things like this all the time, and most of them you never hear about. That's just the way he is.

Of course, when you're as popular as he is there are some things you can't do, much as you'd like to. For one thing, Micky would really like to know more of his fans, and whenever there are lots of them around the entrance of the studios he always wants to talk to them. But most of the time he can't because he's got so much to do and there are so many of them. Whenever he gets the chance, though, there he is, meeting and talking with them. And, if he can do anything for them, he will. There aren't many like Micky.

I know Micky will be around for a long time. He hasn't let anything go to his head and he still wants to be good just as badly as he did in Denver. Micky has got what it takes to stay on top as long as he likes.

MONKEES ARCHIVES 1

MONKEES ARCHIVES 1

MARILYN . MARILYN . MARILYN . MARILYN . MARILYN . MARILYN . MARILYN . MARILYN .
MARILYN . MARILYN . MARILYN . MARILYN . MARILYN . MARILYN . MARILYN . MARILYN .
MARILYN . MARILYN . MARILYN . MARILYN . MARILYN . MARILYN . MARILYN . MARILYN .
MARILYN . MARILYN . MARILYN . MARILYN . MARILYN . MARILYN . MARILYN . MARILYN .
MARILYN . MARILYN . MARILYN . MARILYN . MARILYN . MARILYN . MARILYN . MARILYN .
MARILYN . MARILYN . MARILYN . MARILYN . MARILYN . MARILYN . MARILYN . MARILYN .
MARILYN . MARILYN . MARILYN . MARILYN . MARILYN . MARILYN . MARILYN . MARILYN .
MARILYN . MARILYN . MARILYN . MARILYN . MARILYN . MARILYN . MARILYN . MARILYN .
MARILYN . MARILYN . MARILYN . MARILYN . MARILYN . MARILYN . MARILYN . MARILYN .

MARILYN SCHLOSSBERG The GIRL BEHIND THE MONKEES

When David Jones has finally decided on the coffee table he wants for his new house, but hardly has the time to order it, he asks Marilyn and it's done in a jiffy. If Peter has to film all day but his Swedish sports car needs repair, he asks Marilyn if she won't make the necessary calls, and it's done.

Mike's favorite Aunt from Texas is trying to call Mike on the set and can't get through, she calls Marilyn and before long Mike and his Auntie are chatting away. Out at the front gate, the guard isn't sure if the young lady who says she's Micky's sister really is Coco Dolenz. Marilyn has a look, makes the okay, and Coco can now visit Micky.

Who's this wonder girl who does more than can be imagined for our four heroes? She's Marilyn Schlossberg, formally titled as Production Assistant for the Monkees Show, but actually her job's more of a girl-Friday—Saturday—Sunday, etc. for Davy, Peter, Micky or Mike.

To find out more about Marilyn's exciting life, we asked her to tell us a little about herself:

What experience did you have before you began working for the Monkees?

I went to Boston University and when I finished there, I went to New York to get a job. I had no previous knowledge of show business and had no desire to get into the entertainment field. I was actually interested in the publishing field. I had lunch with a friend of mine who offered me a job at Channel 13 in New York, which I took. There I worked on the "Play of the Week."

What exactly is the role of a production assistant?

Somewhat of a coordinator of all the work. You work with the cast, the director, everyone. After my job at Channel 13, I worked for a film company; then I worked for NBC and the production assistant on "Car 54, Where Are You?" Later I did some casting. I worked on the "Pawnbroker" movie and also on the World's Fair.

How did you get the job with the Monkees?

I heard about the job opening and I went in to see and they hired me. I joined the staff two months before they began to film the show.

Did you have a part in organizing the Monkee Fan Club?

I helped organize it with the various national fan club presidents. We set up several hundred chapters around the country. On the summer tour we meet with the chapters in the various cities. Some of the fans come in and see the Monkees and we send some to the concerts as guests of the Monkees.

(Continued on page 60)

MONKEES ARCHIVES 1

Marilyn Schlossberg (Continued)

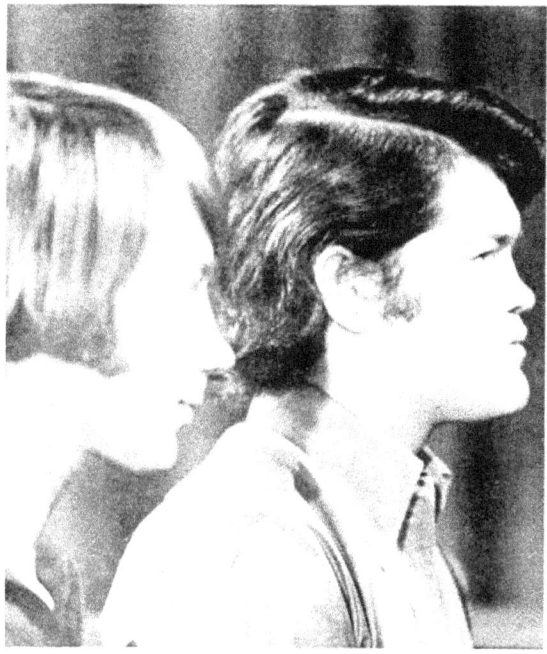

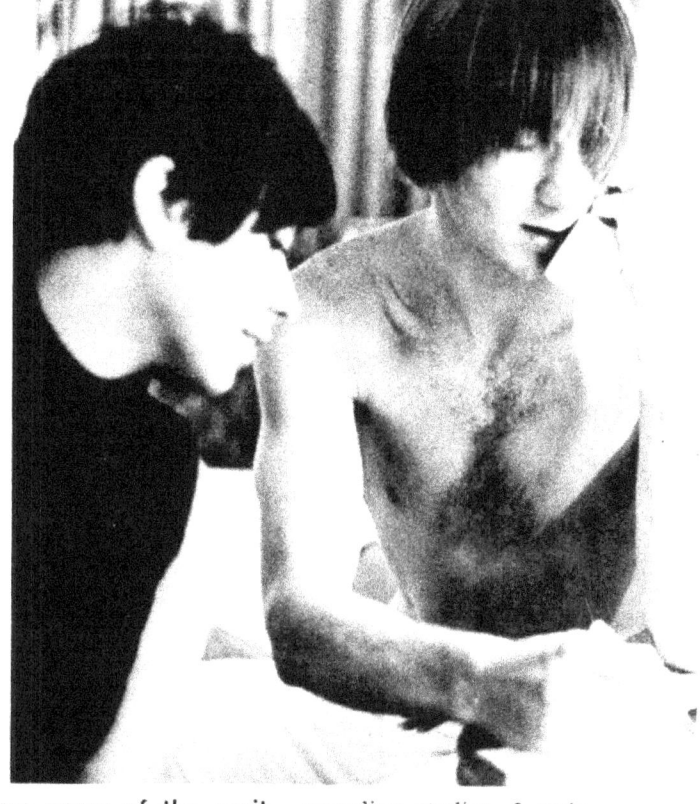

MARILYN (right) helps Peter with some of his personal business affairs.

How are they chosen?

We send a letter to each chapter before the tour starts, inviting them to select a given number of their members to meet the boys and then another group to receive tickets. We write to the fan club presidents in all the cities that we visit.

Did you ever dream the Monkees would be as big as they are?

It was hard to imagine anything being that big. I knew it was unique. I also knew Bob Rafaelson from Boston and New York and I knew he was very creative. But it's very, very hard to imagine anything as big as the Monkees.

How is the Monkee Club different from other fan clubs?

First of all, they meet their fans as they go from city to city. This, itself is very unusual. Also, the Monkees had a great deal to say in how it was set up. Even now when they're really busy, they still take time to keep a close contact with the fan club activities.

What are some of the exciting things that have happened to you because of your job?

I'm involved in so many different areas that the boys are involved in, it's hard to say. I work on the TV show, their recordings, concerts, fan clubs. I spend a great deal of time with them other than business hours.

What are some of the other things you do for them?

If the Monkees need something or want something done on the TV show, they come to me. And I, in turn, would get it set up for them or make requests to have things done.

I take care of their cars (in addition to borrowing them). If they have any problems with them I call the dealers and have the cars repaired—things like putting in tape recorders. I also keep in touch with their families to see if they need anything or if they try to reach the boys.

What part do you have in their recording?

I help set up the schedules and I work very closely with their recording studios. I make sure they keep on schedule, which often means waking them up in the morning by phone.

What was your job on their summer tour?

I was the publicist for the tour. I oversee the New York press conference which was set up in advance through Screen Gems New York offices.

Have there been any problems on tour?

No, the press conference went smoothly. The one in London was excellent. It went very well; and it was the largest press conference that England has ever had.

Occasionally I run into the problem of not being admitted to the hotel. I seem to look several years younger than I am, and have been mistaken as a fan. I carry identification with me at all times.

It's happened at concerts too, but usually the boys rescue me. But it's all worth it, because it's always new and exciting. It's a job that's impossible to describe.

MONKEES ARCHIVES 1

GENIE's ADVENTURES IN GROOVYLAND

(Genie the Tailor got her first break when she designed the new Raider costumes, and now she designs for all the top stars.)

MY VISIT TO A MONKEES' CONCERT

I looked at the clock and realized how late I was! Time for the Monkee concert at the Hollywood Bowl, and here I was dreaming again. Always dreaming. I must get back to reality, I thought, as I tried to find something to wear. The dogs were sleeping on the costumes, and the white cat was rolled up in the suspenders. Fine thing, I thought, white hairs on black suspenders. What will the Sundowners say? I had just finished making the Sundowners' costumes for the Bowl show.

I ran downstairs into the garage, and thought, Morris, don't fail me now. I'm late, and I must get to the concert! Morris made a special effort and when we got into the very heavy traffic with millions of people all trying to get into the Bowl, I pushed my special airborne button, and Morris sailed over all the cars right to the stage. I was very embarrassed, landing right on the stage like that. Good thing nobody's in the theatre, yet, I thought. Heh, heh, heh. Very funny.

Just then a voice called out over the loudspeaker, "Genie the Tailor, what do you mean by landing your helicopter right in the middle of the stage? We're trying to set up the instruments!" I was so embarrassed, and Morris turned pink instead of green, because he was embarrassed too. "He's not a helicopter," I said, "he's a car!" and I parked him on the side of the stage near the water. Hah, I thought, I've got the best parking place in the whole theatre.

The Sundowners' costumes were made of satin and they kept swooshing and sliding all the way down to the dressing room. I just couldn't keep a grip on them. That's the last I'll make of satin, I thought, unless I put them on a leash.

I was walking the costumes downstairs, and trying not to trip on the long sleeves, when who crossed my path but a very friendly gentleman with eyeglasses. "Ho, ho, Genie the Tailor, how are you?" It was Bob Rafaelson, one of the Monkee producers. "I'm just fine, thank you," I said, "but I'm trying to keep a grip on this satin." "Just keep a grip on yourself and you'll be all right," he said. "Here's a ticket to the concert, by the way." Ooooh, I just couldn't believe it. How lucky can a girl be? Now I could sit outside and watch the concert like a regular calm normal person at a concert.

But first, I had to dress my boys. They looked so cute in their suspenders. They looked even cuter in the rest of the costume. I went upstairs and Micky rushed out of his dressing room, all dressed up in cranberry velveteen. "What do you think of our new costumes, Genie the Tailor?" said Micky. "Oh, they're beautiful," I said, and thought to myself, "Oh, I wish I had made them!" Mike Nesmith came out of the dressing room and played his guitar and sang to himself. "Gee", I thought, "I wish I could sing like that." Of course, that would really be strange, wouldn't it, if I sang like Mike Nesmith? Oh well.

Realizing I had an actual ticket in my hot little hand, I ran out to the front of the theatre to watch the concert. I never saw so many people in one place in my life! I was filled with horror as I imagined what it would be like if I had to make all their clothes for that night! Work, work, work. My, my.

Just then the concert began. The boys were so beautiful I couldn't believe it. And then Micky sang "Randy Scouse Git", which he wrote, and played the kettle drums, and then he smiled. All the lights went out but you could see everything because his smile was so bright it lit the whole theatre and all the countryside around. I never saw such a smile in my life.

Peter sang "Auntie Grizelda" and looked like a little clown and Davy sang "I want to be Free" and Mike sang "Sunny Girlfriend" and they played up a storm and everybody was so happy because they were so beautiful! And then Micky jumped into the water that separates the audience from the stage! I ran backstage in time to get him a towel, but too late, he was dripping wet and ran into his dressing room to change. They all came out on stage to do their final number, and as they came off, my mind was reeling I was so excited, I practically jumped up and down!

I was packing all the Sundowners' costumes in my bag to have them cleaned, and counting suspenders, when I felt a gentle hand on my shoulder. I turned around, to find a golden god standing next to me. "Why, Peter Tork", I said. "Genie the Tailor", said Peter, "I've seen the costumes you made for the Sundowners for tonight's concert, and I just want to say, could you make me a pair of pants?"

* * *

I just couldn't believe it was real. My dream had come true. Am I dreaming or not?

THE SUNDOWNERS' costumes were made of satin. They were very thrilled to be able to tour with the Monkees and they really put on a great show. The Monkees have been very good about giving talented groups lots of exposure.

MONKEES ARCHIVES 1

GIRLS in the GROOVE with the MONKEES

Everyone's always starting stories about how the Monkees love this girl or that girl, and usually these rumors are totally false. There are a few girls that the Monkees really dig. They aren't necessarily girls that the Monkees date, but they do have a special place in the hearts of each Monkee. So, meet the group.

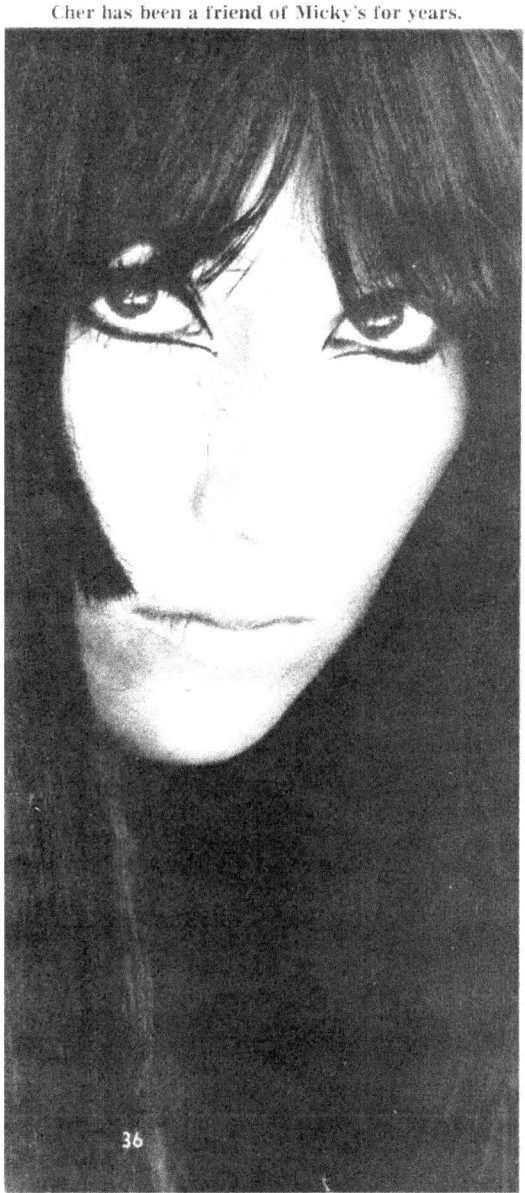

Cher has been a friend of Micky's for years.

LYNN RANDELL knocked the boys out on their tour this year.

SAMANTHA is admired by all the boys... especially Micky.

MONKEES ARCHIVES 1

PHYLLIS is Mike's lovely wife. The others are looking for wives to equal her.

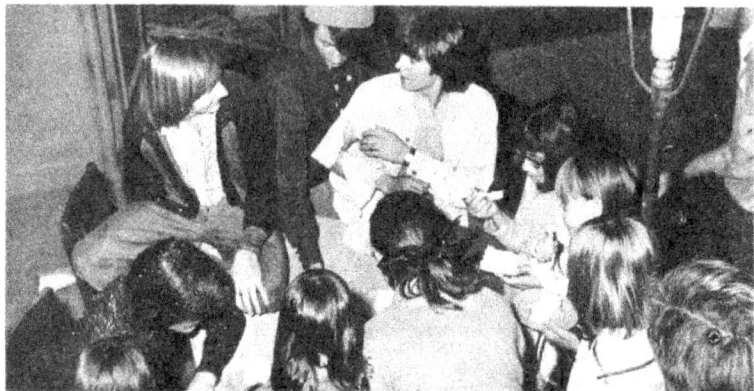

COCO is almost like a Monkee mascot. When she's not around the Monkees miss her.

ANN MOSES is a close friend who writes about the Monkees.

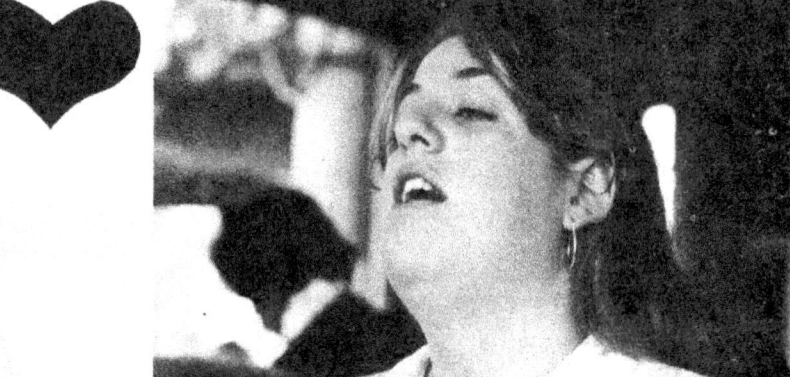

MAMA CASS sings a song the way the Monkees like it sung.

GENIE THE TAILOR makes groovy clothes for Peter.

MONKEES ARCHIVES 1

A MIDSUMMER'S NIGHT WITH THE MONKEES

MIKE MICKY & PETER

U.S. TOUR 2013

MONKEES ARCHIVES 1

The moral behind the

By ROBERT FULFORD
Star staff writer

How did the Monkees get that way? The Star's Robert Fulford analyzes a sociological phenomenon made up of Davy, Mickey, Peter and Mike (above).

Mike Nesmith, the Monkee who wears the wool hat, has said that he's honored rather than insulted when anyone says that the Monkees copy the Marx Brothers. But how honored can you be?

By now it's obvious that the Monkees —the big teenage smash on TV and records this season—have copied not only the Marx Brothers but everybody else whose material suited the producers' convenience. Robert Rafelson and Bertcn Schneider, the Monkees' creators, have ransacked modern pop culture with all the joy of thieves let loose in a jewelry museum.

The Monkees' success—their concert tomorrow night at Maple Leaf Gardens was sold out weeks ago (to the tune of $82,000)—is based on the artistic equivalent of grand larceny.

There lives among us today the notion that contemporary young people are somehow more clever than their parents were, that they tend to see through the tricks of the adult world. This idea takes a bad beating from the success of the Monkees. Their story, if it proves anything, proves that youngsters can be sold a bogus product as easily as they can be sold the real thing.

The Monkees' TV show is a hit on both North American and British networks and their most popular record— the attractively vigorous I'm a Believer—has made its way to the top of the charts on both continents. Yet the Monkees are totally synthetic.

Unlike other groups, which come together through accidents of personal history or the exercise of personal taste, the Monkees were manufactured.

Many of their fans know the main outlines of the story: How, in the fall of 1965, Rafelson and Schneider advertised for performers, auditioned 437 of them, and chose Davy Jones, Micky Dolenz, Peter Tork and Mike Nesmith. How these four young men were then trained in "spontaneous" comic techniques by an instructor who had worked with the Premise, the satirical group. How they were liberally assisted, on both TV soundtrack and records, by musicians and even singers who had skills they did not possess. How the result was then tested and sold, like a detergent, to the consumers.

The fact that all of this could happen so fast is easily explained: The Monkees' creators used nothing but pre-tested material.

There are two Hollywood producers who claim Rafelson and Schneider stole their idea and who are suing for $6,000,000. In the context, the idea is ridiculous. For surely if everyone victimized by the Monkees decides to sue, the litigation will crowd the calendar of every civil court in Los Angeles.

First, Rafelson and Schneider lifted the vocal style of the early, innocent Beatles records and even gave their group a name—a misspelled common word—parallel to that of the Beatles.

Second, they stole outright the cinematic style of Richard Lester, who directed both Beatles movies and who had himself borrowed the techniques of both TV commercials and French New Wave cinema. This style—it involves jump-cuts, speedups, slow motion, and surrealistic effects that would be meaningless in any but the zaniest contexts—was only yesterday regarded as fresh and free. Today, on TV, it looks stale and flat. Mass culture eats its inspirations quickly.

These two borrowings are constants in the lives of the Monkees. Other forms of thievery change from show to show. This week, for instance, you could see clearly at least one traditional Hollywood gag, at least one sequence Olsen and Johnson would have recognized as their own, and at least one outright plot theft.

There was a sequence involving a bed coming out of a wall in inconvenient ways: Chaplin did it first in a silent just about half a century ago, and various comedy directors have used it since.

There was a chase scene which kept gathering new and more outlandish participants each time the chasers and the chasees hove into view. What started out as a chase involving a Monkee, a husband and a wife ended up with a football player in full uniform, an Olympic torch-bearer, a nearly naked woman, and a full-size ape. It was pure Olsen and Johnson.

Then there was the plot. You may recall that in Bells Are Ringing, the Broadway show, the heroine found herself operating an answering service that was being used as a front by some bookies. In this week's show the Monkees found themselves operating an answering service that was being used as a front by some bookies. The difference was that in the original, the bookies masked their bets as orders for classical records; this time, the bookies masked their bets as bookings for pop music groups. (The Monkees' show has four people described as script and story editors, but obviously they are

For the kids' own views

Monkees: Crime *can* pay

not trying to make reputations for artistic creativity.)

Would it be fair to suggest, then, that the Monkees have so far failed to find their own style? It would be more than fair, but the interesting fact is that it doesn't matter.

The Monkees, after all, are directed straight at an audience that never heard of Olsen and Johnson, probably never saw Bells Are Ringing, and know Chaplin only as a distant name. This is an audience, furthermore, that regards early Beatles as traditional culture and can hardly be surprised when a new group follows the Beatles style.

More important, the Monkees format is designed both to appeal to the youngest generation now watching early evening TV (Kellogg's breakfast food is a sponsor) and to accommodate all the old-hat material that the writers care to cram into it.

The format is porous and the plots are pointless.

But young people, brought up on the choppy style of TV commercials, reared in the era of we-interrupt-this-commercial-to-bring-you - another - bit-of-movie, find it easy to take.

And this goes for fairly small children as well as teenyboppers. My 9 year-old and my seven-year-old dig the Monkees. The 7-year-old doesn't understand half the jokes, but then she's used to watching TV she only half understands. That, too, is part of her generation's experience.

Myself, I think the Monkees on TV are awful. Even this week's surrealistic ending was flat—surrealism is a style that requires something like genius, and there's no genius working on this show.

The verbal jokes are, if anything, worse. In a typical one, a Monkee is found missing. "Hey, do you think there's been foul play?" asks a second Monkee. "I don't know," says a third. "I didn't see the game." It sounds as if it were made up on the spot, which indeed much of it is.

Aside from the open style and the borrowed material (and the considera-

of the Monkees, see Page 27

HERE'S LOOKING AT YOU, TORONTO!

ble charm of the four actors), there is a further reason for the Monkees' overwhelming success. They are simple and innocent.

In a period when folk rock is frequently as obscure as modern poetry, when the Beatles themselves write lyrics that require decoding, the Monkees appeal on the most basic level: They sing love songs.

The Beatles, still popular, look to older and hipper adolescents for their fans; they are no longer the lovable long-haired dolls they were in 1963; they have grown in sophistication with their audience.

But the Monkees aim straight at the unsophisticated early adolescent, the sort of kid who wants to be with something but can't quite make out what the Beatles are all about.

In his bewilderment he turns eagerly to these four good-natured, fun-loving Monkees—a package of mass culture created expressly to suit his needs.

MONKEES ARCHIVES 1

MONKEES ARCHIVES 1

Mike Nesmith sings; Peter Tork backs him on guitar; drummer is Mickey Dolenz and organist is Davy Jones in movie, "Head," at Lyric.

Utah-Made Movie Slated

"Head," a motion picture partially produced at Valley Music Hall, opens today at the Lyric Theater and Woodland Drive-in. It is on the same bill as "Pendulum," a suspense-police adventure movie.

"Head" stars The Monkees, Victor Mature, Annette Funicello and features many performers from television. Among cast members are Vito Scotti, a comedian who has been appearing this season on Flying Nun, and Sonny Liston, former heavyweight boxing champion.

The segment that was filmed in Utah, was produced last summer. A crowd of teens that was so large that the Valley Music Hall could not accommodate all of them, was on hand for the production. Many faces of Utah teens will be seen in the crowd as the Monkees are shown playing their selections. They have 6 new songs in the film.

"Head" is a comedy with many unusual settings, such as a sewage disposal plant.

MONKEES ARCHIVES 1

it's VOX for the Monkees at Wembley
Perfectionists buy VOX

SO CUT OUT THIS COUPON NOW!

Please send me full details of Vox Solid State amplifiers and organs

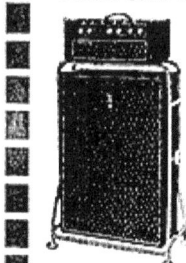

Vox Supreme solid state amplifier. 200 watt peak-power output. Speaker unit: four 12" Vox heavy duty loudspeakers plus two high frequency exponential metal horns, crossover network. Twin channel, four inputs. Reversible amp section. Complete with stand. Amp unit: 23½" x 9½" x 11". Speaker unit: 27½" x 40" x 11½".

Vox Continental original portable organ, sparked off the organ trend with beat groups everywhere. Sparkling vitality and zingy tone give it an instantly recognizable sound. Fully transistorised. Operates with any amplifier. Frequency range from 16' x 8' x 4' IV rank mixture (2⅔', 2', 1⅗', 1') operated from 4 harmonic and 2-tone selector drawbars.

Jennings Musical Industries Ltd
Vox Works, off West Street, Erith
Kent, England

Name

Address

Group

MONKEES ARCHIVES 1

COME ON EVERYONE!

50 LATEST MONKEES LPs TO WIN EVERY WEEK
FROM JUNE 5TH TO AUG 7TH

in the easy **CYDRAX** "Spot-the-Pops" Contest! With a FREE Monkees iron-on transfer for every entrant!

© 1967 Raybert Productions Inc. trademark of Screen Gems Inc. Whiteways Cyder Co. Ltd authorised user

Here's a swinging can't-lose contest from CYDRAX, top-favourite family thirst-quencher... just by entering you get a FREE 4" long Monkees transfer for your shirt or tee-shirt (you just iron it on)!

And you could easily win the latest MONKEES LP.

There are 50 to win every week, from June 5th to August 7th. All you do: say what you think will be the first four pops in the next issue of the Melody Maker after you send your entry, plus why you think apple-goodness CYDRAX is such a swinging drink. You can send in as many entries as you like—right through the competition period; but each one must be accompanied by two labels from big bottles (that is flagons or the new big no-deposit bottles, *not* split sizes) of Cydrax or Peardrax. So keep those entries swinging in.

Remember, you've a chance to win every week till August 7th.

Important! Entries will be opened every Monday from June 5th to August 7th 1967, and compared with the Top Pops charts published in the following Thursday's Melody Maker. 50 prizes of Monkees LPs will be awarded to those entrants whose entries are correct and who in the opinion of the judges submit the most original and interesting reasons why they like Cydrax. The judges' decision will be final and no correspondence entered into. The competition is open to all residents of Great Britain and Northern Ireland other than employees or families of employees of Whiteway's, their advertising agents and the Melody Maker.

 **and PEARDRAX**

Entry form to "Cydrax Spot-the-Pops Contest",
Whiteway's, Hele, nr. Exeter, Devon.

I enclose 2 labels from flagons or no-deposit bottles of Cydrax/Peardrax and a stamped addressed envelope for my Monkees transfer. My selection for the first four Top of the Pops next week is:

1st ....
2nd ....
3rd ....
4th ....

Complete this sentence in 10 words or less: "I like drinking CYDRAX because ...."

Date entry sent ....
Name ....
Address ....

MONKEES ARCHIVES 1

who is david jones?

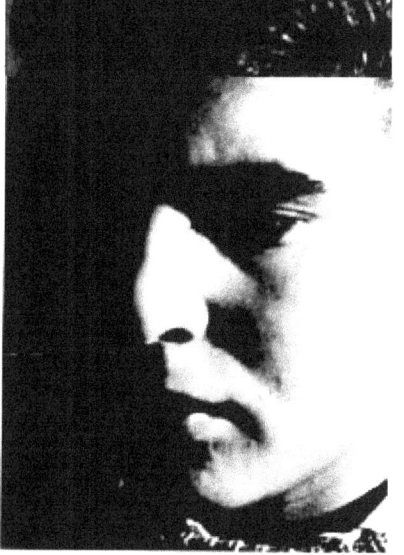

DAVID JONES is the British teen-age stage sensation—the "Artful Dodger" of the Broadway and London productions of "Oliver"!

DAVID JONES is already a teen-age favorite— his fan club membership is in the thousands and he has been featured in teen magazines reaching hundreds of thousands!

DAVID JONES' first record is on Colpix — an exciting new single now breaking nationally!

DREAM GIRL
b/w
TAKE ME TO PARADISE   CP 764

Colpix Records • 1347 North Cahuenga Boulevard • Hollywood, California

WIN A GUEST ROLE on "THE MONKEES" TV SHOW
and this customized PONTIAC GTO!

©1967, Raybert Productions, Inc.

Kellogg's TV Screen-Stakes

Spencer Lloyd Peet Collection

1,516 PRIZES GIVEN AWAY!

- **GRAND PRIZE**—All-expense-paid, 7-day trip to Hollywood to appear on "The Monkees" NBC-TV show, plus a 1968 Pontiac GTO Convertible*. This customized GTO has a 360 H.P. engine, 4-speed transmission with Hurst shifter, rally gauge instruments, tachometer, and other exciting sports car features.
- **15 MORE BIG PRIZES OF PONTIAC GTO HARDTOPS**—each with all the great sports car features described above for the GTO Convertible.
- **1,500 CONSOLATION PRIZES**—
"Monkees" LP Albums.

*If winner of one of the Pontiac GTO prizes is a minor, Kellogg's reserves the right to award car to winner's parent or guardian.

Be a winner...nothing to buy ...easy to enter!

Picture yourself winning a guest role on one of "The Monkees" NBC-TV shows, and this fabulous new Pontiac GTO Convertible. Or, maybe you'll win one of the GTO Hardtop or "Monkees" Record Album prizes. You have 1,516 chances to win! Enter often—the more you enter, the better your chances are! Don't wait—all "TV Screen-stakes" entries must be postmarked before May 5, 1968.

GET DETAILS ON SPECIAL KELLOGG'S® RICE KRISPIES® AND RAISIN BRAN® PACKAGES, OR ON FREE STORE ENTRY FORMS AT YOUR GROCER'S!

"Screen-stakes" void in Wisconsin and wherever else prohibited by law.

©1968 by Kellogg Company

GET "AUTOGRAPHED" PICTURES OF "THE MONKEES" ON SPECIAL KELLOGG'S PUFFA PUFFA RICE AND OKs® PACKAGES, TOO!

MONKEES ARCHIVES 1

MONKEES ARCHIVES 1

We Three Monkees...
Davy Jones, Micky Dolenz and Peter Tork

present

"Christmas Is My Time Of Year"

produced by Chip Douglas

An expression of friendship and togetherness to make the holidays a little brighter for all of us.

"The hottest Christmas record in a decade!"
Just ask KHJ – Los Angeles

MONKEES ARCHIVES 1

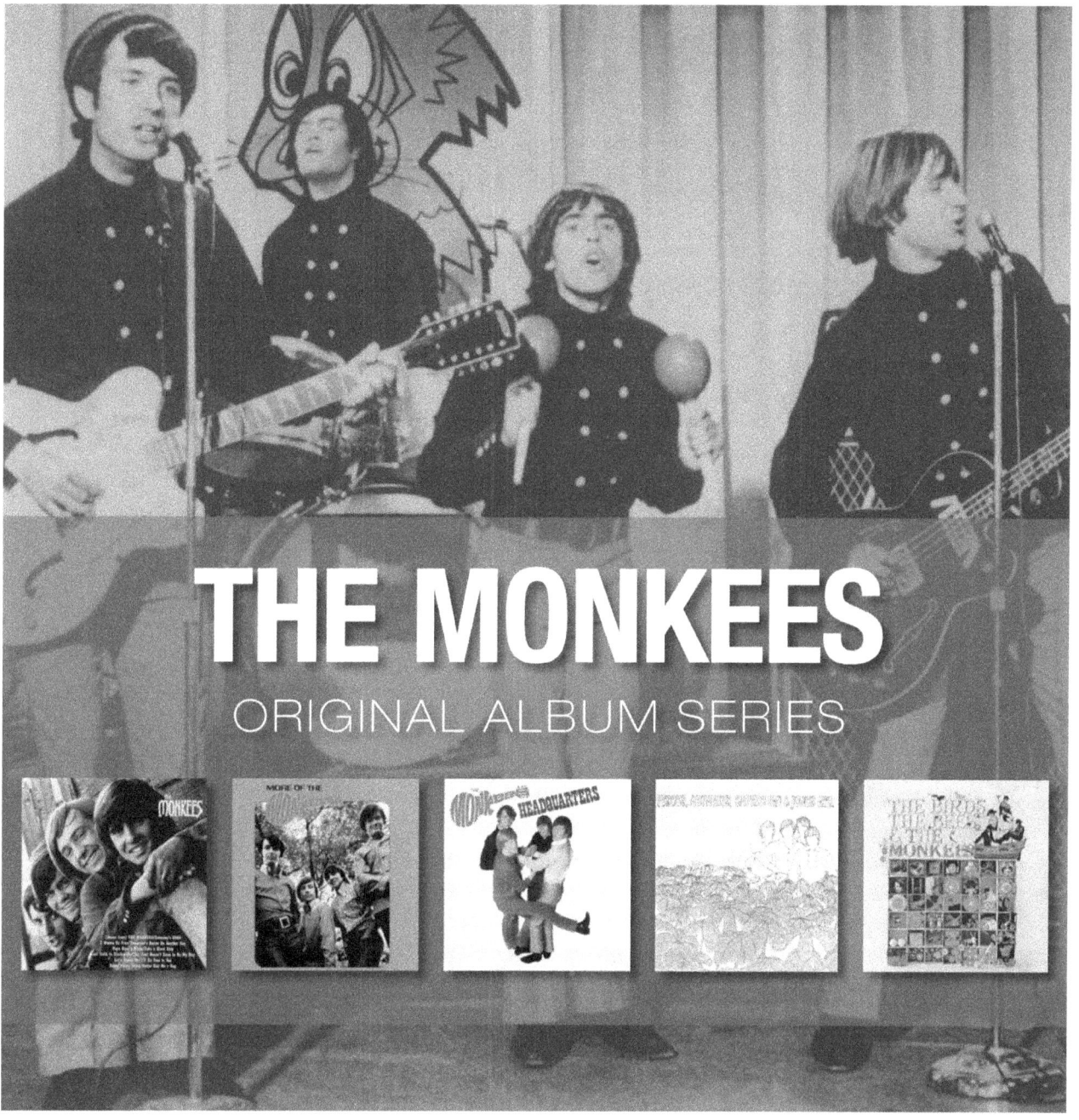

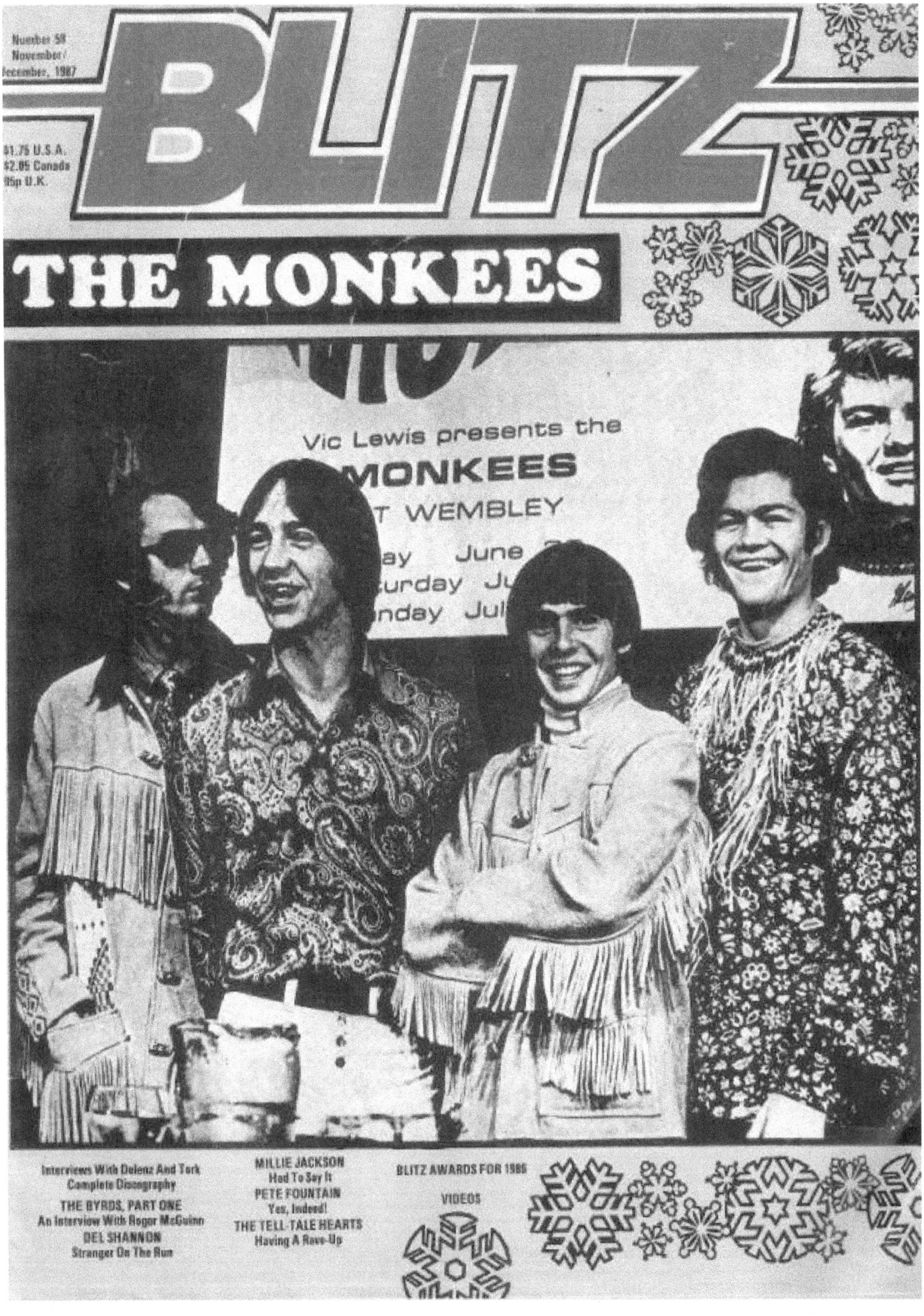
Number 58
November/
December, 1987
BLITZ
$1.75 U.S.A.
$2.05 Canada
95p U.K.
THE MONKEES
Vic Lewis presents the
MONKEES
T WEMBLEY
June
Interviews With Dolenz And Tork
Complete Discography
THE BYRDS, PART ONE
An Interview With Roger McGuinn
DEL SHANNON
Stranger On The Run
MILLIE JACKSON
Had To Say It
PETE FOUNTAIN
Yes, Indeed!
THE TELL-TALE HEARTS
Having A Rave-Up
BLITZ AWARDS FOR 1986
VIDEOS

MONKEES ARCHIVES 1

Reunion of the century: The Monkees after their triumphant performance at the Greek Theatre in Los Angeles, 07 September 1986 (left to right): Peter Tork, David Jones, Michael Nesmith and Micky Dolenz.

LISTEN TO THE BAND!

BY MARY ANNE CASSATA AND MIKE McDOWELL

For many years, it has been touted in the pages of this publication that the ultimate miracle in the constantly metamorphosizing world of rock and roll would be the reformation of its all-time greatest band, the Monkees. Their pioneering endeavors in the fields of garage band rock, experimental rock, country rock, musical theatre and other areas too numerous to mention have earned the Monkees (Michael Nesmith-lead guitar; Peter Tork-keyboards, bass, David Jones-bass, percussion; Micky Dolenz-drums, synthesizer) status as innovators nonpareil. And the comparatively tepid state of the rock and roll movement in the wake of the Monkees' dissolution in 1970 only served to illustrate the necessity of a focal point of their calibre.

Fortunately, that ultimate miracle happened in 1986, as Peter Tork, Micky Dolenz and David Jones reunited for an enormously successful worldwide Monkees reunion tour. The resultant mania earned the band another chart album with Arista's *Then And Now* compilation and a hit single with Dolenz and Tork's collaboration on the Mosquitos' *That Was Then, This Is Now*. Unfortunately, lead guitarist Michael Nesmith's demanding schedule in the film industry did not permit his participation in the tour (although he did grace a wildly appreciative audience at Los Angeles' Greek Theatre on 07 September 1986 with his presence by sitting in on lead guitar with the band for *Pleasant Valley Sunday* and *Listen To The Band*, an event that many in that capacity crowd would doubtlessly concur was rock and roll's finest moment ever). In Nesmith's absence, bassist Peter Tork assumed the role of lead guitarist.

The triumphant return of the Monkees into the rock and roll hierarchy has seen the re-emergence of numerous artifacts indigenous to their heritage. Magazines such as *Creem* have devoted entire issues to them, while others like *Tiger Beat* have re-printed late 1960s Monkees commemorative issues of their publication. Rhino Records' re-releases of the Monkees' nine original albums for the Colgems label have all enjoyed substantive runs on the national album charts. Their 1966-1968 television series is garnering commendable ratings in national syndication. And numerous rare concert and television clips have been circulating amongst video collectors. In the latter category, the most fascinating item has been their NBC television special, *33⅓ Revolutions Per Monkee*, filmed in November 1968 and broadcast in early 1969. With guest appearances from the Clara Ward Singers, Little Richard, the Buddy Miles Express, Jerry Lee Lewis, Fats Domino and Julie Driscoll, Brian Auger And The Trinity (the latter who duets with Micky Dolenz on a jazz/funk version of *I'm A Believer*), the Monkees in the span of a one-hour television special offer a bizarre and virulent assessment of the recording industry and the socio-political climate of late 1960s America and manage to incorporate a number of noteworthy musical selections into the proceedings, including the vitriolic *Wind Up Man*, Tork's existential *Thou Makest Demands On Me*, Nesmith's brilliant country-rocker, *The Only Thing I Believe That's True*, an improvisational *Listen To The Band* (presented as a jam with the Buddy Miles Express), covers of the Five Du-Tones' *Shake A Tail Feather*, the Diamonds' *Little Darlin'* and Danny And The Juniors' *At The Hop* and Tork's Bach improvisations on the electric piano.

The resurgence of Monkeemania has also spawned a number of new projects within or relating to the band. David Jones has recently completed his autobiography, *They Made A Monkee Out Of Me* (available through Dome Press) and issued a cover of the Swinging Blue Jeans/Chan Romero classic, *Hippy Hippy Shake* b/w *After Your Heart* as a single on the Australian Powderworks label on 30 March. A Jones solo album (tentatively titled *Incredible*) is also imminent. Michael Nesmith guested in a new Whoopi Goldberg film and has made available a new comedy video, *Dr. Duck*, in which he is the focal point. Monkee organizations like the Pisces, Aquarius, Capricorn And Jones Fan Club and the North Beechwood Drive Irregulars and veteran promoters such as Phyllis Rabinowitz and Maggie McManus have been organizing Monkees conventions and memorabilia swap meets across America. The band also plans another national tour for July through October of 1987 (including a return to Los Angeles' Greek Theatre from 21-23 September), in which Michael Nesmith may participate on a limited basis. Best of all, the Monkees (including Nesmith) will soon begin work on a new full length motion picture (scheduled for December, 1987 release) and have spent May and June in the studios recording a brand new album.

These varied activities have made significant demands on the schedules of the Monkees, leaving them with little or no time to pursue extra-curricular activities. However, Blitz's Mary Anne Cassata was fortunate enough to speak with lead guitarist Peter Tork in early December, 1986 in New York City at the conclusion of their national tour. Though under substantial pressure from several sources to honor a variety of personal appearance commitments the same day, Tork recalled the extensive coverage afforded the Monkees in past issues of Blitz (including a lengthy Peter Tork interview in our May-June, 1980 edition) and as such was more than happy to devote a few minutes to relate the following data pursuant to their various undertakings.

Much has happened to the Monkees in the weeks following these interviews. The long-awaited *Heart And Soul* single was finally released in late July. Coupled with Peter Tork's upbeat and immersible *MGBGT* (recorded live in concert), *Heart And Soul* features drummer Micky Dolenz on lead vocals and bears stylistic allegiance to the band's 1986 *That Was Then, This Is Now* single. The Roger Bechirian-produced *Pool It!* followed in mid-August, the Monkees' first album of all-new material since May, 1970. In addition to *Heart And Soul*, *Pool It!* includes a cover of Wreckless Eric's *I'd Go The Whole Wide World*,

MONKEES ARCHIVES 1

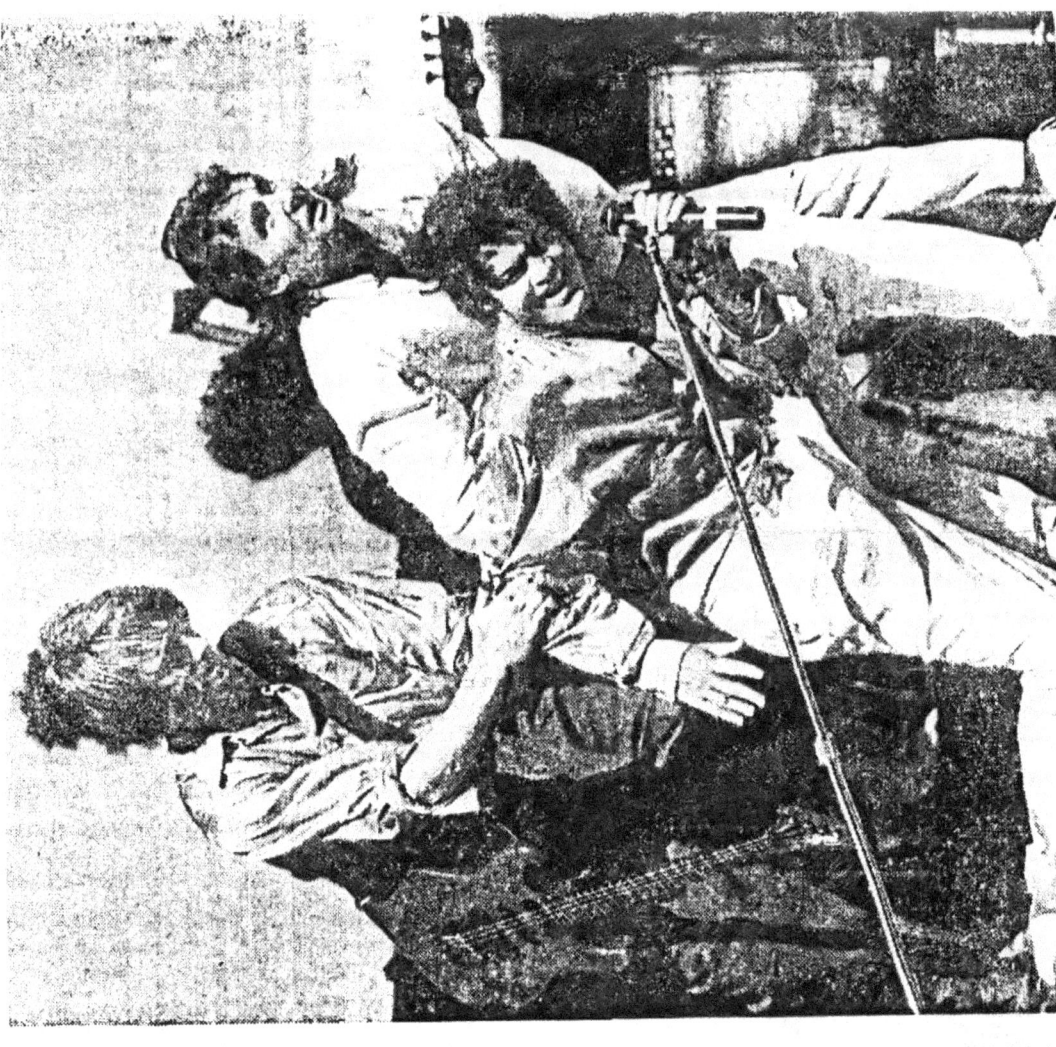

A playful Mickey Dolenz was helped to his feet by Peter Tork (left) and Davy Jones during the first of their two rollicking appearances Sunday at the State Fair.
—Sentinel photo by Brian Poulter

Charming Monkees still a barrel of fun

By Jim Higgins

There they were,
At the State Fair,
With some old hits
And a few gray hairs,
Hey, hey, they're the Monkees,
With some reunion monkeying around,
Kids were so busy screaming,
How could they hear those '60s sounds?

West Allis — If the United States could beam the Monkees around the world, it wouldn't need Radio Free Europe.

Those television and pop music stars of the late '60s could liberate everyone with the goofy and slightly subversive charm they turned Sunday on more than 25,000 people during two concerts at the State Fair Park Grandstand.

Playful Mickey Dolenz, handsome Davy Jones and thoughtful Peter Tork could not roll back time, but turned in a B-plus job of recapturing their spirit.

After brief, unremarkable opening sets by Herman's Hermits, the Grass Roots and Gary Puckett, the three Monkees bounded on stage to a recording of their theme.

Throughout the show, Tork calmly stroked a red guitar, Dolenz occasionally pounded a small kit of electronic drums and Jones tapped his familiar tambourine. But most of the instrumental punch was supplied by a loud eight-piece band that included a four-person horn section.

Dolenz, Tork and Jones concentrated on what they did best — sing and clown around. This pleased a delirious, shrieking crowd, which consisted both of people who were kids when the series aired and people who are kids now.

When Dolenz, the band's best singer, took the lead, the music sounded superb. He delivered one lively vocal after another — "Steppin' Stone," "Last Train to Clarksville," "Goin' Down," "I'm a Believer" and the encore, "Pleasant Valley Sunday."

Dolenz sang with soul, and in his buoyant, high-stepping antics showed he's studied some stage masters, including Little Richard and James Brown.

Scores of youths screamed for Jones, who has traded his baby face for a tanned, lined, mature one. Neither Jones nor Tork displayed Dolenz's vocal ability and stage presence but worked effectively within the talents they had.

The three singers, who might be considered among the founding fathers of rock video, indulged themselves and the crowd in a great deal of silly humor.

With mock anger Dolenz confronted a man in the audience: "Hey! He's not singing!"

"Peter, teach him the words," Jones said to Tork.

Tork, who usually had to play the dummy, replied: "What are they?"

Mike Nesmith, known by fans as the talented, moody Lennon-like Monkee, did not join the reunion. The three Monkees — or someone in their entourage — playfully jabbed their old mate by dressing up a tall, skinny roadie in a wool hat, a Nesmith trademark.

LINDA meets the MONKEES!

16's "Meet Davy & The Monkees Contest Winner"

POW! Here it is — the story and pictures of 16's **Meet The Monkees Contest!** The winner was 15-year-old Linda Thompson of Houston, Texas. Lovely Linda's dream came true — and she wants to share her exciting day in Monkee-land with all the **16**-ers who entered this greatest-ever contest! So come along with Linda to Hollywood, and remember: this time "lucky" Linda won — **next time, it could very well be YOU!**

First stop is "on location" on a set where the Monkees are at work filming their first motion picture. But they are not too busy to greet their "Sweetheart For The Day."

You can bet this pic of Linda with Davy — has a special place in the huge personal photo album of her fab day she received from **16** as a keepsake of her trip!

When the Monkees broke for lunch, Linda and her mom (who accompanied her on the trip) got right in line with them in the studio cafeteria! Here Linda chats with Peter.

Marvelous Micky gave our girl something special to remember him by — a flower. But **she'll** never forget his twinkling eyes and warm smile!

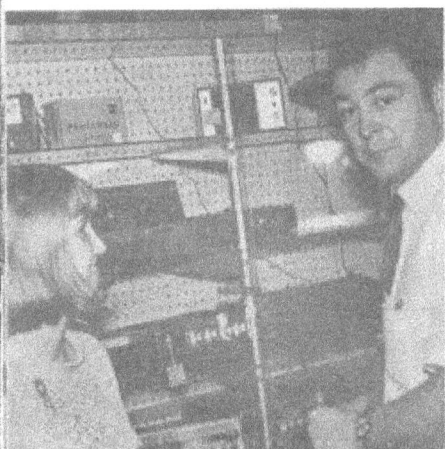

Part of Linda's prize was a $100 shopping spree. The main thing that she wanted was a tape recorder. Here she is purchasing it at Schaeffer's in Hollywood. She spent the rest of the money on souvenirs for the folks back home.

As a soopa-special **16** surprise, our very own Editor-in-Chief, Gloria Stavers, arranged a dinner date for Linda with Chris Crosby. (That's Linda's mom on the left).

Captivating Chris and lovely Linda share their favorite magazine — **16**. Chris took Linda to an exclusive French restaurant in Hollywood — and a great time was had by all!

MONKEES ARCHIVES 1

Advance Information on 1966-67 Programming

The Monkees

theinvisibleagent.wordpress.com

NBC TELEVISION NETWORK

MONKEES ARCHIVES 1

MONKEES ARCHIVES 1

 Advance Information on 1966-67 Programming

The Program and Its Creators

Program Type:
Half-hour, filmed comedy about an unknown quartet of wild, way-out and financially underdeveloped singer-musicians (THE MONKEES) and their efforts to become wilder and further out (and thus famous and rich). In color.

Producing Company:
Screen Gems in association with the NBC Television Network.

Co-Producers: ROBERT RAFELSON and BERTON SCHNEIDER
Robert Rafelson joined Screen Gems in 1964 to develop new television and feature film properties and played an important role in the launching of NBC's The Wackiest Ship in the Army. Earlier he wrote more than 30 adaptations for the highly-acclaimed Play of the Week series and was a writer and associate producer on The DuPont Show of the Month.

Berton Schneider is a former Vice President of Screen Gems with an impressive background in television business affairs. He also served as an assistant to film producer Sam Katzman. THE MONKEES marks his first production venture and his first collaboration with Rafelson.

Pilot Writers: LARRY TUCKER and PAUL MAZURSKY

A successful comedy writing team since their initial collaboration on the Hollywood edition of the highly-praised Second City Revue, Larry Tucker and Paul Mazursky now devote their talents almost exclusively to television. Their first home screen venture was Fractured Flickers. This lead directly to a regular scripting job on CBS' Danny Kaye Show, an assignment for which the pair won a Writers Guild Award. In addition to the weekly Kaye stanza, Tucker and Mazursky have written individual episodes of a number of other full-hour and half-hour series.

Pilot Director: MIKE ELLIOT
A commercial director before his THE MONKEES assignment, Mike Elliot has worked on hundreds of TV product announcements. He has received many awards for his filmed commercials.

NBC TELEVISION NETWORK

NOTE: The program described in this booklet is subject to availability and does not represent a commitment.

MONKEES ARCHIVES 1

MONKEES ARCHIVES 1

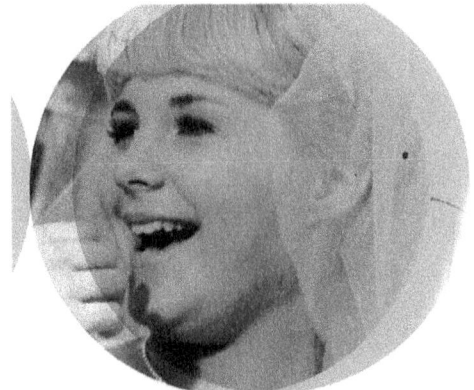

There are four young men who call themselves THE MONKEES. Like their prototypes The Beatles:

> They have musical inclinations and have even been known to play in tune (though admittedly not always playing the *same* tune at the same time).
>
> They sport overlong hairdos and unconventional modes of dress.
>
> They are appreciated by the teenage set, for whom they seem to convey some inner meaning of life, and also by adults still young enough at heart to indulge in the foot-tapping urge.

You could say that The Beatles and THE MONKEES are just alike. You could say it, but you'd be wrong. For underneath the music, the mops and the yeah-yeah-yeah is a basic difference: The Beatles are known in every corner of the globe and are worth $16 million dollars. THE MONKEES are the world's most unknown teenage idols—and at last count their combined wealth totalled $16.87.

Monkee Business

THE MONKEES—Davy, Peter, Mickey and "Wool Hat" (as they would be known to their fans, if they had any)—are the stars of a new half-hour Screen Gems comedy series. Their mutual goal is to become as famous as some of their thicket-headed predecessors, and each weekly episode will be devoted to their efforts in that direction. They have a manager of sorts—a man named Rudy Gunther, who owns the Record Rack music shop—and they do work once in a while. But THE MONKEES are not very typical young men and their week-to-week dealings with a world full of mere mortals will be the source of what promises to become television's wildest and freshest and funniest 30 minutes of tomfoolery.

To complement the zany storylines, the series will adopt a number of the off-beat moviemaking techniques that helped make runaway hits of such unconventional feature films as A Hard Day's Night, Cat Ballou, Dr. Strangelove, Tom Jones and The Knack. Nonsequitorial dialogue will be used. Characters may dress two different ways in one scene. There will be shock, flip and unmatched cuts. Some sequences will be speeded up; others slowed down. Overexposure and underlighting will be utilized to achieve a feeling of uninhibited realism.

The earth has withstood The Beatles, The Animals, The Rolling Stones, Herman's Hermits and Freddy and the Dreamers. But is it ready for THE MONKEES?

YEAH, YEAH, YEAH!!!

theinvisibleagent.wordpress.com

MONKEES ARCHIVES 1

Four Escapees from Animal Land

DAVID JONES as DAVY
PETER TORK as PETER
MICKEY BRADDOCK as MICKEY
MIKE BLESSING as "WOOL HAT"

To cast well-known actors in the pivotal roles on Screen Gems' off-beat new series would have been to imbue the four MONKEES with the personalities of already established stars. Instead, a talent search was initiated to discover four relatively unpublicized young men with the acting and musical talent to fit the roles. The actors who play Davy, Peter, Mickey and "Wool Hat" are the product of that search: four new faces and personalities who *are* THE MONKEES (and whose real-life first names have been given to the respective characters they play).

David Jones, the smallest MONKEE, is a 20-year-old Englishman, who started his professional career as a radio actor for the BBC. His most important credits include Oliver! and Pickwick, two musical comedies in which he played featured roles in London and on Broadway.

Peter Tork, an accomplished musician, who has mastered the ukulele, banjo, guitar, French horn, piano, harp and recorder, is a nightclub entertainer. He is making his television debut on THE MONKEES.

Mickey Braddock, THE MONKEES' drummer, was the star of NBC's Circus Boy series for three years, starting at the age of 10. He also has played occasional episode roles on such series as Peyton Place and Mr. Novak, and has made periodic nightclub appearances.

Mike (Wool Hat) Blessing is a young singer, guitarist and composer, who has enjoyed several successful supperclub and road tour engagements. He is equally adept at folk music and rock and roll.

MONKEES ARCHIVES 1

SEE BEACH BOYS WIVES PIX   Page 4

KFWB/98
HITLINE

CROWELL-COLLIER BROADCASTING
VOL. 2 NO. 10
GREATER LOS ANGELES
OCTOBER 4, 1966

MONKEES TO TAKE OVER!!

"The Monkees" are "the spirit of '66." Asked to explain themselves, they're likely to assume somewhat pained, somewhat incredulous expressions, as if to say, "We know who we are — why don't You?"

For the benefit of the unhip – those not with "the spirit of '66" – "The Monkees" are unknown, young, long-haired, kookily-dressed singing group. They are on a weekly half-hour NBC-TV series in color Monday, concerning the "adventures" of an unknown, young (etc.) singing, guitar strumming foursome making their way — backwards, sideways, upwards, downwards – toward fame and fortune.

They are also the somewhat nonchalant possessor of a brand-new Col Gems recording contract, and their first single will be issued in August on the Colgems label. RCA Victor will manufacture and

old, give or take a year either way. They all have brown hair and brown eyes. Michael is 6'1", Micky is 6', Peter is 5'11" – and Davy is 5'3".

"The Monkees" began as a gleam in the eyes of co-producers Bert Schneider and Robert Rafelson of Raybert Productions, which will film "The Monkees" in association with Screen Gems. A year ago they ran an ad in the Hollywood "Daily Variety" to ferret out four young men who had the personalities they wanted for "The Monkees." They interviewed or tested some 500 aspirants before the real "Monkees" stood out – in the forms of Davy, Micky, Peter and Michael.

The four have all had singing and/or acting experience. Davy Jones, English-born, has been an apprentice jockey and an actor in the Broadway mus-

MONKEES ARCHIVES 1

THE MONKEES are taking over! Watch their antics every Monday night, 7:30 on NBC.

Colgems label. RCA Victor will manufacture and distribute all Colgems products.

"The Monkees" are Davy Jones, Micky Dolenz, Peter Tork and Michael Nesmith. On screen they will be called "Davy Jones," "Micky Dolenz," "Peter Tork" & "Michael Nesmith."

They are all twenty years actor in the Broadway musicals, "Oliver!" (as "The Artful Dodger") and "Pickwick."

Micky Dolenz, son of actor George Dolenz, starred in TV's "Circus Boy," for three years ('55-'58), under the name, "Micky Braddock." He's the drummer of the group.

(Continued on Page 2)

GENE WEED was a big hit at the KFWB Booth at the Los Angeles County Fair. The booth was surrounded by visitors all day, and Gene gave away records and KFWB sweat-shirts. Watch for Larry McCormick's picture in the next issue.

RIGHTEOUS BROTHERS SET FOR THE ROYAL TAHITIAN

The Royal Tahitian announced the signing of the Righteous Brothers for their first return engagement running November 23 thru November 29.

The Righteous Brothers are now ranked second only to the Tijuana Brass in the Country in terms of record hits in one year, and in drawing power on personal appearances.

Their first engagement at the Royal Tahitian was a complete 8-day sellout and they recently completed standing room engagements in such diverse places as the Coconut Grove in Los Angeles, The Latin Casino in New Jersey, and the Cave in Vancouver, B. C.

Although local boys, all of their appearance for the rest of the year are scheduled out-of-state, and out of the Country.

Whether they team as singles or together, the hit

(Continued on Page 6)

The Robbs, regulars on Dick Clark's ABC-TV "Where The Action Is", release their new Mercury single this week entitled "Next Time You See Me", produced by Snuff Garrett. The Robbs will be the first American group to release a single which has the reversed guitar sound made popular by The Beatles. The Robbs, who achieved tremendous national popularity when they appeared in Chicago at Dick Clark's Young World Fair, plan their first personal appearance tour this Fall, packaged by their manager, Tom Parker and will cover eight weeks of one-nighters. The Robbs' new single is destined for the top '10'. Watch for it!

The Grass Roots, starring in Chicken of the Sea's "Crepuscular Happening" at Swing Auditorium, Friday, July 14, at 8:30. You'll want to see this concert with the Grass Roots and four other bands in a battle. Battling will be "Blues in a Bottle", "The Tourquays" and the "Good Feelins", and the "The Smoke". Admission is $1.50 with three Chicken of Sea tuna labels or $3.00 without.

A DAY WITH DAVY
By DIANE DIGIOIA

I won a day with Davy Jones on KFXM and the day began with a flight to Los Angeles. We were met at the airport and taken to the International Hotel where we were shown to our lovely room. At 1:30 we formed in the lobby, there were 21 girls. They were from Hawaii, Ohio, Tennessee, Michigan, Louisiana, etc. We all boarded the bus and were driven to Marineland, where we met Davy.

Everyone at this point began taking pictures with Davy, so I got up there and he put his arm around me, man did I feel good! We all went down to watch the seal and porpoise show, I sat two seats away from Davy. After the show we all went down on the stage area and a photographer took pictures of Davy and the group.

We returned to the bus, including Davy Jones, and we went to a live recording session. On the bus, Davy sang and talked with all the grils. I had gotten motion sickness on the flight, someone told Davy, he asked me how I was feeling, he told me not to feel too bad because he sometimes gets motion sickness also. Now I really felt great! He's so sweet! When we arrived at the studio we met the Beach Boys, the Yellow Balloon, and Don Grady of "My Three Sons". Davy explained how a recording was made and all this time he was looking at just me!

Atfer the tour we went to our pizza party at Michelie's. We had a blast. Then we went across the street and saw a new Monkee film, a real riot! Everyone boarded the bus again, we thought we were going to the hotel, but instead we returned to the studio and were able to meet the rest of the Monkees and get their autographs.

After returning to our hotel we posed with Davy for more pictures. I sat on the couch with him and he put his arm around me, they took the picture, he gave me the Monkee "Headquarters" album and kissed me good night. This is a day I will always remember, I wish all of you could have shared this day with Davy Jones.

July 7, 1967   KFXM "Tiger 59"   p. 2

ED GRrrrrr SEZ . . .

THIS OLE' TIGER has been in a PENSIVE mood lately . . . so took up a little self-instruction in PSYCHOLOGY . . . now that I'm an EXPERT (that's a DRIP under PRESSURE), thought you might be interested in the results of my ANALYSIS of the MOD-BODS . . . rather than going into a detailed PSYCOANALYSIS, I shall just BRAVELY (after all, I AM a TIGER) give you my UNBIASED, UNQUESTIONABLE, LEARNED conclusions as to the BEST and WORST TRAIT in each jock . . . GARY MARSHALL . . . WORST trait: tendency toward ALOOFNESS . . . BEST trait: one of the HARDEST WORKERS in radio . . . CHARLIE WALTERS . . . WORST trait: he can be VERY STUBBORN . . . BEST trait: his AFFABILITY . . . DICK LYONS . . . WORST trait: a tendency to be OVERLY TEMPERMENTAL . . . BEST trait: a very KIND-HEARTED individual . . . DANNY DARE . . . WORST trait: tends to ANTAGONIZE people . . . BEST trait: his HONESTY . . . JOHNNY HELM . . . WORST trait: can be HYPERCRITICAL . . . BEST trait: his DEPENDABILITY . . . CRAIG DENNY . . . WORST trait: his OVEREAGERNESS . . . BEST trait: his SINCERITY . . . of course, you realize this may well be the LAST WEEK you HEAR from EDgrrr . . . the MIGHTY 590 is REALLY ON THE MOVE with the SUPER SUMMER SPECTACULAR . . . already HUNDREDS OF PRIZES won by lucky KFXM'ers . . . and the TIGER has LOTS MORE . . . including CASH, MOTORCYCLES, COLOR TV, TRANSISTOR RADIOS, PHONOGRAPHS and RECORD ALBUMS . . . TOMORROW NIGHT, NUMBER ONE KFXM PRESENTS JAMES BROWN AT SWING AUDITORIUM . . . many FREE PASSES have been won from your CONTEST KING . . . the MODBODS report quite a HAPPENING last Friday night for the COUNT FIVE dance at the RIVERSIDE YOUTH CENTER . . . our FEARLESS LEADER COMPLAINS his IMAGE is being TARNISHED in this column . . . so I promise not to mention AL ANTHONY'S BOOZING anymore . . . DOUBLE "A" spent the long 4th weekend down OCEANSIDE way .

MONKEES ARCHIVES 1

MONKEES ARCHIVES 1

MONKEES ARCHIVES 1

MONKEES ARCHIVES 1

MONKEES ARCHIVES 1

Special Section!! **Monkee Mania!** (Continued)

Hey, Hey – It's The Monkees Reunion!

History Repeats Itself As All The Monkees Gather In L.A.!

Their TV adventures were fun and chock full of giggles, but the Monkees live was always an extra special treat. So thoroughly enjoyable were the songs and the performances, it's no accident that Monkees fans wanted to hear them still twenty years later...

To the month, it was twenty years since the Monkees had gone on the air...

...And so they did when Peter, Davy and Micky got together for a tour sponsored by Chunky candy. Each man packed up his loved ones, housed them in a tour bus or camper and headed down the rock 'n roll trail that eventually led them to...

MONKEES ARCHIVES 1

...One Michael Nesmith who joined them in performance in their former home base of Los Angeles. To the month, it was twenty years since the Monkees had gone on the air and for the older fans there that night...

...It was a thrill to see this foursome together again. For new Monkees fans, those who latched on to this funny troop of rockers by way of MTV's 22½-hour retrospective and all the current reruns, it was a chance to see the original chemistry in action...

...A chance to be involved in a "happening" once more—where you didn't just see and hear the Monkees —you could almost reach out and touch them!

Turn The Page!

MONKEES ARCHIVES 1

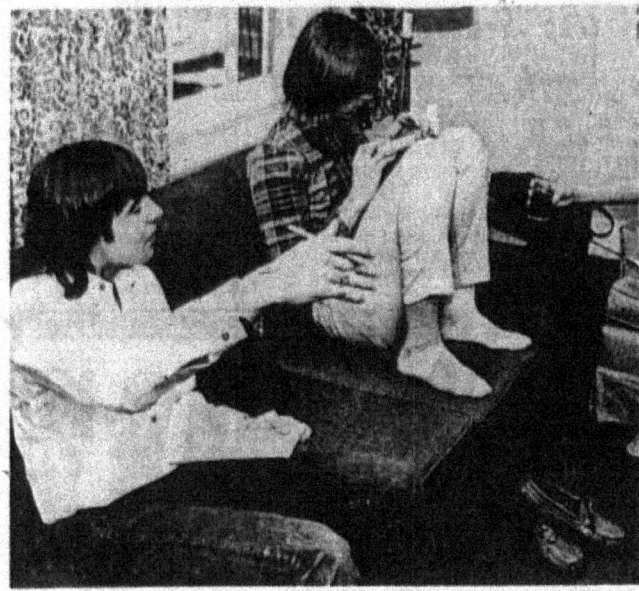
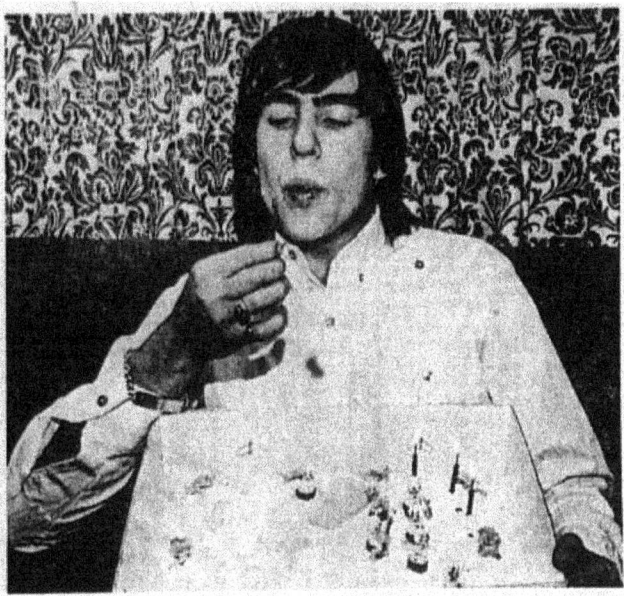

Davy Jones and barefoot Peter Tork answer questions; Davy lights up his birthday cake.

Staff Photos by Frank Jones

Monkees: Hard Workers With Varied Opinions

By Luix Overbea
Staff Reporter

It was a Monkees' world all day yesterday in the Hotel Robert E. Lee. To old folks—say over 25—there seemed to be lots of excitement and too, too many dreamy-eyed teenage girls in the lobby.

Two policemen in crisp uniforms patrolled the lobby with tolerant smiles.

From time to time, a long-hair with boots strolled through the lobby. There were squeals. "Are you with the show?" A shake of the head, and another girl was disappointed. The Monkees were not to be seen in the lobby.

With proper credentials, visitors to the hotel were permitted to ride the elevator to the ninth floor. This floor was Monkeeland.

When television's zany Monkees romped into town very early in the morning, "we were so tired," Davy Jones said, "that we did two hours of wall crawling and wall walking down the hall."

Backs to Wall

That is a kind of walking or crawling with their backs to the wall. "Anyway, we did not wake up anybody but our bosses, and who cares about that?"

Two of the four Monkees, Jones and Peter Tork, showed up for an interview. The other two, Micky Dolenz and Mike (Wool Hat) Nesmith, were at the Memorial Coliseum.

They were setting up for the show. "We have to have our amplifiers just right," Davy said in his clipped British accent. "There are some men paid to set things up, but we strive for perfection."

Jones and Tork—Davy and Peter to their television and record fans — agreed on very few things. They had opposing views on long hair and school.

On long hair:

"I look better with my hair short," Davy said. "My father doesn't like long hair. Without long hair I wouldn't have this job. So I say — people should take us for what we are, not for what's on the outside of the head, but what's in the head."

Long hair means much more to Peter. "I wore my hair long before I became a Monkee," he said. "Long hair stands for something. It says more than millions of short-hair older people have said for years."

School means a lot to Davy and something else to Peter.

"This job is important to me," Davy said. "I left school at 14. That was a big mistake. I regret it. This is the only work I know. I'm clean. I'm neat. I work because I want a job."

Flunked Out Twice

Peter, the son of two college teachers, flunked out of college twice before going into show business. He does not like school. He said:

"Look at it this way. Schools — public, private and colleges — are strictly vocational institutions. Yeah, you got to have degrees if you want to get somewhere.

"If you want to think, you do that someplace else. There is no compulsion for schools to teach knowledge. They do not teach wisdom. They do not teach people how to think."

Davy added that experience is an efficient teacher. He said, "School teaches you off the blackboard. Life teaches you firsthand through people. I have learned more through people in my six years out of school than I would have in 10 years in school."

Today Davy is 21 years old. Today is also Mike's birthday. He is 24. Somebody sent them a joint red and white birthday cake with five candles and "Happy Birthday Davy and Mike."

"Everybody sends cake," Davy said. Peter refused to pose for a picture with the cake.

Davy dresses neatly. He is so finicky that he washes his own socks and laundry.

Peter kicks off his shoes as soon as he enters a room. During the interview he wore mismatched socks, pink and yellow. "Ordinarily I don't wear pastels," he said, "but today I'm tired." He wears mismatched socks in loud colors usually.

This is the Monkees' first personal appearance tour as a group. To them it's "a gas." "It's wonderful to meet teenagers and see what they think of us," Davy said.

"Girls are fine as long as they don't get too close to us," he said. "They try to get on stage and touch you . . . talk to you. We have to be careful."

As a former stage performer in New York, Davy is more at home with the television show than the others. When the group first went on the television screen, it took them five days to film a show. Most of the shows now take 2½ to 3½ days.

They work 12 hours a day on set. "We break every rule of television," Davy said. "People are crowding on the set. Scenes are shot as we feel. This is very hard work."

All four Monkees are salaried actors. They do not get extra pay from the current personal appearance tour taking them to 10 cities on one-night stands.

"We collect for ourselves only on records," Davy said. They have two million-seller records and one million-seller album to their credit. A new album is coming out Jan. 15.

Their personal appearances have been more taxing than they expected. In spite of the two officers in the lobby, two policemen on the ninth floor and one plainsclothesman at large, people seemed to pour in and out of the room continuously.

Everybody wanted autographs. The Monkees also gave away their album to interviewers. When reporters entered the room Davy offered them coffee or Coke.

The press conference ended with a reminder to the Monkees that they were scheduled to tour a local tobacco plant.

A Monkee's Advice: Relax

By ROM WEATHERMAN
Staff Reporter

Chrisee Amen, 13 going on 14, didn't exactly have one of her "Monkee attacks" when she visited the Monkees yesterday in their hotel suite here. But she was pretty fluttery.

Chrisee, a daughter of Mr. and Mrs. Ralph Amen of 100 Friendship Circle, is a devoted Monkee fan who sometimes sighs ecstatically over their records and TV performances. That's what her 6-year-old brother Eric calls "a Monkee attack."

A reporter accompanied Chrisee to a Monkee press conference to record her reaction upon meeting her idols face to face.

The room in the Hotel Robert E. Lee was somewhat in disarray. It had just been vacated by a gaggle of teen-age girls who had been admitted to the presence of the Monkees for some reason or other. People were milling around. The telephone kept ringing.

Chrisee's reaction after gazing at Davy Jones, the British member of the troupe, was to whisper in amazement: "He's so calm!"

Monkee Refreshment

Davy served Chrisee a Coke. And she had a moment of anguish over whether to drink it or take it home for a souvenir. She decided to drink it.

Chrisee didn't seem to mind that two of the Monkees, Micky Dolenz and Mike Nesmith, were absent. They had gone on to Memorial Coliseum to tune up all that electronic music equipment. The Monkees performed last night before a crowd of about 8,200.

But there was Davy as big as life. And in a few minutes in came Peter Tork, the shy Monkee who turned out not to be shy at all.

Chrisee managed to get out a question: "When are you getting out another album?"

"January the fifteenth," said Davy.

Chrisee sat, looked and listened.

She had only one bad moment. That came when Peter moved over and sat on the arm of her chair for a photograph. The chair tipped a bit.

"If you want to be a human being, relax," Peter advised.

He asked the photographer if he wanted a gimmick and took off Chrisee's glasses and put them on himself. Someone told Chrisee to look at Peter.

"But I can't even see him," Chrisee wailed. She recovered her glasses.

Someone told her to ask Peter a question.

"How old will you be on your next birthday?" Chrisee got out.

"Twenty-five," said Peter.

Peter said it might make Chrisee too tense if he

Chrisee and Peter

put his arm around her. But he did, and the picture was made.

"It's all over — now you can relax," Peter said. But she never did.

She was nearly breathless when she descended on the elevator and rejoined her family in the hotel lobby. She clutched a Monkee record album which Davy and Peter had autographed and on which Peter had drawn a picture of a monkey.

Chrisee said she would keep it always and never forget.

MONKEES ARCHIVES 1

Micky Dolenz

Staff Photos by Frank Jones

Peter Tork

Mike Nesmith

Davy Jones

Noisy Crowd Here Shows They All 'Luv the Monkees'

By Luix Overbea
Staff Reporter

Move over Beatles, the Monkees are here. Some 8,200 screaming fans, most of them teen-agers, screeched their devotion to the television quartet's stage shenanigans at Memorial Coliseum last night.

There was not a quiet moment nor a dark spot in the house from the moment the Monkees, clad in continental fitting gray suits, black boots, paisley ties and pastel green shirts, bounced on stage at 9:10 p.m. until they left their fans limp with thrills one hour later.

Squealing admirers cramped themselves solidly in the aisles all the way from the rear to the stage. Only the wooden horses and 40 policemen separated the throng from the performers.

Flash bulbs squirted their eye-blinking lights, as camera bugs squinted, focused and snapped what they hope will be once-in-a-lifetime memories.

The Monkees opened with their 'Last Train to Clarksville.' The blinking cameras gave the impression of flashing lightning. The crush was on up front, but little by little policemen shoved the crowd back.

Holding down center stage was little Davy Jones, swinging a tamborine or flicking marimbas. Several Davy signs were waved from the crown. Flanking Davy were Mike (Wool Hat) Nesmith to his right and Peter Tork, both plunking highly amplified sound from shiny guitars.

Reigning high from the center was Micky Dolenz and his gleaming drums.

"This is not a rock 'n' roll show," Davy said in a pre-

The Monkees outline a variety of opinions at a press conference. Page 3.

show interview. But the group opened with three rockers.

Then came folk time with "I Want to Be Free." Sounds of ecstasy reached a crescendo as the huge screen above the stage flashed color slides of scenes supporting each song.

Policemen and some adults in the crowd checked the cotton in their ears as the din grew louder when they sang "Sweet Young Thing" from their album. The teen-agers joined the Monkees in singing each song, clapping their hands, and making noise, noise, noise.

A big sign, "We Luv the Monkees," expressed the crowd's sentiments.

After 10 selections, each Monkee did a solo. Micky got happy, left the drummer's stand, and sang and danced "What Did I Do" or something that sounded like that. The more he gyrated, the happier the crowd was.

The other Monkees left the stage to change costumes. Another group came on stage to support the singers.

Peter returned with a banjo. He sang a folk tune. Mike recalled memories of Bo Diddley with "I'm a Lover." Davy did a show tune — and was brought

See Crowd, P. 9, Col. 4

Officer restrains teen photographers near the stage.

Crowd 'Luvs the Monkees'

Continued From Page 1

back for a "Happy birthday to you" from the crowd.

Micky returned with a pink jacket screaming the old Ray Charles hit, "I Got a Woman."

The crowd's frenzy cooled for a minute while the Monkees made another change, then returned for the finale.

Can the Monkees really sing? Who knows when nobody really heard them? They are good showmen. They entertained the crowd, not with the usual rock 'n' roll routines, but with their unique personalities, which have made their television show so popular.

They were even more entertaining because they presented three talented supporting acts. The first was Jewel Akins of "The Birds and the Bees" note. Then came Bobby Hart.

A surprise followed. They were the Apollas, a swinging girls trio from Los Angeles. They excited the crowd with their singing, although fans were impatient for the stars.

Immediately after the show the Monkees left the arena and rushed out of town for their next stop. They dashed the hopes of fans who wanted to get backstage — even reporters could not break the security guard.

Out front in the lobby, barkers sold thousands of programs and hundreds of Monkee pins at a dollar each. A special display for Vox Teen Beat, a magazine, had a sellout, and there were plenty of lookers at a brand of guitar the Monkees play.

A tremendous amplifying set-up made it possible for everyone, even in the darkest most distant corners of the Coliseum, to hear what was going on.

The night with the Monkees was delightful fun for those who could stand the noise.

Bad Year for Police

MANILA (AP) — This was a bad year for Philippine policemen. From January to November 639 were arrested on charges ranging from robbery to murder, the National Bureau of Investigation reported.

MONKEES ARCHIVES 1

DAVY, 21, is all swagger, frug and hugs. He swaggers and brags, frugs whenever, wherever music's going. Big on hugs. Hugs everyone: producers, buddies, chicks—especially chicks. Fabulous sunburst smile. Fabulous steely little body—five and a quarter feet of it. "I'm shorter than the other guys," he pipes, in his Manchester English, "but I'm making as much money." Knows what he wants: Money. "I'm gonna make a couple hundred thousand, then I'm gonna get outta here and set up a riding stable at home. I want to be a jockey again. That's what I want." Of his fellow Monkees: "I'd kill for any one of those guys. I would."

MIKE, 24, is funny. He just stands there and it's funny—or opens his mouth and says something (anything) in his native Texas Twang, and that's funny. No smiling. Deadpan. "What did you do before The Monkees?" he was asked once. "Ah was a failure," he said on cue. Mike came to LA after college with a wife, a baby and $3.65, then banged around for a while as a folk singer. "Ah got this here guitar for Christmas one year," he says, "an' Ah got tired of just goin' plunk, plunk, plunk on the darn thing. Sooo, Ah jes' made up a little song." He makes up a lot of little songs now. Of the show, he says: "We'll do OK—if the crick don't rise."

MONKEES ARCHIVES 1

VOL. 2, NO. 42   OCTOBER 21, 1966   SAN BERNARDINO/RIVERSIDE, CALIFORNIA

Monkees' Car at KFXM Show

Custom Car Show November 4, 5 & 6

Gary Marshall (he's the one with the tie) and Edgrrrr made a Hollywood visit this weeks to see the famous "Monkees" car, a muchly modified GTO pictured here. This car used on the Monkees TV show will be a part of the KFXM Car Show next month.

The annual KFXM Inland Empire Custom Car Fair is to be held Nov. 4-6, at the National Orange Show grounds, San Bernardino. Since this will be the only show of its kind in the Inland Empire this year, the NCCCA is throwing its entire weight behind the event to make it outstanding. Movie-TV cars, such as the Bat-Mobile, the Green Hornet, the Monkees' Car, the Phyllis Diller Car, and a half dozen more, will highlight the three day automotive extravaganza. KFXM will remote broadcast daily while more than 150 custom cars, hot rods, dragsters, dragboats, and customized motocycles valued at over $1,000,000 will be shown to the public under the theme of "Safety and Assistance on the Road." The six facets stressed by the NCCCA are listed as safety, assistance on the road, power, speed, beauty, and advanced engineering. The Custom Car Fair is designed to appeal to people from seven to seventy. It is interesting, educational and has something for every member of the family. In addition there are continuous racing movies, a continuous Walt Disney cartoon show, nine teenage style shows, a Miss Teen and a Junior Teen Contest, a Model Car show, a battle of bands, and numerous action events. The National Custom Car Club Association represents over 21,000 member clubs and nearly a million individual members.

MONKEES ARCHIVES 1

Observer Photo by Bill McCallister

Jones, Dolenz And Nesmith Clown It Up In Motel

Monkees-Musical Hysteria Teen Bliss

Earlier Story On Page 14A

A Review
By ROBBIE HOOKER
Observer Staff Writer

Take several thousand slightly daffy teenagers; add nine popular recording groups—and what you've got is a place full of gum-chewing, hand-clapping; fan-waving, mildly hysterical folks.

That was the scene Wednesday night at the Charlotte Coliseum, where a bundle of mop-topped pop entertainers paraded before a full house of WAYS' fourth birthday, and 12,060 persons — the Coliseum cpacity — came to celebrate.

Not all of them actually listened.

A number of the teens, when they weren't marching up to the foot of the stage to pop flashbulbs in their idols' faces, ambled around in the aisles and clogged the exits.

Between acts, they talked loudly and hailed friends.

Around the stage, half a records, announced and then sang its biggest seller "Things Go Better With Coke."

Biggest hiit of the night, however, were the Monkees, the American answer to the Beatles. And the bill of fare also included a "special mystery guest" who, not surprisingly, turned out not unlike all the others.

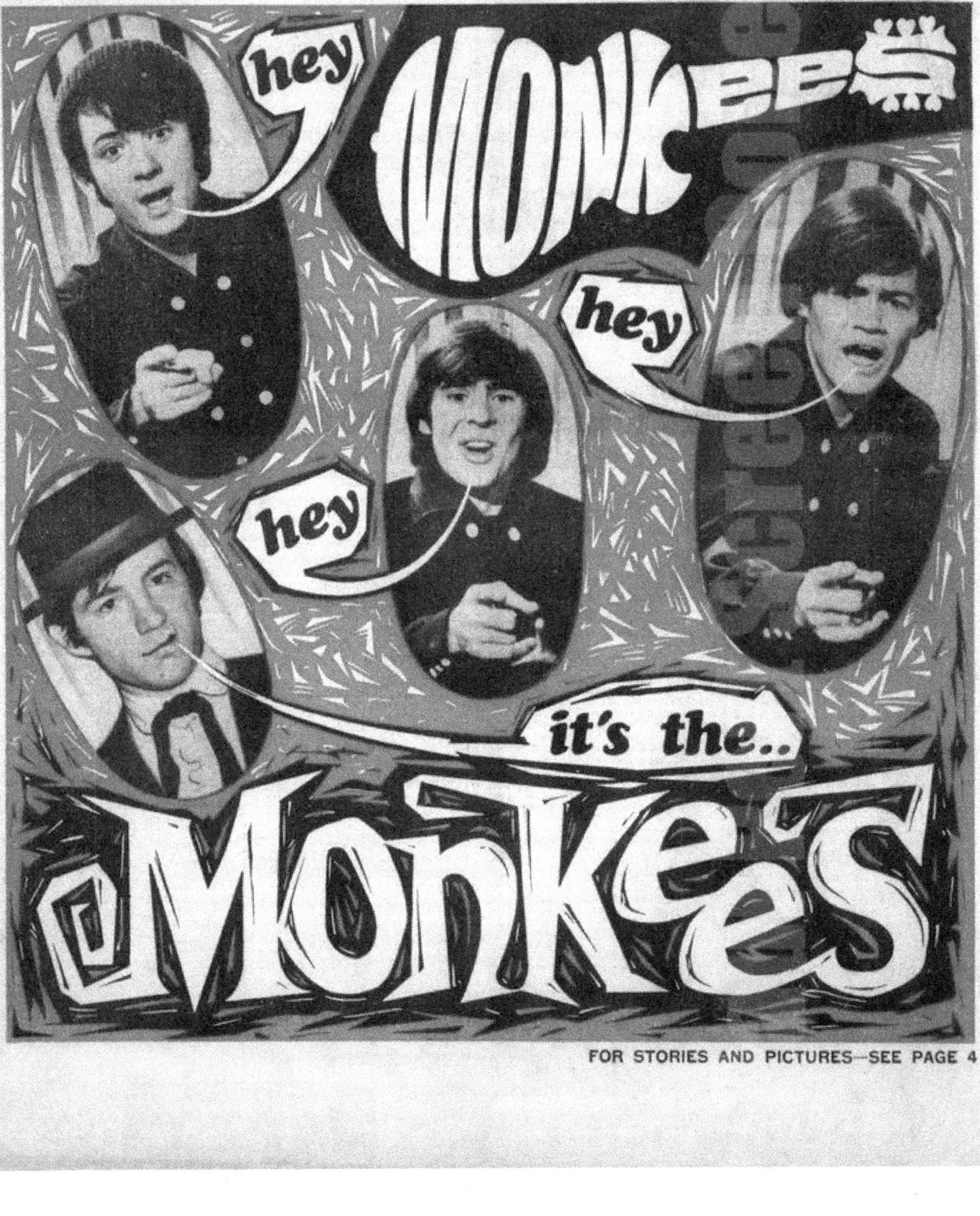
Radio Times (incorporating World-Radio) February 9, 1967. Vol. 174: No. 2257.

FEBRUARY 11—17

Radio Times

SIXPENCE

NORTH OF ENGLAND EDITION

BBC-1

tv

BBC-2

hey
MONKEES
hey
hey
it's the..
Monkees

FOR STORIES AND PICTURES—SEE PAGE 4

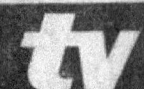

MONKEES ARCHIVES 1

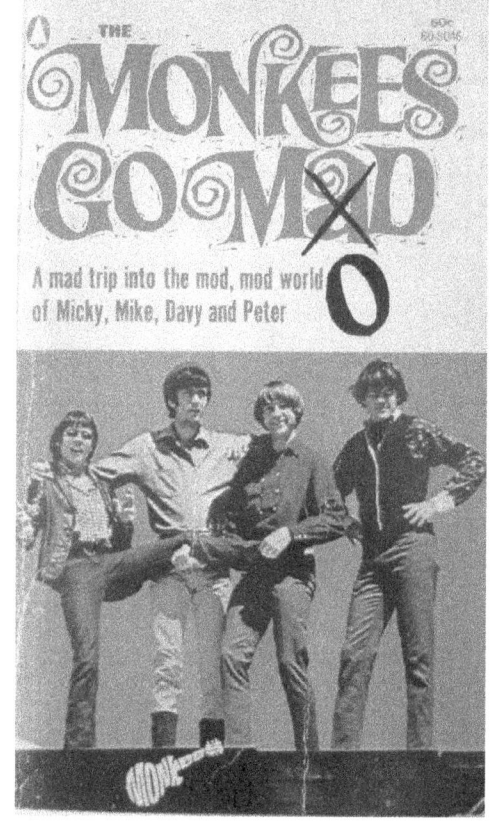

MONKEES ARCHIVES 1

MONKEES ARCHIVES 1

MONKEES ARCHIVES 1

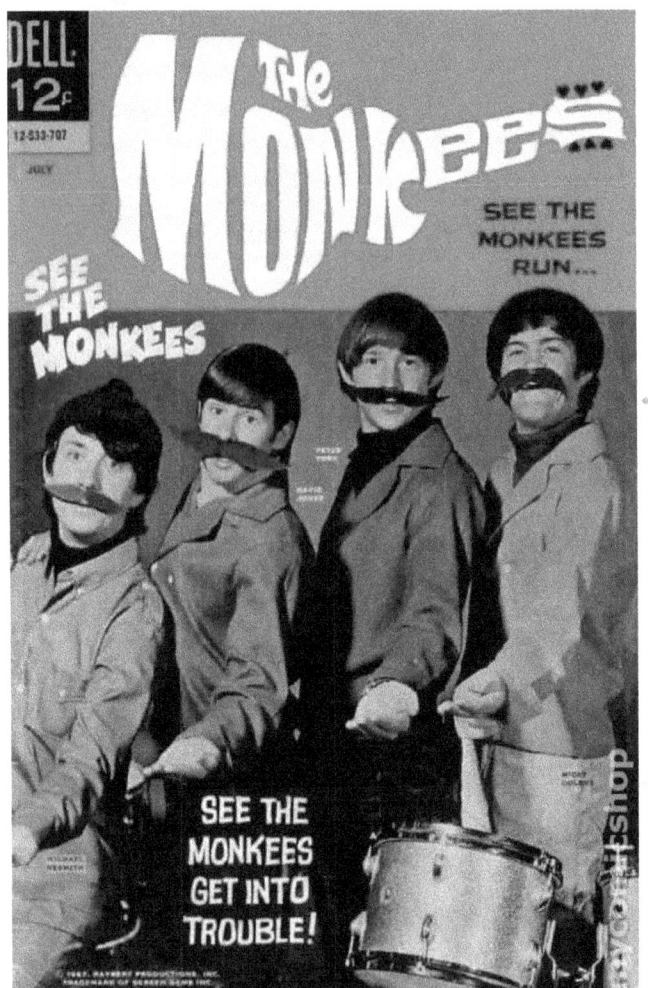
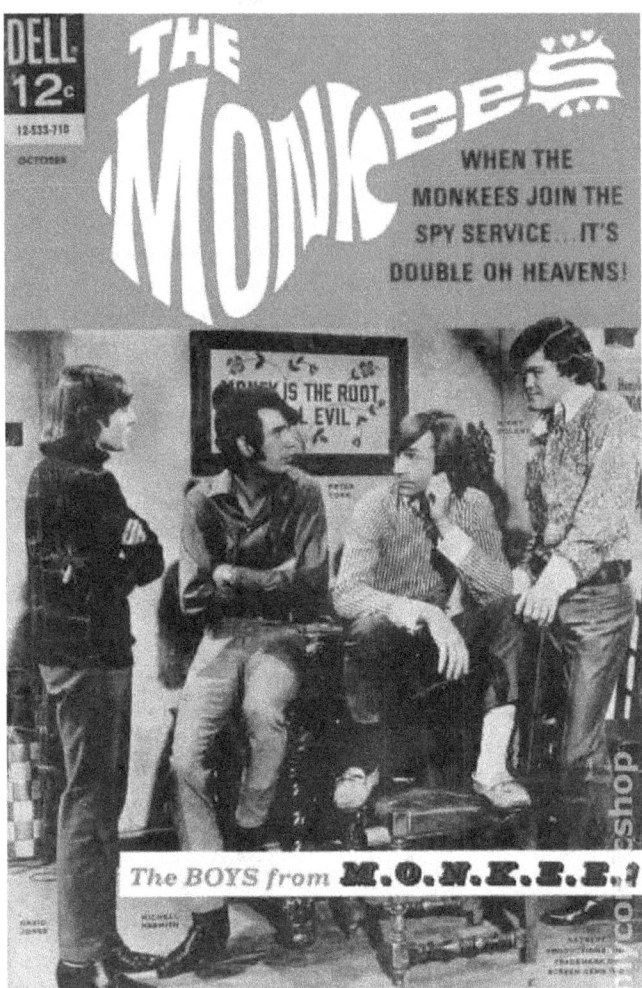

MONKEES ARCHIVES 1

MONKEES ARCHIVES 1

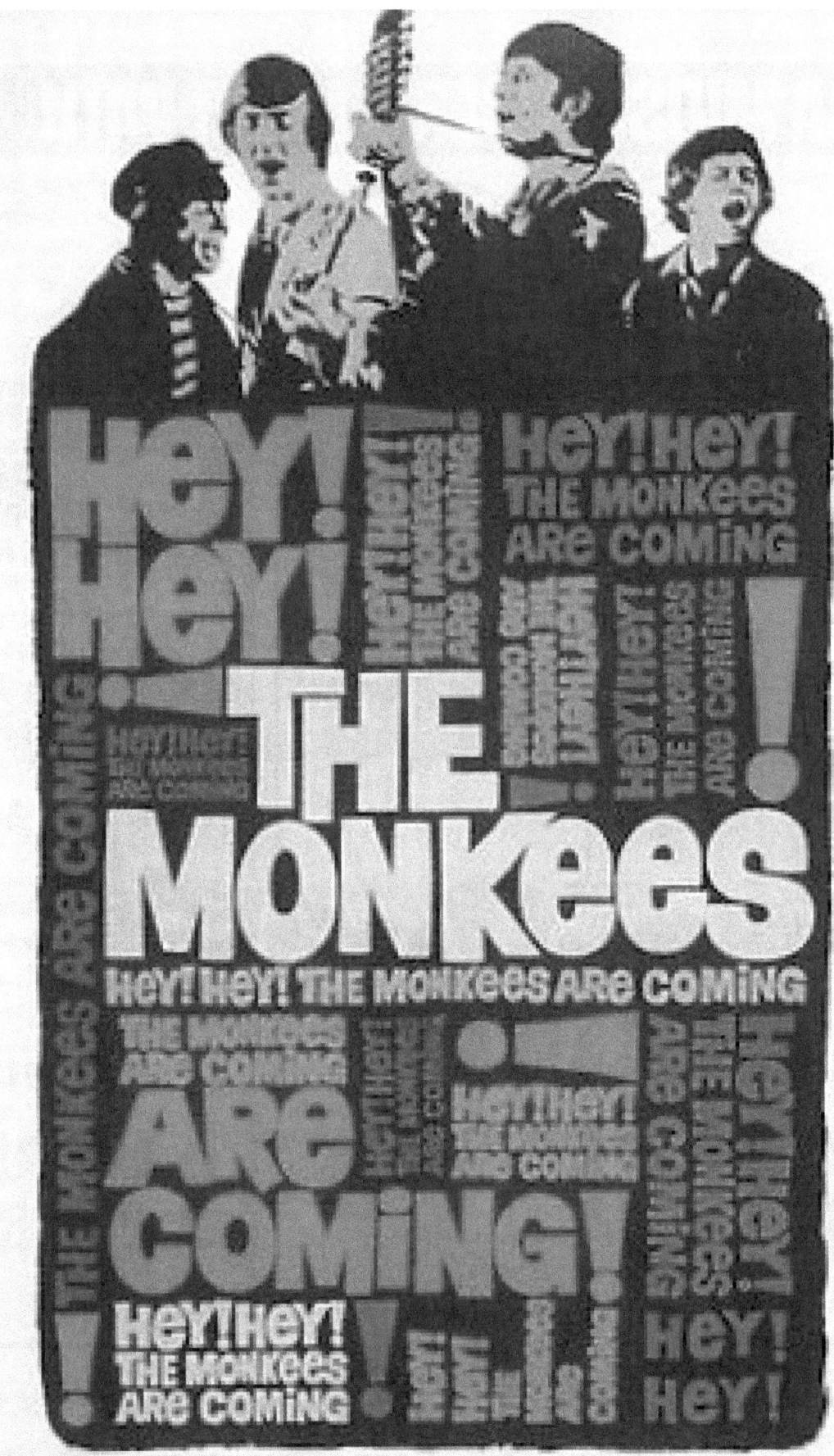

MONKEES ARCHIVES 1

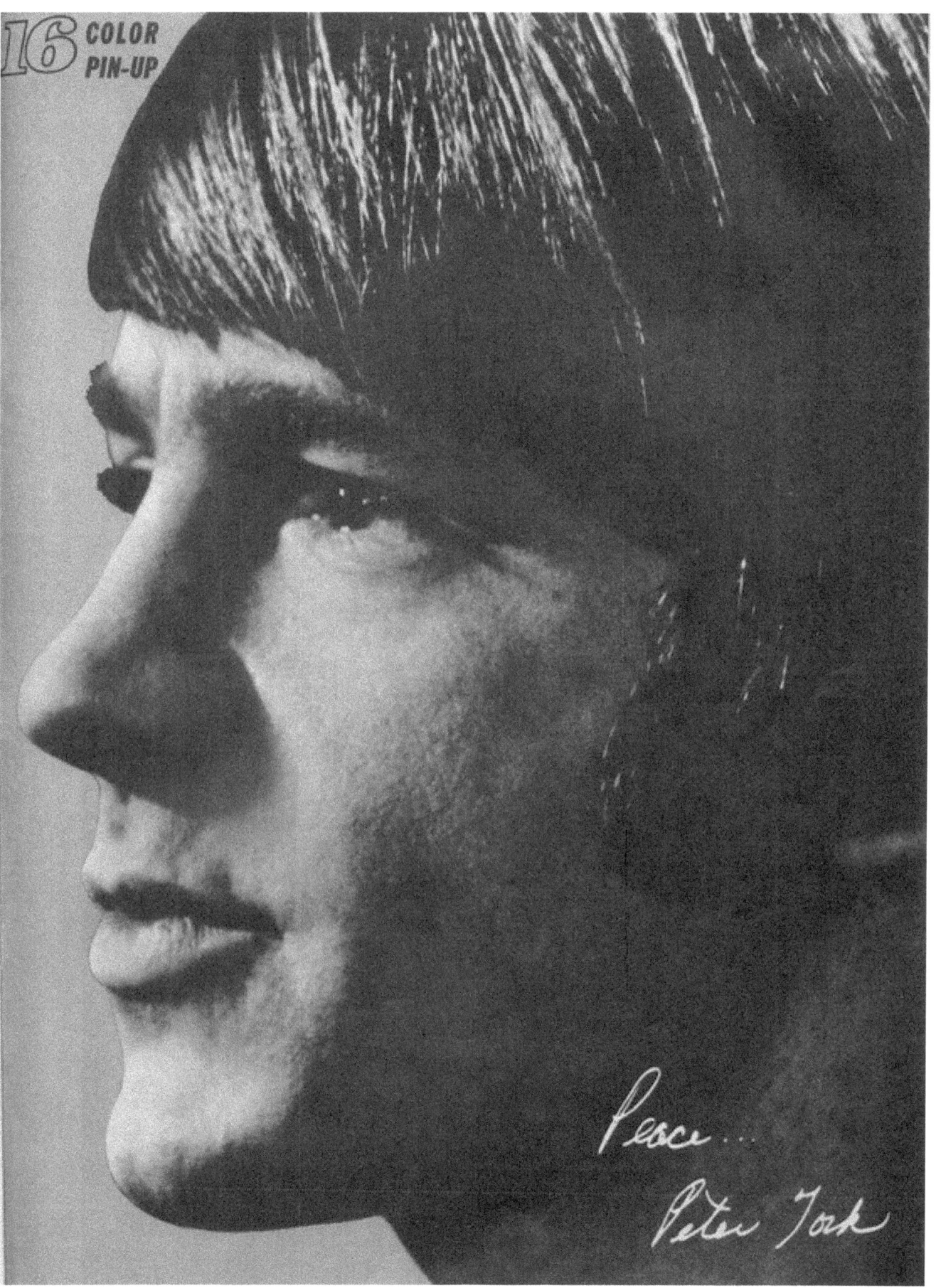

MONKEES ARCHIVES 1

MONKEES ARCHIVES 1

MONKEES ARCHIVES 1

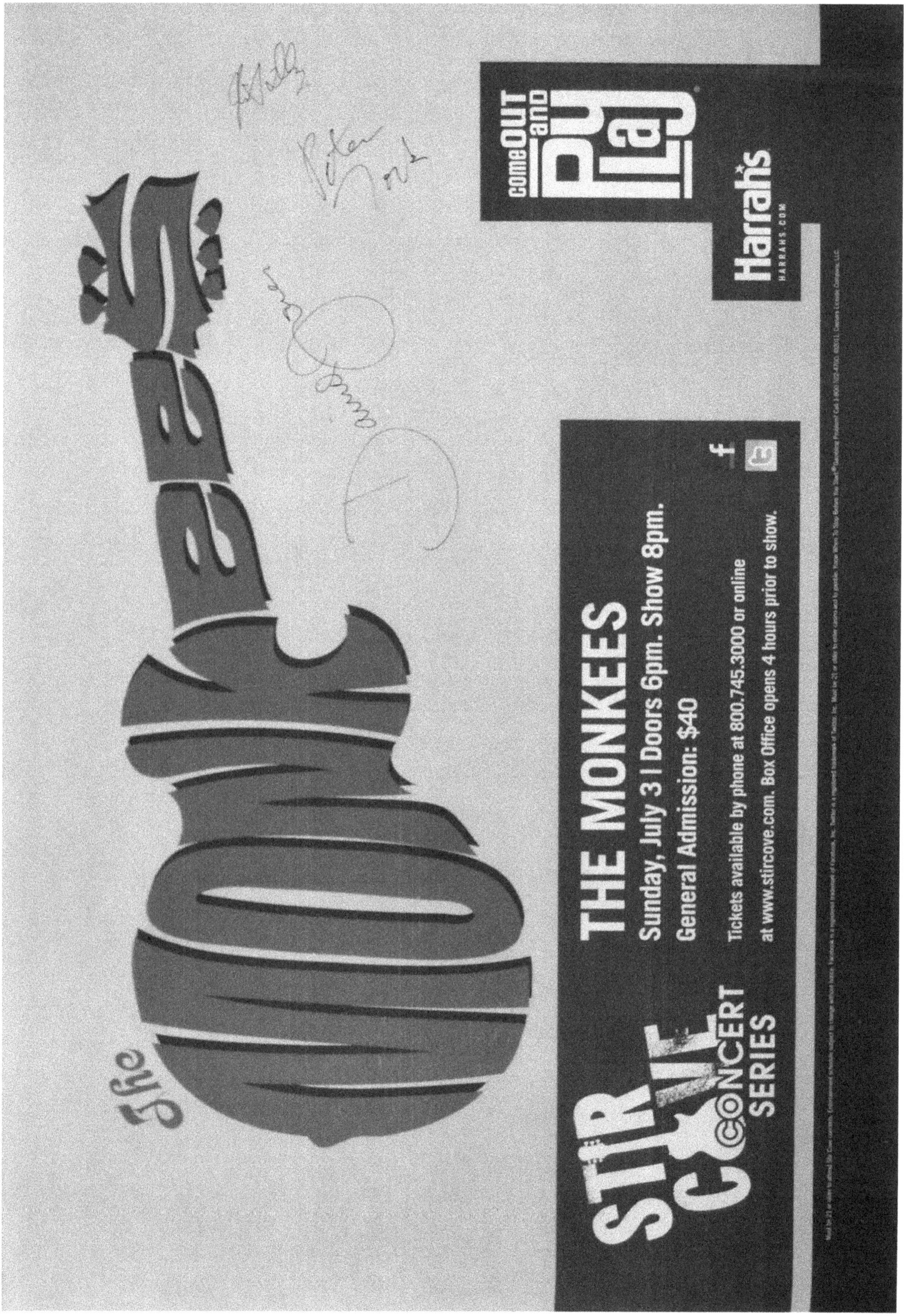

MONKEES ARCHIVES 1

THE MONKEES

Sunday, July 3 | Doors 6pm. Show 8pm.

General Admission: $40

Tickets available by phone at 800.745.3000 or online at www.stircove.com. Box Office opens 4 hours prior to show.

Stir Cove Concert Series

MONKEES ARCHIVES 1

MONKEES ARCHIVES 1

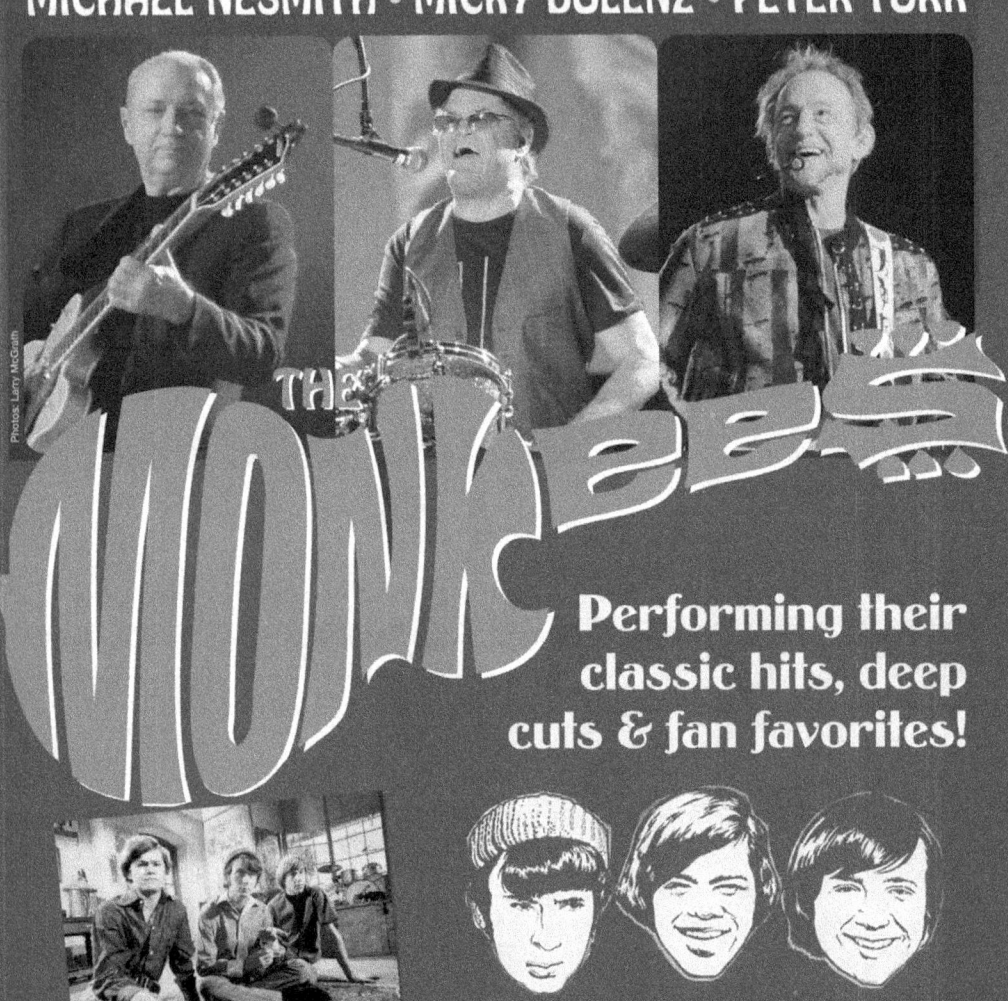

MONKEES ARCHIVES 1

MONKEES ARCHIVES 1

MONKEES ARCHIVES 1

MONKEES ARCHIVES 1

MONKEES ARCHIVES 1

MONKEE NEWS

OFFICIAL PUBLICATION OF THE MONKEES FAN CLUB • DECEMBER 1967

THE MONKEES take a moment from their busy filming schedule to look over the NEW Fan Club Booklet, now available to renewal memberships as well as to new members.

Hits Million Mark

The new Monkee album, "Pisces, Aquarius, Capricorn & Jones Ltd." has sold over one million copies. The new single "Daydream Believer" and "Goin' Down" has hit over 1½ million.

Only 1968 members eligible to order exclusive Monkee merchandise shown on pages 4 and 5. Be sure to renew your membership when you place your order!

NEW MONKEE MEMBERSHIP KIT AVAILABLE NOW

The time is now! The ALL NEW Monkees National Fan Club membership kit is now ready and available to all of you who renew your Fan Club memberships.

The new exciting book (each page perforated for easy framing) contains dozens of never-seen-before pictures, in both color and black and white. It is packed full of other surprises that will thrill every Monkee fan.

Of course, NEW members will also receive the kit, but as a current member of the National Fan Club, you are getting this advance announcement.

Renewal Due

The renewal dues are only $1.50 and here are just a few of the things you will receive in your NEW kit.

**Booklet packed full of new never-seen-before pictures.
**Your personal membership identification card.
**Official Monkee Pen
**Membership button
**Monkee school book cover

New Color Pin Up

The big news is the inclusion of the 4 large color pin ups in this year's NEW kit. The only people that will be able to get these pictures are fan club members.

So, The Time Is Now!

Fill out the membership form and mail with $1.50 today. Be one of the first in your school to have your NEW kit.

MONKEE FAN CLUB
BOX 88
LOS ANGELES, CALIFORNIA 90051

Enclosed is my check (or) money order for $1.50. Please enroll me as a 1968 member of the official Monkees Fan Club and send me the exciting ALL NEW Fan Club Kit.

NAME _____
STREET ADDRESS _____
CITY _____ STATE _____ ZIP _____
PHONE _____ AGE _____ CHAPTER NO. _____

MONKEE NEWS

Monkees Insist On Doing Own Stunts

When a multi-million dollar property, such as THE MONKEES, insist on doing all their own stunt work for their weekly television series, nerves get a bit tense with the production staff. But, Davy, Peter, Mike and Micky would have it no other way; and without guidelines or nets that are so often used under such circumstances.

One of the more precarious situations occurred in the recent filming of "Hitting the High Seas" when the situation took them aboard a three-masted sailing schooner about 15 miles out into the Pacific Ocean. Contending with choppy waters and a rolling ship, the four boys climbed the rigging, walked the plank and swung around the ship in Tarzan style. The only casualty was a touch of sea sickness . . . not with the Monkees, but with the production crew watching all the cavorting.

"The Wild Monkees" episode sees the boys in a motorcycle drag race, and of course the four stars did their own riding, much to the frustrations of the stunt riders that were hired for the show and had to stand by and watch.

Jumping from tree-to-tree in a celluloid jungle can get dangerous when so much depends on split-second timing and rendezvousing mid-air with a rope that is swung to them by a prop man. After watching them in the recent "Monkees Marooned" episode, one can understand Peter's retort to an interview question when asked if he spent any time working out in a gym . . . "who needs it?" he replied, "we get all the workout we need just doing the show!"

Actually, no one should really be surprised or startled at the fact that the Monkees insist on doing their own stunt work when they realize that complete individuality has always been their by-word. All four of the boys sincerely and seriously believe that they must perform in the mode that is expected of them by their fans; whether it be flying from tree-to-tree, hanging from a ship's mast or playing their own music for their record releases and TV show.

"Besides," notes Micky, "it's no worse than driving home on the Hollywood Freeway!"

DAVY, in a split-second maneuver, grabs a vine mid-air as it was swung to him by a prop man during the shooting of "Monkees Marooned."

Only 1968 members eligible to order exclusive Monkee merchandise shown on pages 4 and 5. Be sure to renew your membership when you place your order!

MICKY slips off his motorcycle during the race in "Wild Monkees." While stunt men were hired for this sequence, they stood by and were not used.

THEY FLY THROUGH THE AIR . . . Peter and Micky are seen high above the deck of the schooner used in the filming of the "Hitting the High Seas" episode.

MONKEE NEWS

This past summer, while on their concert tour, The Monkees filmed sequences for their tv series in Paris, Chicago and New York; all of which are being incorporated in future shows.

❧

... Tentative plans call for filming a feature-length movie in Japan, Australia and New Zealand this coming Spring. This filming will be scheduled along with an extensive concert tour of these countries.

❧

... Monkee fans continue to show their loyalty as evidenced by the 65,000 pieces of fan mail received each week.

❧

... Peter has decided to take Japanese lessons with an eye toward the up-coming visit to Japan. All the boys have already recorded promotion spots in Japanese with the help of a Berlitz language teacher.

❧

A hobby that started with Mike has now been taken on by all the boys—cars! Mike now owns a Buick Riviera, a Pontiac GTO, a Jeep, a truck and his two latest, a Cadillac limousine and a specially-built Mini-Cooper. The Mini was ordered in London during their Summer Concert Tour and is the most elaborate Mini ever made! Davy has a yellow GTO convertible and a black Cadillac. In a few weeks, he'll be receiving his new steel-grey Honda sports car. He's having it imported from Paris and since there are very few of them in this country, his Los Angeles fans can be pretty sure that when they see that car, Davy will be in the driver's seat. He's also having a custom-made racing car built, but all details on that are still a secret. A maroon GTO and a red, white and blue Volkswagen bus are currently occupying Micky's garage, but it looks like there will soon be another addition. Micky fell in love with the double-decker buses while in England, and has been trying to make arrangements to get one shipped to him in Hollywood. Meanwhile, he is busy building himself a gyro-copter. That's a single passenger helicopter like the one used in the James Bond movies. Peter is now alternating between his burgundy GTO, his maroon Mercedes-Benz sedan and his bright red MGB-GT. Now we're really sure that his favorite colors are in the red family...

The Monkees bought one more car, but this time it was for someone else. They bought Marilyn Schlossberg, their production assistant, a white MGB sports car for her birthday. It was quite a surprise and naturally this birthday turned out to be the most exciting she's ever had.

❧

Davy and Peter flew to New York on October 20 for the grand opening of Davy's new East Indian shop in Greenwich Village. The name of the shop is "Zilch" and is located at 217 Thompson Street. Throngs of fans have been busy buying up the groovy clothes and accessories and it sure looks like another successful venture for Davy Jones.

❧

Mike's wife, Phyllis, is expecting her second child in late December. Imagine having two children as marvelous as Christian!

❧

The new Monkee album, "Pisces, Aquarius, Capricorn & Jones Ltd." has three songs written or co-written by two of the Monkees. Mike wrote "Daily Nightly" and co-wrote "Don't Call on Me." Davy Jones and three other writers did "Hard to Believe," together. The new 45 single included "Goin' Down," with music by all four of the Monkees.

❧

... This season The Monkees television show can be seen in 39 countries, plus the United States. These include most of South America and Europe, plus Iran, Liberia, Hong Kong, Singapore and Malta, to name a few. There's no doubt that the group is now almost as popular in all four corners of the world as they are back home.

❧

MONKEE NEWS

PAGE 10

GIRLS! GIRLS! GIRLS! GIRLS! GIRLS! GIRLS!

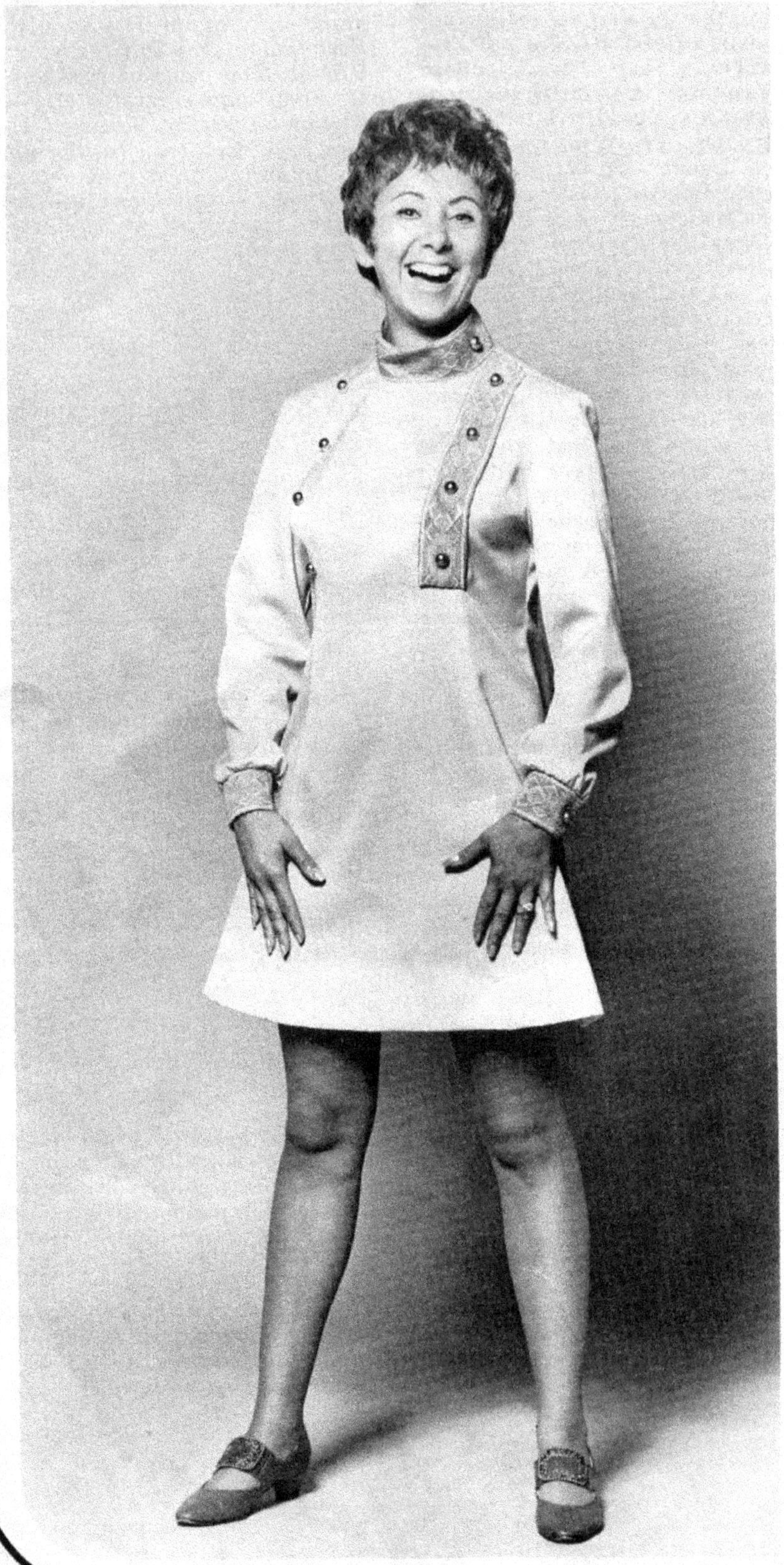

THIS DRESS IS AVAILABLE ONLY TO MEMBERS OF THE MONKEES OFFICIAL FAN CLUB.

BE THE ENVY OF EVERY GIRL IN SCHOOL

Only by mailing in the coupon can you get this specially-designed dress. It comes in three bright colors, BLUE, YELLOW or GREEN and has the exciting new Indian-inspired look. The braided collar and cuffs are individually matched for each color and the gently swinging skirt provides an ideal fit. Remember this dress is not sold in any retail store, so mail in your order immediately. $14.95

YELLOW—GREEN—BLUE
Sizes 3/4—5/6—7/8—9/10—11/12

Now you can have the most exclusive Monkee item ever made

$14.95

BE SURE TO WATCH THE MONKEES CHRISTMAS SHOW AND SEE YOUR DRESS ON TV

MONKEES ARCHIVES 1

♪ MONKEE NEWS ♪   PAGE U

Your Own Monkee Poster

This multi-color official poster comes in two sizes. The extra large size is 30x40 inches and sells for $2.00. The smaller size is 17x22 inches and is only $1.00. See the order blank on this page.

Brand New And A Blast!

Tell the world you are a Monkee fan with the authentic Monkee sweat shirt, showing pictures of each of the Monkees.

A lot of the groovy kids use the shirts to collect autographs of their fave people. A low, low $3.00. Three sizes to pick from, but don't forget the "in" kids wear them big.

Monkee Shades

Set off with a heavy mod golden chain, authentic Monkee shades are designed for real swinging fans. Cost is only a low $1.98.

Official Monkee Jewelry

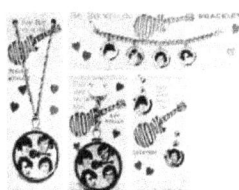

Hey! What great Christmas gifts. The best part is that each item is only $1.00.

The In Thing is Tatus

Really be with the in crowd by wearing a tatu of your favorite Monkee... or all four.

Each set contains individual photos of Davy, Micky, Mike and Peter — and autographed! $1.00 for the set.

In case Mom asks, they wash off, but not too easily.

MONKEES FAN CLUB
BOX 2
LOS ANGELES, CALIFORNIA 90051

Allow Four Weeks Delivery

I AM A 1968 MONKEE FAN CLUB MEMBER. PLEASE RUSH THE FOLLOWING MONKEE MERCHANDISE. ENCLOSED IS THE PROPER AMOUNT BY CHECK (OR) MONEY ORDER. ALL POSTAGE PREPAID.

ITEM			Quantity	Amount
EXCLUSIVE MONKEE DRESS ☐ YELLOW ☐ BLUE ☐ GREEN — SIZES ☐ ¾ ☐ ⅚ ☐ ⅞ ☐ ⁹⁄₁₀ ☐ ¹¹⁄₁₂				
JEWELRY Earrings ☐ Necklace ☐ Bracelet ☐ Key Chain ☐				
POSTER 30"x40" ☐ 17"x22" ☐				
TATU Package ☐				
SWEATSHIRT	Small ☐ White ☐	Med ☐ Blue ☐	Large ☐ Yellow ☐	
SUNGLASSES ☐				
		ADD 5% IN CALIFORNIA FOR STATE TAX		
			TOTAL	

NAME _____ AGE _____

STREET ADDRESS _____

CITY _____ STATE _____ ZIP _____

MONKEES ARCHIVES 1

♫ MONKEE NEWS ♫ PAGE 01

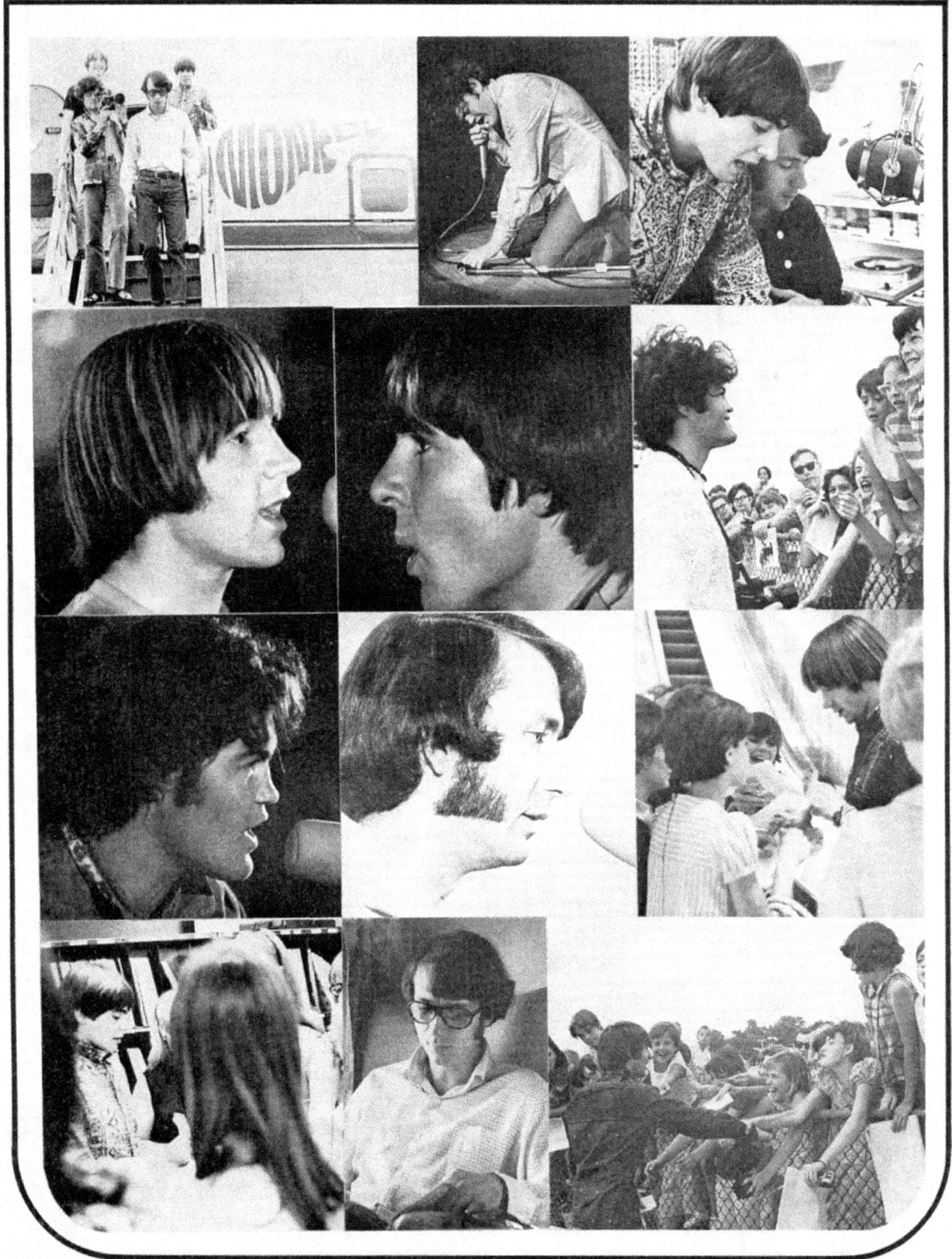

WELCOME TO THE monkee club

Dear Club Member:

We are delighted to welcome you to the official National Monkee Club. Davy, Mike, Micky and Peter are really great guys and I'm sure you're going to enjoy "meeting" them through their fan club. In the future you will be receiving notices and bulletins informing you of the up-coming events of The Monkees ... their television shows, records, and personal appearances.

If you're interested in forming a chapter of the National Monkee Club in your vicinity or school, all you have to do is have at least 12 people who are also members of the National Monkee Club. Each chapter elects its own officers - President, Vice-President, Secretary, Treasurer - and sends back the enclosed Chapter List filled out (together, of course, with the proper membership fees for all the new members). Please type or print the list clearly.

Naturally, you can belong to only one chapter - but get as many members as possible, because there will be a prize awarded to the largest chapter organized. AND each Monday night, your chapter will have a chance of receiving a phone call direct from your favorite Monkee.

I look forward to hearing from you soon - and so do Davy, Mike, Peter and Micky. And you'll be hearing from us again very shortly.

Sincerely yours,

Lynn Martin

Lynn Martin
President
National Monkee Club

MONKEES ARCHIVES 1

MONKEES ARCHIVES 1

MONKEES CLUB BRANCHES OPEN

WEST CALDWELL, N. J.—The first in a national chain of Monkees Clubs was opened here last Friday (27). Some 35 clubs will open in the next few months. Winners of talent contests in each club, which will be located in small cities for the most part, will play at other Monkees Clubs. Screen Gems, and Colgems, the Monkees recording label, will have first refusal on signing talent for recordings and publishing. Entertainment International, a subsidiary of Spectrum, Ltd., is handling licensing of the teen-age night clubs. The firm's address is 725 Park Avenue, East Orange, N. J.

DAVID JONES
The Artful Dodger

David Jones was born in Manchester, England and joined the cast of the original London production of *Oliver!* on May 7, 1962. Although his only previous stage assignment was the role of Michael in a touring version of *Peter Pan,* he had already enjoyed a considerably active career on radio and television. On the radio program, "There is a Happy Land," he had the longest part ever written for a teenager.

MONKEES ARCHIVES 1

MONKEES ARCHIVES 1

NEWSLETTER

HOLLYWOOD, CALIFORNIA   JULY, 1967

MICKY

Dear Monkee Club Member:

Here it is, your own private and confidential newsletter direct from The Monkees to the members of their only official national club.

Right now The Monkees are in Hollywood filming episodes for next season's television show. The network has already ordered enough programs to keep the show on the air until at least the middle of 1968, so Micky, Davy, Peter and Mike have a lot of work ahead of them!

At the end of June, the boys leave for a quick weekend of concerts in London, and then return to the United States for a personal appearance summer tour. The dates of the tour are listed below along with the radio station sponsoring the concert. Listen to the station for all the information on how to get your tickets. If The Monkees are coming to a city near you, don't miss the concert. The boys are on stage for almost an hour, play and sing more than a dozen songs, along with a background of film, giant pictures, and even psychedelic lights. It's the most amazing concert you'll ever see!

July 8 - Jacksonville, Fla. (WAPE)
July 9 - Miami Beach, Fla. (WQAM)
July 11 - Charlotte, N.C. (WAYS)
July 12 - Greensboro, N.C. (WCOG)
July 14 - New York City (WMCA)
July 15 - New York City (WMCA)
July 16 - New York City (WMCA)
July 20 - Buffalo, N.Y. (WKBW)
July 21 - Baltimore, Md. (WCAO)
July 22 - Boston, Mass. (WBZ)
July 23 - Phila., Pa. (WFIL)
July 27 - Rochester, N.Y. (WBBF)
July 28 - Cinn., Ohio (WSAI)
July 29 - Detroit, Mich. (WKNR)
July 30 - Chicago, Ill. (WLS)
Aug. 2 - Milwaukee, Wis. (WRIT)
Aug. 4 - St. Paul, Minn. (KDWB)
Aug. 5 - St. Louis, Mo. (KXOK)
Aug. 6 - Des Moines, Iowa (KIOA)
Aug. 9 - Dallas, Texas (KVIL)
Aug. 10 - Houston, Texas (KNUZ)
Aug. 11 - Shreveport, La. (KEEL)
Aug. 12 - Mobile, Ala. (KABB)
Aug. 17 - Memphis, Tenn. (WMPS)
Aug. 18 - Tulsa, Okla. (KAKC)
Aug. 19 - Denver, Colo. (KIMN)
Aug. 25 - Seattle, Wash. (KJR)
Aug. 26 - Portland, Ore. (KISN)
Aug. 27 - Spokanne, Wash. (NJRB)

In every city The Monkees appear, they will be meeting personally with members of the local Chapter of the Monkee Club, and taking some more lucky members to the concert as The Monkees' personal guests. Letters to the chapter presidents with all the details have already been mailed, and The Monkees are looking forward to meeting as many of their club members as possible.

For those cities that The Monkees can't visit personally on this tour, the four boys will be making personal phone calls to select chapter meetings. Among the clubs that have already received personal phone calls from The Monkees are:

Chapter #128 - Arabi, La.
Chapter #139 - Buffalo, N.Y.
Chapter #124 - Memphis, Tenn.
Chapter #110 - Honolulu, Hawaii

There have been a lot of silly rumors about Davy being drafted. As a British citizen living permanently in the United States, David

DAVY

does have to register with his local draft board. The board is now reviewing his draft status, but it will be many months before David is called for even a physical examination, so it's much too soon to worry about him going into the army.

The Monkees' new album "HEADQUARTERS" is now in record stores everywhere. Davy, Micky, Peter and Mike spent almost a whole month at RCA's recording studios in Hollywood playing and singing the 14 songs on the album, even writing a good number of them. You can help The Monkees by asking your favorite disc jockey and radio stations to feature songs from the album, and by playing the record for your friends.

Songs from the album will also be heard on The Monkees' summer

(continued on back)

MIKE

PETER

MONKEES ARCHIVES 1

MONKEES ARCHIVES 1

all about... *Peter Tork*

Peter's real name is Peter Thorkelson and he was raised in Connecticut where his father is Associate Professor of Economics at the University of Connecticut.

Although Peter spent 3 years at Carleton College in Minnesota preparing for a teaching career, his first love has always been music. In fact, so much so that he plays guitar, ukelele, 5-string banjo, bass, piano and French horn—and plays them all well!

After deciding to devote all of his time to his favorite subject, Peter left college and began his musical career in N.Y.C.'s Greenwich Village, performing as singer-musician in various hide-aways that always welcomed new music. When money became something of a necessity, he toured with the Phoenix Singers as accompanist, but The Village was his "scene" until a little over a year ago when he hit Los Angeles.

He had been on the West Coast only two months and was playing at the Golden Bear in Huntington Beach when a buddy of his told him about the audition ad. Peter went back to Hollywood, auditioned and was quickly chosen as one of the four Monkees.

He was born in Washington, D.C., February 13; he is 5'10", weighs 152 pounds and has brown hair and eyes. His one and only hobby is quite obvious—Music!

MONKEES ARCHIVES 1

all about... *David Jones*

David Jones was born in Manchester, England, on December 30, and left home—with the full blessing of his dad—at the age of 14½. He headed for England's Newmarket Racetrack as a jockey trainee...and soon became a very good jockey.

Between riding jobs, he discovered life among England's young set and explored the places—such as The Cellar—from which the great new musical sounds were coming.

His first acting job was playing a juvenile delinquent in a radio drama on the BBC. This led to a steady job on a daytime series reading the "Morning Story" for six months. All during this time, he continued at the racetrack. Then came his winning the role of the Artful Dodger in the theatrical production of "Oliver", which won him many admiring fans. His next show was "Pickwick", which won him special acclaim from the American critics.

Davy has lived in the United States five years now, but makes frequent visits to England to see his family.

He has brown hair and brown eyes and his favorite hobbies are horseback riding, swimming, and fishing.

MONKEES ARCHIVES 1

all about... *Micky Dolenz*

Micky, a native of Los Angeles, is not a newcomer to the entertainment field. He is the son of the late actor, George Dolenz, and began his own acting career at the age of ten as the star of the long-running TV series, "Circus Boy".

After attending public schools in the San Fernando Valley, Micky entered Valley College and then L. A. Technical Trade, pursuing a possible architectural career. But music won out, and he left to become lead singer with a group called The Missing Links. During his stay with The Links, he also made appearances acting in TV series such as "Peyton Place" and "Mr. Novak."

Then came the audition ad for "The Monkees" and his talents as a singer-comic won him a starring role.

Micky is 6' tall and very lean and athletic. He has brown hair and eyes and was born on March 8. Micky's hobbies, with girls always listed first, include just about anything from water skiing to electronics.

MONKEES ARCHIVES 1

all about... Mike Nesmith

Mike is a self-taught guitar player who couldn't play a note until he was about 19 years old. And since he couldn't read music, he composed his own material—some of which can now be heard both in "The Monkees" TV series and on their record album.

He was born in Dallas, Texas, and graduated from San Antonio College, where his musical talents took over. After college and a stay in the Air Force he moved to L.A. and teamed with bass player John London and together they toured Southern California. They eventually added a drummer to the group, but the draft board quickly broke up the promising trio.

Mike's next stop was Ledbetter's, a folk club in L.A., where he developed his own following by singing and playing his own material. A year ago, his friends urged him to attend a "Madness Audition" for a new TV series. Dressed in Levis and wearing his now-famous green wool hat, he was quickly recognized as a born "Monkee" and got the part.

Mike was born December 30, is 6'2", weighs 155 pounds and has dark brown hair and eyes. All his hobbies include things that move fast—flying, motorcycling, racing cars.

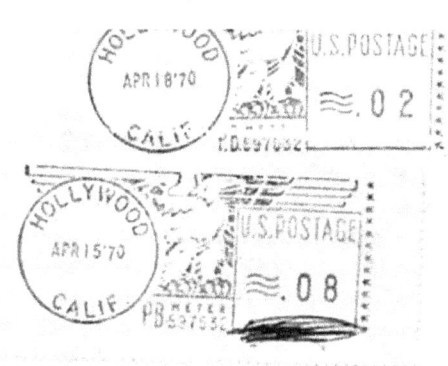

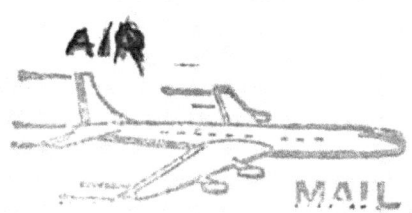

A SPECIAL NOTE TO MONKEE FAN CLUB MEMBERS:

Micky and David asked that I drop you a note and tell you about the new MONKEES record . . . OH MY, OH MY. It was just released and we hope you will be hearing it on your favorite radio station.

You can help make their new record a big hit. Telephone, or write your favorite disc jockey and ask them to play the record. **If they don't, keep calling.**

In case your local record store hasn't stocked OH MY, OH MY yet they can order it by referring to COLGEMS Record No. 66-5011 distributed by RCA.

Let's all pitch in and help the new MONKEES record become a big hit.

Joan Davis
MONKEES NATIONAL FAN CLUB

MONKEES ARCHIVES 1

MONKEES GO WILD WITH FAVE STARS!!

The madcap Monkees each picked a popular personality of their choice and personally interviewed them on a segment of **The Monkees** show. Here is Mike Nesmith (left) with his choice—Frank Zappa of The Mothers Of Invention.

Mike and Frank again. They changed clothing—Frank put on Mike's famous wool hat and Mike put on a "fright wig," moustache and beard. Here you see them as themselves again.

Frank performed the song **Mother People** and Mike directed a make-believe orchestra. They topped off their get-together by breaking up and completely dismantling this car.

Micky's guest was Elektra Records' recording artist Tim Buckley. Here is Tim strumming a tasty guitar accompaniment while Micky hums a tune.

Another shot of Tim singing **Song Of The Siren**. Micky has been a fan of Tim's for quite some time and he had a ball interviewing and performing with him.

Davy chose Charlie Small, a jazz piano player and singer whom he has long admired. Charlie performed **A Girl Named Love**. (Peter's choice—Pete Seeger—was unable to appear.)

MONKEES ARCHIVES 1

MONKEES ARCHIVES 1

WIN

©1967, Raybert Productions, Inc.

a Guest Role on "THE MONKEES" NBC-TV SHOW
and this PONTIAC GTO for Dad!

1968 Pontiac GTO Convertible with 360 H.P. engine, 4-speed transmission with Hurst shifter, radio, heavy-duty suspension, dual exhausts, tachometer, rally gauge instruments, mag-type wheels, wide-oval tires, and other exciting sports car features!

THE "MONKEEMOBILE" YOU SEE ON THE TV SHOW IS A SPECIAL GTO!

1,516 PRIZES GIVEN AWAY IN
Kellogg's TV SCREEN-STAKES

GRAND PRIZE

A Guest Role on "The Monkees" TV Show and this Pontiac GTO Convertible!

KIDS! Picture yourself as the Grand Prize Winner of an all-expense-paid, 7-day trip to Hollywood to appear on "The Monkees" NBC-TV Show. (Mom or Dad can go along with all expenses paid, too!) You also win the Pontiac GTO Convertible described above.

15 MORE BIG PRIZES —
Pontiac GTO Hardtops

The next 15 prize winners get one of these dashing 1968 GTO Hardtops. Each has all the exciting features of the GTO Convertible above.

PLUS — 1,500 CONSOLATION PRIZES

 "Monkees" Record Albums

◀ COMPLETE RULES ON SIDE OF PACKAGE

Nothing to buy...easy to enter, here's how:

1. Fill in the Official Entry Form on the back of this package, or use the Free Entry Form available at your grocer's; or print your name and address and the words "KELLOGG'S RICE KRISPIES AND RAISIN BRAN" in plain block letters on a 3" x 5" sheet of paper.
2. Enter as often as you wish, but you must mail each entry in a separate envelope to the address given below.
3. The 1,516 "TV Screen-stakes" prize winners will be determined by a random drawing (see Rule 5 on side of package).

USE ENTRY FORM BELOW OR FREE ENTRY FORMS AVAILABLE ON STORE PADS AT YOUR GROCER'S!

Official Kellogg's "TV Screen-stakes" Entry Form
MAIL TO: KELLOGG'S TV SCREEN-STAKES
BOX 756, HINSDALE, ILLINOIS 60523

Please enter me in Kellogg's Rice Krispies and Raisin Bran "TV Screen-stakes".

PRINT PLAINLY - PLEASE INCLUDE ZIP CODE

NAME ....

ADDRESS ....

CITY ....

STATE .... ZIP CODE ....
All entries must be postmarked before midnight, May 5, 1968, and received by midnight, May 15, 1968. NO PURCHASE REQUIRED.

MONKEES ARCHIVES 1

MONKEES ARCHIVES 1

The Monkees

遂に来

マイク・ネスミス

デーヴィー・ジョーンズ

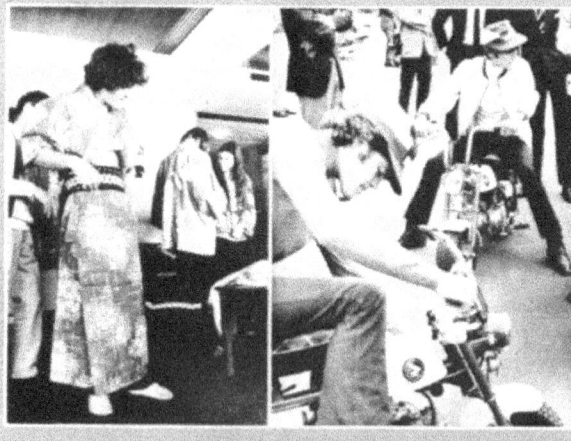

右二面は演奏合間にくつろぐ一行
右上は羽田空港で飛行機のタラップに立った四人

何度か来日を伝えられながら、ファンの期待を裏切ってきたザ・モンキーズが、遂に日本公演のため、9月30日午後1時7分羽田着のカンタス航空機で来日した。ミッキー・ドレンツ、ピーター・トーク、デーヴィー・ジョーンズ、マイク・ネスミスの順でタラップに現われたモンキーズは、約1000人の警官による万全の警備のうちに宿舎の東京・赤坂のホテル・ニュー・ジャパンに直行した。

記者会見は10月2日午後1時から、ホテルの大宴会場で行なわれた。ザ・ビートルズやS・コネリーに匹敵する大規模なものだった。

☆　☆　☆　☆　☆

待ちに待った舞台演奏は10月3日東京・武道館ての公演からスタ

MONKEES ARCHIVES 1

WHAT IS A MONKEE FAN?

Find out if you qualify in the fastest growing club in the world!

A Monkee fan is someone who's in love: in love with life and with four great guys who give life meaning. The Monkees know how to live, truly and well, and Monkee fans look to them to show the way.

A Monkee fan loves laughter and good times and knows that the Monkees have found ways to put these things into everyday life. No matter what the situation, a Monkee fan knows that if the Monkees suddenly appeared, everything would be super-groovy again. The Monkees would find some way to take the un-grooviness out and put bounce and laughter back in.

MONKEES CARE

A Monkee fan knows beyond any doubt that the Monkees really care about her. She isn't just "another fan" to 'any one of them, she's someone they want very much to know and talk to and groove with. Lots of times there just isn't any way to accomplish this, but Monkee fans know that if there was a way, the Monkees would be there.

A Monkee fan dreams constantly of the day she'll finally meet them. She knows that it's got to happen someday—they meet so many, many fans and her turn just has to come up. So she dreams and plans and gets ready for that day because she knows that it will be the most important day in her life.

A Monkee fan fills her walls with pictures and her bookcases with scrapbooks of the greatest four alive. She reads everything about them that she can trust, knowing that when people get famous there are always other people who want to put them down. She realizes that there will always be rumors, false stories and all sorts of un-groovy things going around and the only thing a fan can do is have faith in the guys she loves and not believe the stories.

Instead, she thinks about the great things she knows the Monkees are. She learns from them for she knows that they have worked very hard to get where they are and that on the way they have learned many things. She's able to trust the things the Monkees tell her because she knows they're true.

A Monkee fan spends a half-hour every week in heaven. When the Monkees are on, nothing interferes. All her thoughts, her emotions, everything she has is directed toward the four people she sees on the TV screen. She knows that they feel how intensely she loves them because sometimes she'll be watching one of them on the screen and he'll get a gleam in his eye and she'll know that he's understood.

MONKEES ARCHIVES 1

Mike, like the other Monkees, flipped out over photography during the tour! On stage, off stage, backstage! Anywhere and everywhere, the guys would pull out their Instamatics and take pics of each other and everyone else within camera range!

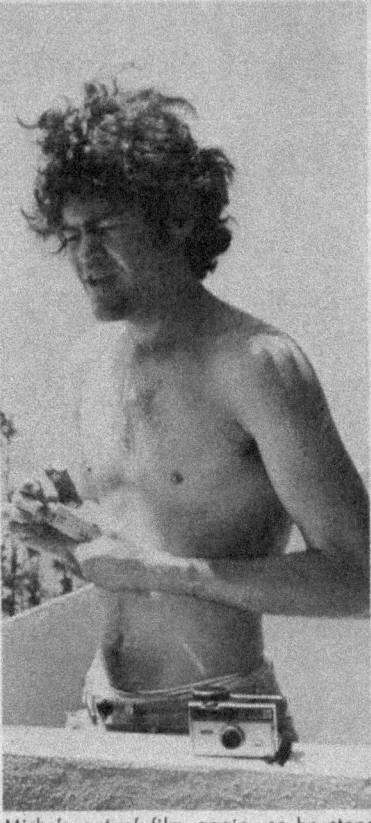

Micky's out of film again, so he steps out on the balcony to flick in a new roll.

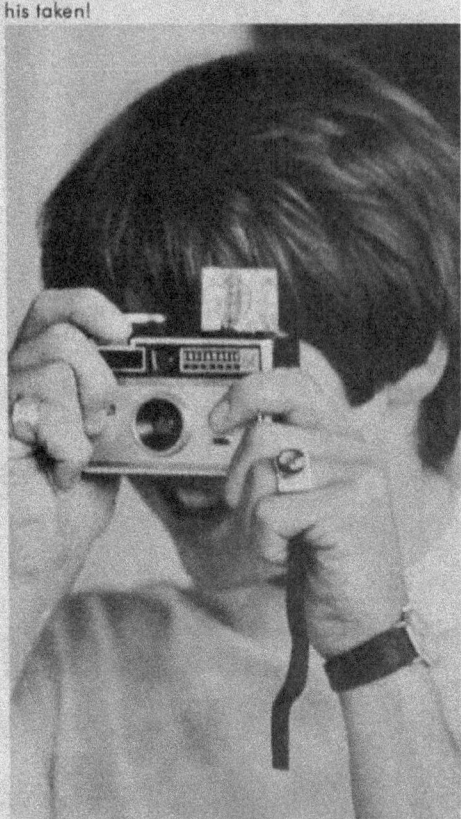

There must be millions of pics of Davy 'round the world! Now he switches sides, and is taking a pic, instead of having his taken!

THE MONKEES FLICK OUT!

Cameras in hand, Micky and Davy compare notes in their hotel hall.

"Is the lens long enough, Peter?" "I guess so. I'm standing in Miami and I can see the Empire State Building!"

MONKEES ARCHIVES 1

Bright Spot in TV Season
That's The Monkees, Youth Knows

By JOAN CROSBY

NEW YORK—(NEA)—They are four high-spirited young men with thick thatches of hair who were brought together by a television producer and told, "You are The Monkees."

They are a bright spot in a television season that leaves much to be desired, snapping off vocal and sight gags on their imaginative NBC-TV series based in style, with no apology, on the two movies made by The Beatles.

The Monkees, who even sound like The Beatles on their Colgems album, Meet the Monkees, and on their hit single "Last Train to Clarksville," were patterned after the British group. Again, no apology is needed.

The boys, who have caught on with teen-agers, adults and several important television critics (there seems no middle ground with The Monkees; you either love them or can't stand them), are Davey Jones, the only English one in the group and a show-stealer on Broadway when he played The Artful Dodger in the musical, "Oliver"; Micky Dolenz who, as Mickey Braddock was a child star on television in the Frontier Circus series; and newcomers Mike Nesmith and Peter Tork.

"I wish I had a drink of water," Davey Jones said, sitting at a lunch table in the group's Plaza Hotel suite (the staid hotel had not been told it was housing a—horrors—switched-on singing group; reservations were made for "four actors").

"Are you thirsty?" asked Mike Nesmith.

"No, I want to see if my neck leaks," Jones replied.

An interview with them is not a question and answer session. It's more an attempt to preserve sanity and dignity while laughing and trying to write down what they are saying.

"Did you know we're breaking up on Tuesday?" Nesmith asked, "did you know I'm really small and cute and Davey is really very tall?" (Davey is 5 feet 3 and the other boys are tall.)

"Do you know, while we're sitting her talking, I'm getting mad because I got kicked out of Disneyland because I have long hair?" Dolenz asked.

"Our show is going to go higher and higher in humor," Jones said. "We are trying to take Peyton Place's audience away."

"Mike wore a hat as a trademark," Tork said, "but as soon as he had to wear it, he got tired of it. So he began wearing a bowler in public."

"I'm having the original hat bronzed," Nesmith said.

"We're doing a story about a kid who is tossed out of Disney land because he has long hair," Dolenz said.

"Micky has a monorail mind," Tork said.

"Tell your readers to picket Disneyland," Jones said.

"Don't pick it, it will never heal," from Tork.

Peter picked up his guitar and began to sing. "Peter sings at the drop of a hat," Davey said, dropping Mike's green wool hat. They all joined in for a pretty chorus. Then Micky, his young face looking very pathetic, said, "When they wouldn't let me in Disneyland, they didn't ask me any questions or talk to me or even try to find out what kind of a person I am. They just looked at my long hair, knocked the gun out of my hand and told me to get lost."

★ ★ ★

THE LATEST—The Monkees (left to right) are Mike Nesmith, Micky Dolenz, Peter Tork and Davey Jones.

MONKEES ARCHIVES 1

EXTRA! THE NEW

ALL THE NEWS THAT'S FIT TO

Vol. 1, No. 1 Special To Freakout, U.S.A!

MICKY'S DREAM GIRL

Micky smiles for our fotog.

Micky Dolenz will expect a lot from his dream girl–because he will give a lot in return. First of all, the gal who captures Micky's heart must have a tremendous sense of humor. She must be able to take a practical joke and be ready to hand some out.

This dream girl will have to be ready for anything, like getting dunked in a pool, getting a pie in her face, riding a bike, car, plane, anything that Micky may decide he digs at the particular moment.

Secondly, she must never loose her cool. His chick was to be real hip. She must never hit that panicsville button, even if she has to fake her way through a situation. So, chicks, that means she must also be ready for adventure any time of the day or night.

He loves the names Debbie and Dawn, but if you have a name like Beatrice, Hermine, Zelda or Stella, Micky could learn to dig that, too. After all, a guy doesn't fall in love with a name, he flips for the girl.

If you wanted to be his dream girl you would have to dig Pontiac GTO cars. Like, well, they're the only thing on the road as far as Micky is concerned. They move, they have neat lines, and the motor really purrs, baby.

Micky loves photography as a hobby. He will go to endless efforts getting the right angle or shot, so don't be surprised if he asked you to hang from a cliff or dangle from the Empire State Building (just as long as you don't make a splash on Broadway).

Now we get to the clothes scene. Micky loves casual clothes as you can see from all his photos, but when the occasion calls for it, he steps out looking like he's advertising for **Esquire** mag or something. He wears a tux when he has to and he has some really cool suits. He prefers the double breasted ones.

The dream girl in his life will have to like the outdoors and be pretty good at swimming and certain sports. Whenever he is not shooting and has time, you'll find this cool fellow soaking up some ultra violet rays on the beach or lying around a pool listening to music and reading. He has learned how to relax. His chick will have to do the same.

Micky loves his family. His girl would have to get along with his sisters or she could never be happy. They are all very close and there is a tremendous bond between them. A girl would have to understand this and not be jealous of Micky's family. Some chicks make the fatal mistake of thinking a guy is all theirs, you know, private property, hands off, he belongs to me. Oh, this is endsville for some girls and they can't see it. Fellows have friends and family, too. You've got to learn to accept this facet of their life.

Micky is looking for a girl who is idealistic and with high moral standards. He likes gals who are affectionate and all that jazz, but he feels marriage is a sacred thing. His standards are very high and he expects the same thing from the gal with whom he walks down the aisle and you'd better believe that or you're out of the picture for good. If you're not the clean cut type you might as well bug out right away. He wants a real nice gal, she can't be gross and she can't have a trashmouth. He won't put up with vulgarity; she can't be a dorf either, in other words, he wants a well rounded and adjusted person like himself. He won't settle for less and you can't blame him.

So there you have it, always keep your cool, dig movies, sports, cars, photography, outdoors, indoors, television, relaxation and all that jazz. It turns out to be a pretty nice combination.

We have declared open hunting season on Micky Dolenz and may the best gal win. He is clever and moves fast. He doesn't let any grass grow under his feet, so you'll have to use real subtle tactics. Good luck, chicks.

MIKE'S TEEN MARRIAGE FORMULA

"For in its innermost depths, youth is lonelier than old age."

I can still remember the morning I received a letter from Phyllis with that beautiful quotation from Anne Frank's Diary written across the bottom of the page as a P.S. after the regular "Love."

I suppose, that that was the moment when I decided that I was going to ask her to marry me.

Sure, it was a stupid decision! By what your parents, and ours, call adult standards, we were stupid, reckless kids–risking our entire futures because of an adolescent crush.

But parents have a way of forgetting how stupid, reckless and lonely they were when they were our age....

And how bright the future can look, if you have the courage to face it!

That "if you have the courage to face it" is the Big Guy. Without it, you're nowhere!

Let's face facts. Marriage is not the easiest gig in the world to play–particularly when you're young. It's not at all like dating or going steady. It means that you are ready to take responsibility for your life, plus somebody else's, seven days a week. And that's not easy!

But it **can** be done!

If you have the courage to say: "Yes. We are going to get up-tight with each other. Like, we're people, right? So, now what do we do? How do we make it work, for ourselves, and for each other?"

If you have the courage to ask yourself those kinds of questions, and try to answer them, you don't need my or Phyllis' formula for a successful teen marriage. You've already found it.

Pass it on.

— Mike Nesmith

Mike studies the playback of a recording, seeing if it sounds right.

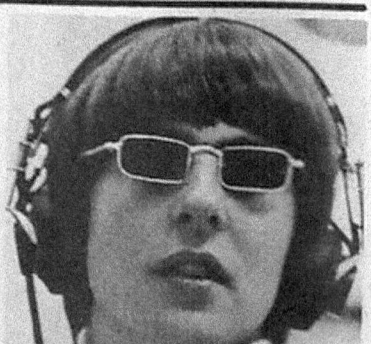

Davy and his famous Monkee Shades.

MONKEES ARCHIVES 1

MONKEY TIMES
PRINT ABOUT MONKEY BUSINESS

World's Best Monkey News

THE BAD SCENE DAVY TRIES TO FORGET

For David Thomas Jones, better known to his adoring fans as Davy Jones, life wasn't always a success story. Davy was born in Manchester, England, in 1946, right after World War II had ended.

There was a time in Davy's life where he was a really mixed up boy. He left home for two long years. Now he is trying to forget he ever did this terrible thing to his parents and three sisters, Lynda, Hazel and Beryl. Sometimes when you're a teen you think you're so absolutely right, then later on, after much heartache and torment, you find out you were all wrong.

This is what happened to Davy Jones back in England some years ago, but Davy had the courage to admit he made a mistake and come back home. His parents, being understanding, forgave him, as did his sisters. The only person who didn't forgive Davy was Davy himself. It is just now, after a year of success, that he can really think about it and not get the creeps.

Davy is only 5'3" tall. For a long time he was self-conscious of this. He thought that, to be a real he-man, you must be tall and rugged. While he was out in the world on his own he found out the truth. It is what is inside that counts, not just what the world sees. He has also found out that a person all wrapped up in just himself makes a pretty small package.

All the other Monkees are tall, but now it doesn't bother Davy. From the very beginning of their relationship, Peter, Mike and Micky took Davy for what he was; a real groovy fellow, who is a lot of fun. Not only that, he can be relied upon when a guy really needs him. This is what counts.

Dave was once a jockey. He still has dreams about riding horses and winning races. The career of a jockey is a short-lived one, to be sure. There is a tremendous amount of competition, not to mention the danger involved. Davy got his fill of this and went on to different vocations, until one day, he realized he wanted to be an actor. It was something that just had to be.

Davy read a long time ago that famous quote of J. Sherma's, **The best prophet of** the future is the past. The past with all its turmoil and heartaches has been a good teacher for Davy. He has learned many things from his teenage mistakes. Davy is not afraid to **admit** these mistakes either.

It has taken him a long while to forget the past–it was a real bad scene. Now he has emerged a cool guy who loves clothes, plays golf, lifts weights, collects coins, rides horses at his leisure for fun, digs blondes and sports cars, digs motorcycles. We could go on and on.

The truth is, that some teens make a mess of their youth and go on to make a bigger mess of their adult life as well. They don't have the courage or the stamina to straighten themselves out and admit that maybe they were wrong, that their parents were only trying to help. This is the true test of a real man, when he can admit that he did make some mistakes in his younger life.

Davy shares a pad with Micky Dolenz now. His phone bill is high, we mean really high because of his calls to England to his folks. He hasn't forgotten them, in fact, he is making up for the two years he lost with them. Years that taught him so many things.

Davy loves to date girls, and he is particularly partial to blondes but digs all girls. During his years away from home he found out to his dismay that not all birds are nice, some just after money, prestige. It was really a jolt to his ego. There are many girls who just make the scene for what they can get. Now Davy can spot these gals without any trouble. His heart was broken more than once when he found out a chick was just going out with him because he was in the limelight.

Working with Peter, Mike and Micky have taught him a great deal about life, too. These fellows are on the ball and they don't miss a trick. They stick together like glue; which is an unbeatable combination, to say the least.

They help and teach one another, but no one will ever make Davy forget those two years away from home. They are buried in his heart as a constant reminder and he will not make the same mistakes again.

GOSSIP CORNER

Gossip is always interesting to read but when it's about THE MONKEES, wow! There's no need to go into the oft-repeated nonsense that they don't play their own instruments or sing all of their songs. This has been proven false–and you can rest assured that they do everything that they are supposed to do.

Reports that MICKY DOLENZ still suffers pain from a dreaded bone disease contracted when he was much younger are true–to a point. The pain is not generally very intense but it is there nevertheless. And Micky walks with an ever-so-slight limp. It's something that probably will be with him until the day he dies. No cure is known, and it's ironic that the disease has been officially arrested for many years but the damage it did to his bone structure causes the pain just mentioned.

What in the world is Micky doing? Talk about getting carried away!

PETER TORK'S "God is love" motto (discussed in a story elsewhere in this newspaper) is not a phony affectation but a sincere, deeply-felt philosophy. Peter is the third most-popular member of THE MONKEES and it's interesting to note that many more of his fans are in the older class–quite a few adults, as a matter of fact–while MICKY, MIKE NESMITH and DAVY draw in predominantly younger fans.

And it is refreshing to see a group that doesn't disclaim awareness of spiritual values and religious belief. PETER is quite religious, and MICKY is fairly so as is DAVY. MIKE is somewhat less religious than the others but certainly not an atheist and none of them would ever consider making remarks such as JOHN LENNON'S quotes. That's one reason why THE MONKEES are so popular. Their fans seem to sense how warm and honest and decent they are.

Nothing can, for a change, be overstated respective to MICKY'S devotion to his late

MONKEES ARCHIVES 1

STOP PRESS...STOP PRESS...STOP

FLYING MONKEE

Micky has been very busy recently putting together the helicopter that he bought a few weeks ago. It's a Gyrocopter, exactly the same as the one-man helicopter that James Bond used in "You only Live Twice", and he's assembling it in the living room of his home.

Any day now, the other residents of Laurel Canyon are expecting to see a flying Monkee zooming around the hills.

PETER MOVING SOON

As all of you know very well, Peter has never been particularly interested in material things. He is much more concerned with people and his music and has lived in the same house, a couple of miles from the studios, ever since the Monkees hit the headlines. But, finally, he's accepted that he must move to a bigger house otherwise all his instruments, recording equipment and so on, will overflow into the street. So right now he's looking around for a larger place.

HOUSE AND RANCH FOR DAVY

Davy has just bought a small English type house in the Hollywood hills, near Sunset Boulevard.

It's a two storey building with two bedrooms and a bathroom upstairs and a living room, dining room, kitchen, bathroom and study downstairs.

Davy tells us that there's a fabulous view right across Los Angeles from any of the windows on one side of the house.

New Single delayed

When the master tape of the new Monkees single did not arrive in this country in time for its reported release on October 13, frantic telephone calls and cables revealed that the Monkees had still not given the O.K. to both sides of their new record.

They did finally agree the titles on October 24 and Screen Gems in this country received a cable from America confirming that the titles would be "Daydream Believer" and "Going Down". A release date was immediately fixed for mid-November.

How do you like Micky's new hair style?

Hilary, one of the girls who was with Micky in Hyde Park during the Monkees summer visit to this country, has sent us this picture of the two of them which was taken by a friend.

MONKEES ARCHIVES 1

Come to Mike's House

THE NESMITH HOUSE is situated high in the Hollywood Hills and is considered one of the most luxurious homes in Hollywood. It was designed by one of the leading architects in the U.S., who lived there himself before Mike and Phyllis bought the home for their own. Since they moved in, they have completely remodeled and redecorated the house to give it warmth and **really** make it "their" home. Even though Mike's house is secluded, and is enclosed by bushes, a wall and an electric gate with closed circuit TV — so that all visitors can be screened — **you** have a special invitation to come along and visit the Nesmiths at home.

Inside the house, we find Mike deep in thought—resting on the sofa in his living room, next to a beautiful stone fireplace.

This is the organ, located on the other side of the living room. Here Mike composes most of his tunes.

Mike stands next to his stereo center, where he listens to the playbacks. The stereo center is one of Mike's pride and joys.

MONKEES ARCHIVES 1

The game room includes a pin-ball machine, which supplies lots of fun for Mike's friends. Mike is seated at the Nesmiths' 12-foot dining table.

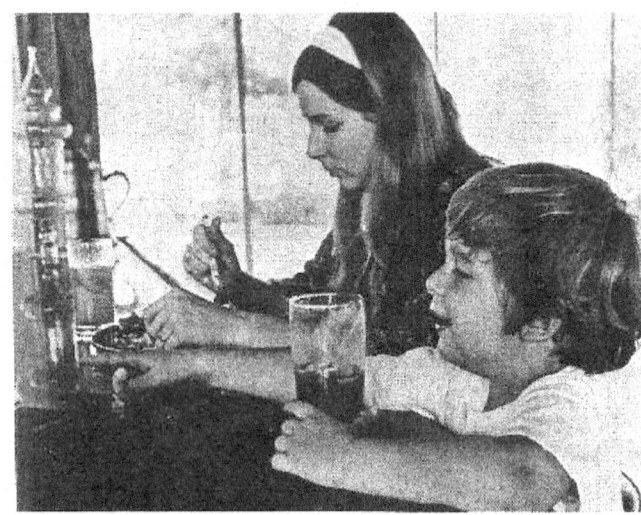

Here are Phyllis and Christian, enjoying a snack at the soda fountain which was built into the den.

Christian shows you the garden and the magnificent views from every side of the Nesmiths' home. But he's more interested in introducing you to someone else—

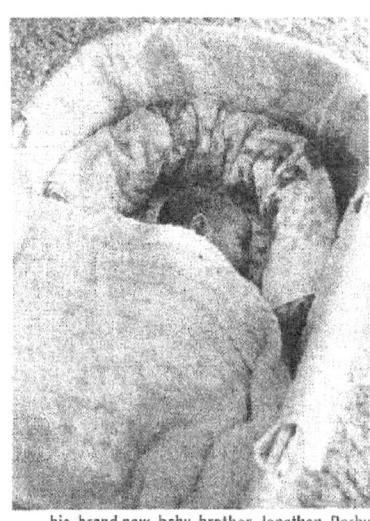

—his brand-new baby brother Jonathan Darby, who spends most of his time sleeping.

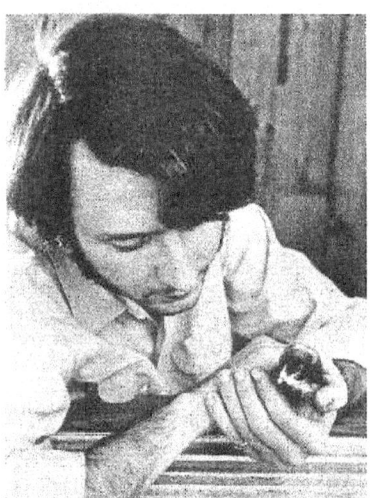

What have we here—**another** addition to the Nesmith family?! Mike shows you a Texas Prairie Chicken which was given to him by a fan, and explains that these birds are very, very rare.

Mike's 1967 Cadillac has one-way black windows and a stereo. However, Christian prefers his own form of transportation — his convertible tricycle!

Mike's fabulous swimming pool is both **inside** and **outside** the house! You merely swim under the glass partition if you want some sun and water sports!

Mike isn't just reading — he's seated in one of the two "stereo" chairs in his den. The chair has two speakers, and Mike listens to the music while relaxing.

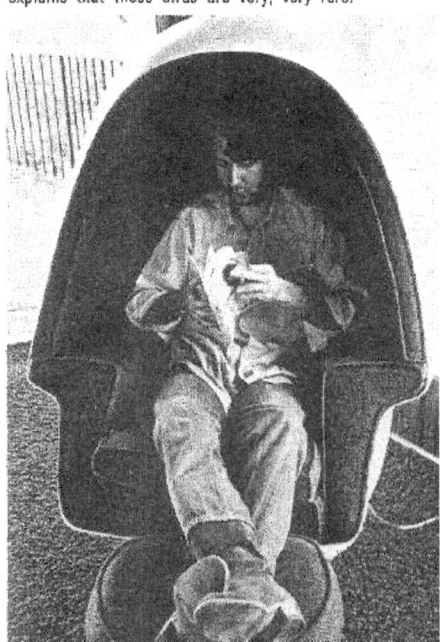

MONKEES ARCHIVES 1

MY LIFE with the MONKEES

by David Price

That Wild Canadian Weekend!

Everything was very exciting because the Monkees were on their way to Winnipeg for the first concert they were to give in Canada. The flight there was pretty calm and nothing much happened until we touched down. It was freezing cold in Winnipeg (17 degrees) and there were tons of kids standing on one of the large airport decks waiting for the Monkees in all that cold and snow. They had been standing for hours just to catch a glimpse of the Monkees.

The plane landed on the field and as the limousine pulled up next to the plane, the kids started waving. The guys got off and started waving back and then got in the limousine to go to the hotel where they could more or less relax.

Mike

We were staying at the Fort Garry Hotel on the sixth floor and, naturally, there was nothing to do. Mike put on his old sweatshirt and went walking all over the hotel. Well, the hotel staff took one look at long-haired Mike in this sweatshirt and went into a dither. They just didn't know what to think of this strange looking creature. Not that Mike looked strange or anything, because he just couldn't, but the people in Winnipeg are very conservative and not used to people with long hair in weird looking sweatshirts walking around the lobby of one of their best hotels. Another thing the long hair did was totally confuse all the fans and everyone else. If you had long hair your chances of being attacked for an autograph were excellent. A lot of us had a terrible time trying to explain that we weren't the Monkees. It finally got to the point where we would run the other way whenever we saw an eager face with a pencil and a piece of paper in its hand.

Sold Out

The performance at Winnipeg was an afternoon show and naturally I had to be there early to help set things up. At eight o'clock in the morning the tickets for the concert went on sale and at 11 a.m., three hours later, the entire stadium was sold out! The capacity of that place is 12,000 and there were 12,500 people who had tickets. The management had sold an extra 500 tickets for standing room only, so the audience was composed of 12,500 stamping, screaming, frantic people, and to see them from the stage was just unbelievable.

There had been lots of tension on the trip, because of a prediction that had been made. Someone had predicted that the Monkees were going to be killed while performing in Canada and so to avoid that, Mike asked me, and his friend Charlie Rockett and Phyllis' brother, Bruce

GOING PLACES with Davy Jones, Mike and Peter is really a gas for me. Below you see Peter and Mike on the plane on the way to Canada. This weekend was one of the most hectic but most fun we've had on these Monkee tours. Every morning when I wake up I can't help but wonder how long everything will keep being great!

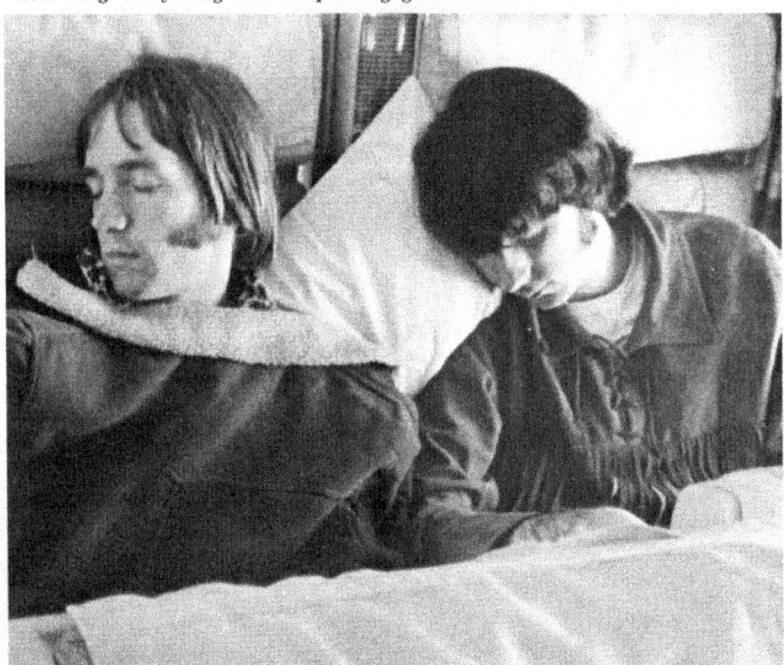

MONKEES ARCHIVES 1

Barbour, to make sure that any packages that landed on stage were thrown off again because one of them might contain a bomb. Now, none of us, and I want to make that very clear, none of us really believe in predictions of doom, but we all wanted to be on the safe side so everyone in the Monkee party was extra careful and great pains were taken to see that they were completely protected. Naturally the prediction didn't come true, but just the same everyone was very tight about the whole thing.

The Show

The Monkees arrived at the auditorium about half an hour before the concert and were slipped back stage. The show is an unbelievable thing. As you look at the stage you see one phony amplifier on either side of the stage and just before the Monkees come on, the lights dim twice. The third time, the lights go out and the Monkees race onstage and hide in the amplifiers.

The audience knew that something was happening but they didn't know just what it was and they were absolutely frantic. Then, over the loud speaker blasted their theme song, "Hey, Hey We're The Monkees" and the lights went up. Suddenly, right in the middle of the song, The Monkees came crashing out of the phony amps and ran toward their instruments. They picked them up and started playing "Last Train To Clarksville". Davy was playing the electric key board base on stage during this concert and used it in their second song, "Kind Of Girl I Could Love". The guys are gradually adding new songs to their concerts and the next song they did was one from their third album, "Sunny Girlfriend".

Solos By All

Then the lights dimmed and all the guys left the stage. The audience howled for more and then Peter came back onstage with a banjo in his hand and played folk songs for the audience. He sang his heart out for them and for his family and parents who were in Winnipeg to see him. Peter was very happy this trip because for the first time, he got to do a stand-up solo without having to play an instrument and that solo was "Auntie Grizelda". He thought that was an outasite thing to let him do. He really dug it and so did the audience.

After Peter was through, he left the stage and Mike came out on stage backed by the "Candy Store Prophets". He sang Bo Diddley for the crowd and they really went wild. Mike would stand there very quietly just singing a line and then all of a sudden he would just go wild with the harmonica and marracas. He danced around the stage like nothing I've

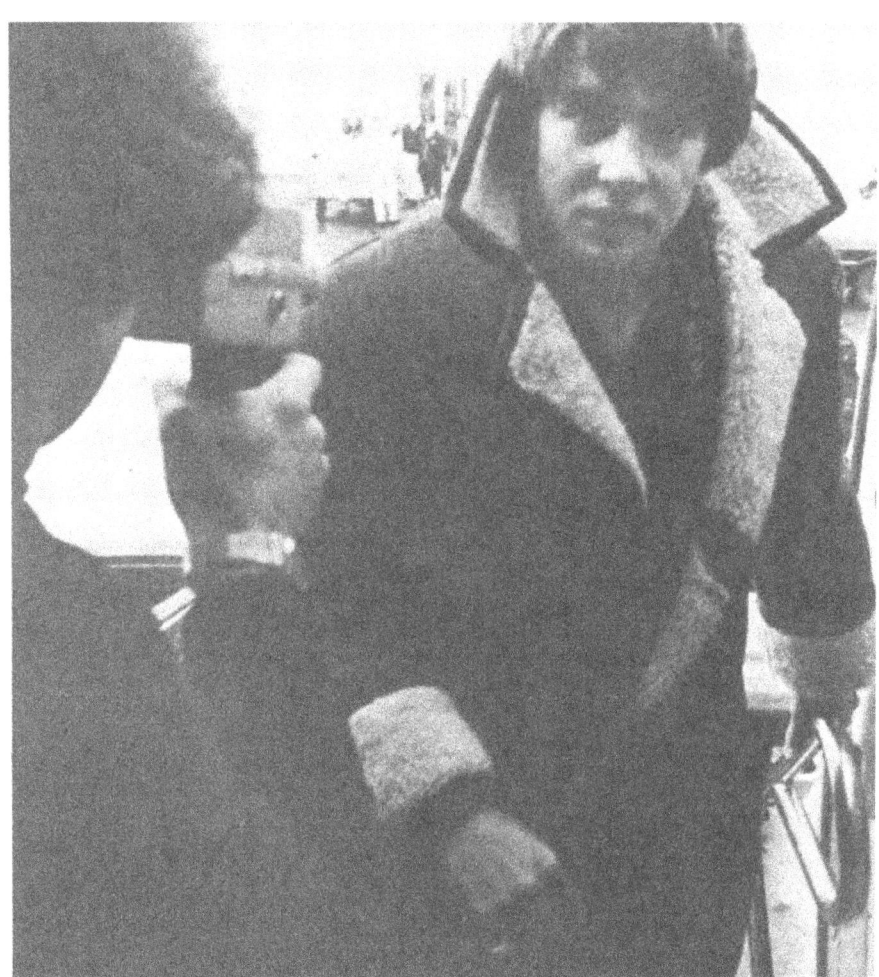

DAVY'S probably the most eager traveler. He loves to fly and see different parts of the world. Of course he's been doing it since he was a very small child. Micky, below, loves to perform and each time he gets center stage, his performance is better. If the Monkees ever break up, Micky will be a star on his own.

MONKEES ARCHIVES 1

(Continued)

ever seen before and the audience was right there with him going absolutely crazy.

"Lookout Here Comes Tomorrow" brought Davy Jones on stage and the audience went mad. They really dug him. The Canadian audiences were fantastic!

When Davy was through, it was Micky's turn and on he came, with his hair combed straight back. He stepped up to the microphone, took it in his hand and as the rhythm and blues pulse of a James Brown song hit the audience—so did Micky. He was just unbelievable! He really tore that place up. Toward the end of the song the strobe lights were flashing on him and he went down on his knees and was sobbing into the microphone with his head a few inches from the stage floor, when Mike came walking out on stage with Micky's coat and put it over his shoulders. He helped Micky up and walked him to the exit. Just as they got there, Micky suddenly broke free and ran back to the microphone. Actually, he slid on one knee for about the last ten feet and then he started right in again and really wailed that song. Then Mike came back and tried to get him off stage again and once more Micky broke free and ran back to the microphone. This time instead of sliding on his knees he did a complete flip in the air and the audience went screaming wild!! As soon as the show was over, the Monkees tore back to the hotel.

Mr. Stewardess

Later we caught a plane to Toronto. We left Winnipeg in the middle of a blizzard and everyone was very uneasy—so naturally, Mike did his best to put everyone at ease. The Stewardess was giving a speech about safety precautions on a plane and how the crew was there to make the flight as comfortable as possible for everyone. Mike stood up in the middle of this whole speech and went through her whole routine. He demonstrated the oxygen mask and the way he did it and the voice he used were priceless.

After he was through showing everyone how to wear safety belts and how to use the mask and what to do in case of a crash—dive out of the plane head first—he calmly went down the aisle asking everyone if they preferred coffee, tea or milk. The whole routine completely cracked everybody up.

Cards and Noisemakers

A massive card game got going shortly after this routine and great fortunes were won and lost. Naturally, Davy won a bunch of fortunes and everyone else started trying to figure out how to get out of paying him.

Suddenly someone had an idea and started playing their noise maker. I guess he figured that if he played loud enough he wouldn't hear Davy when he tried to collect his massive fortune. The reason we all had noisemakers on that plane is because it was a Monkee Rule that if you didn't have a noise maker of some kind like a penny whistle or a hummazoo you couldn't get on the plane, so everyone had a noisemaker. We all started playing the noisemaking games and we played them all the way to Toronto which annoyed the pilot no end. Some of us played marches and Peter's group played Beatle songs, while Mike's group competed with the Stone songs. Mike also sat there and let loose with an imitation of a jet crashing or an auto race. Micky slept and with all that noise I really don't know how he did it. We had a ball while Davy tried to be heard so he could collect his fortunes from the card game. Unfortunately he didn't have any luck because we couldn't hear him and we were all broke.

The Landing

When we landed there were thousands of kids all over and we made a mad dash for the limousines and tore off to the hotel—the King Edward. There were thousands of kids standing around below and we were on the eighth floor. Every once in awhile one of the guys would go over to the window and wave and the sound you'd hear would be enough to rattle the building.

Over the Edge

Finally Mike got bored and decided to call CHUM radio. He got a disc jockey on the phone and all the guys yakked it up for awhile and talked to all the people over the air. Then Mike said, "We have something you've just got to hear". So, the disc jockey got his tape recorder going and all four of the guys went over to the window while I held the phone. When they got to the window, Mike, Peter and Micky picked Davy up and swung him out the window. He was hanging on by his feet. The crowd went crazy and I'd swear you could hear that mob 500 miles away. It was ear shattering and Davy didn't help much either. He was yelling the loudest at Mike and the rest of them. "Don't you dare drop me! Be careful" and generally pleading that they hold on tight because he didn't really "feel like dropping in to see the mob from eight stories up, fellows". Finally the guys pulled Davy back in and they talked to the disc jockey some more and then hung up.

"Come On Up"

Mike seemed to have a thing for that window because he went walking back over to it, turned to us and

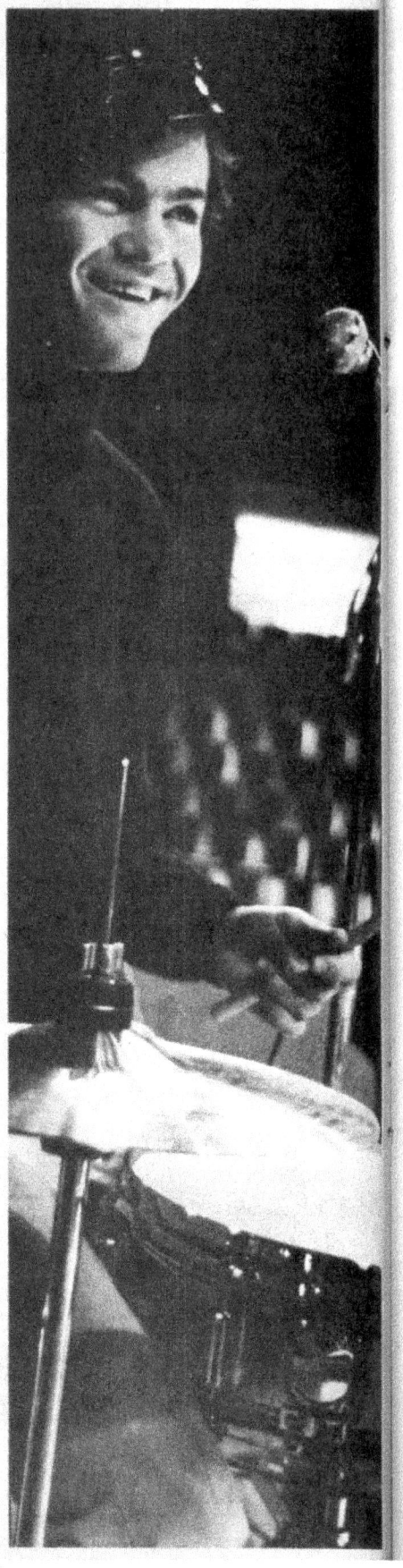

MONKEES ARCHIVES 1

smiled and we **knew** something was really going to let loose. He stood at the window, leaned out, looked very quietly at the crowd, and then yelled with accompanying arm movements, "Come On Up!" Pandemonium broke loose and so did 500 kids —right through the police lines. You can bet that entire scene was total bedlam!!

The Mountie Hat

The next morning everyone was served a huge meal and we all sat around and gabbed about nothing until it was time to leave for the auditorium. On the way to the show, Phyllis' brother, Bruce, managed to talk a Mountie out of his hat. It was one of those three tiered jobs, all fur, with a great big red band around it. Bruce gave it to Micky to add to his collection of police hats and Micky thought that was an outasite thing for Bruce to do. He just loves that groovy hat.

Missing Banjo

When we got to the auditorium, Bruce and I found that Peter's banjo was missing and so we had to find a replacement and quick. Fortunately, Ric Klein came up with one and so the show was saved. The crowd was just totally unbelievable and 23 people were hurt after falling off a wall into a barbed wire fence. We were still uptight about that prediction for the Monkees, so Mike issued orders again that anyone who tried to get on the stage should be removed as fast as possible. A couple of people tried to get on the stage but they were removed very quickly and the show went without incident.

Back Home

Later that evening we all left for the airport to catch our flight back to Los Angeles. The Monkees took the limousine. The rest of us were in a truck playing our noise makers. The kids must have thought that we had the Monkees with us—especially when they heard the noisemakers. Anyway they all tore after us—tons of them racing with the truck. What really got us was one kid who must have raced with the truck for about two miles along the runway.

The Great Pillow Fight

Once aboard the plane everyone tried to relax. Suddenly someone hit Davy with a pillow and Davy let loose! He started throwing pillows like a mad man and everyone got into it—even Mike. Mike of course wasn't throwing any pillows — he had more important things to do like planning strategy. This consisted of finding two loose seat belts and waylaying anyone who came down the aisle by handcuffing them to the nearest seat with the seat belts. As he handcuffed them he casually informed them that—"You are now under arrest. A Mountie always gets his man." By this time the "Great Pillow Fight" was in full swing and the entire plane was involved, stewardesses and all. It was pure bedlam. Someone got a brilliant idea and wet some of the pillows down which made them a lot heavier and wow—did that ever hurt. Those little white fluffy pillows became heavy solid four ton bricks. About that time we all decided to call it quits and a card game began—again with Davy winning great fortunes and the rest of us losing.

The rest of the flight was peaceful and when we landed everyone agreed that it was a wildly fantastic tour and that the audiences were outasite. They all really dug the Canadian audiences and are looking forward to another tour there in the future. In the meantime they'll be busy filming their show, cutting an album and touring other parts of the world. Naturally I'll do my best to cover all of these events for you in future issues of Tiger Beat and The Monkee Spec so be watching for them soon.

MONKEES ARCHIVES 1

"WITH THE MONKEES AT HOLLYWOOD BOWL"

BY LYNNE RANDELL

IF YOU READ the latest *16 Spec*, you shared some of the excitement I felt the first time I appeared in a concert with the Monkees (their concert in Wichita, Kan.). But I guess nothing will be as unforgettable to me as doing the world-famous Hollywood Bowl with them! First off, 17,500 kids showed up that night, breaking the attendance record for the Bowl! The opening acts were the Sundowners, Ike & Tina Turner and then me (backed up by the Sundowners).

When I showed up at the Bowl for rehearsal, I nearly dropped dead. It looked like the biggest thing in the whole world. The grooviest part of rehearsal, of course, was watching the Monkees prepare for the big show. They rehearsed like mad for ages — in the studio, in rented halls and, finally, in the Bowl itself. I don't have to tell you how conscientious they are, for you can see *that* in any performance Micky, Mike, Peter and Davy give. At 8 o'clock on the big night things started right on time. When Bobby Trip, a KHJ "Boss Jock," introduced me — and very nicely too, thanks, sir — my heart was beating like a big bass drum, but the Sundowners and the audience were so great that I soon forgot my stage fright and really had a ball.

However, the *real* ball came during the second half of the show, when the Monkees dashed on stage in maroon velvet, double-breasted suits with bell-bottom pants, white shirts and patent leather boots. There was so much screaming and excitement that you could hardly hear the music. When giant pictures of the Monkees were played against a huge screen on the stage, the audience went completely wild and I stood in the wings jumping up and down and screaming right along with them. For their solo numbers, Peter wore a white sweater with tight white slacks; Mike wore a gorgeous white double-breasted suit and a shirt trimmed with white lace; Davy wore a stunning tuxedo with a dress shirt and no tie; and Micky wore a bright paisley shirt with red hipsters.

The wildest thing that happened all night came at the end of Micky's "James Brown imitation." As he finished his ". . . one more time!" frenzy for the third time, Micky suddenly leaped into the air and landed with an enormous splash in the fountain that separates the audience from the stage at the Bowl! The lights went off — and in split seconds he had jumped up and was changing backstage for the grand finale. The Monkees wore pin-striped pants and velvet Monkee shirts, and finished off a perfect evening by singing *Shades Of Gray* while beautiful waving colored lights drifted across the screen above them.

After the show, there was a special very private party for the Monkees and their friends. I was honored to be invited. I sat like a person in a dream watching Mike (with Phyllis), Davy, Peter and Micky greet such guests as Sally Field, Keith Allison, David Winters, David Pearl, Gloria Stavers, Tad Diltz and all the Monkee-folk from Screen Gems. The clincher came when I was told that evening by Steve Blauner that I was going to be signed to the entire Monkee Stateside tour. Wow, am I lucky! So stay tuned to *16* for more Monkee news from me as I share with you the fun and excitement of my new life in the fabulous world of Micky, Mike, Peter and Davy.

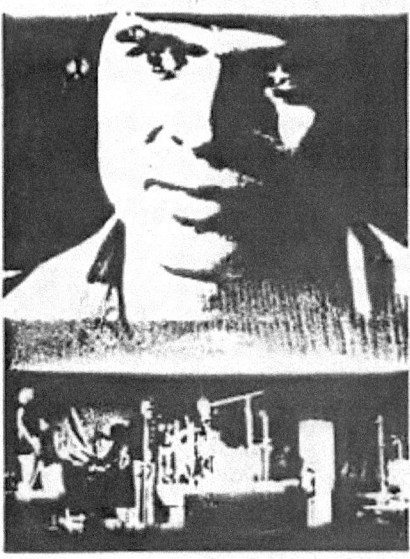
Davy in the sky with diamonds!

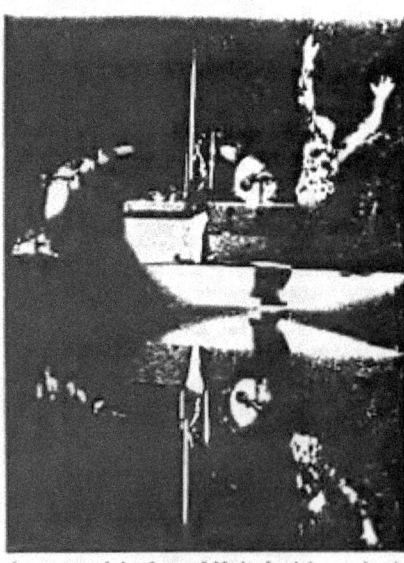
A second before Micky's big splash!

MONKEES ARCHIVES 1

WE MET THE MONKEES IN HAWAII!

BY COLLEEN SAKAI AND EILEEN UCHIMA

HAVE YOU EVER lost your head in a cloud, a lovely, puffy, pink and white cloud as soft and sweet as a misty dream? Well, it happened to us! Both of us lost our heads in just this way when the Monkees came to Hawaii — and we haven't recovered them yet!

Our names, as you've doubtless already noted, are Colleen Sakai and Eileen Uchima, and we are students at University High School in Honolulu. On the day before Davy, Micky, Peter and Mike made their scheduled appearance at the Honolulu International Center Arena as guest stars of the *Miss K-POI Pageant*, we not only met all four boys but actually interviewed them! Needless to say, it was an experience neither of us will ever forget. All of the Monkees are adorable — yet each is so different from the others. When you read what the boys said in answer to our questions, you'll see just what we mean:

What do you think of Hawaii? And what do you like best about Hawaii?
Davy: I love it. I like it all.
Peter: I loved the drive I took up to Tantalus. And I like the mixing of the races. This is really the melting pot of the world.
Mike: I like it a lot — the whole island.
Micky: I've been here before and I liked it.
If you had a wish, what would you wish for?
Peter: More wishes.
Davy: To live in Hawaii.
Have you tried surfing here yet?
Davy: I've been surfing all morning. It's great!
Peter: I'm scared of surfing.
Davy: I'm going to teach you how to surf before we leave here.
Peter *(preening)*: I can't answer that. Ask Davy — he'll tell you.
(Davy gives Peter a sneer.)
Which one of you is the cutest?
Micky: *I'm* the cutest. Ask the others if I'm not.
Davy, Peter and Mike *(in a chorus)*: Whaaa — ?
Describe yourself, Peter.
Peter: I'm sure of myself. I know what I can do.
Teasingly: You mean you're conceited?
Peter: No! Certainly not!
Peter, describe Micky.
Peter: Big chin, little nose, happy smile — and he's *skinny!!*
Micky, describe Peter.
Micky: Big nose — and he's UGLY!! *(They laugh).*
Micky, a magazine (not 16 Magazine) reported that you don't like girls who laugh at your jokes. Is this true?
Micky: Whaa-tt?? I was misquoted. I don't like girls who laugh *a lot.*
What do you think of your fans?
Peter: If it weren't for them, we wouldn't be here.
Mike: We love them — one and all.
Do you like fans who throw things at you?
Mike: I like it when they throw flowers —
Davy: And I'like it when they throw money! *(He laughs and the others join in.)*
What do you think of kids who try to get to see you backstage?
Davy: If they can, it's swell.
What do you think of girls who go to buy their tickets six or more hours before the show opens? Would you do it?
Micky: It's a gas.
Davy: I would.
Mike: It's swell. I would do it if it was for a show I wanted to see.

That's all the questions and answers we have space for, but we have given you at least a sample of the fun we had interviewing the Monkees — and the fun *they* had in return!

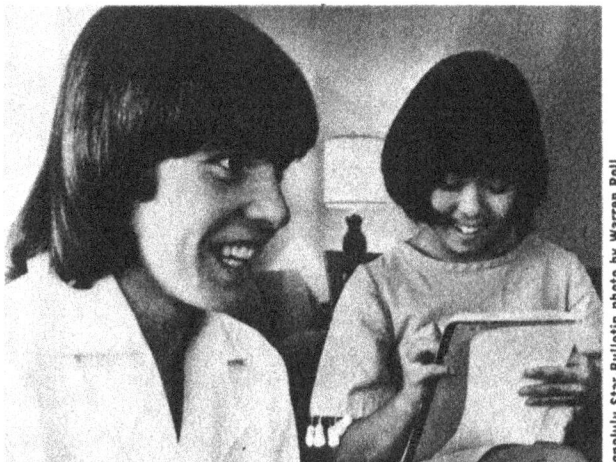
Davy and Eileen.

Colleen, Peter and Micky.

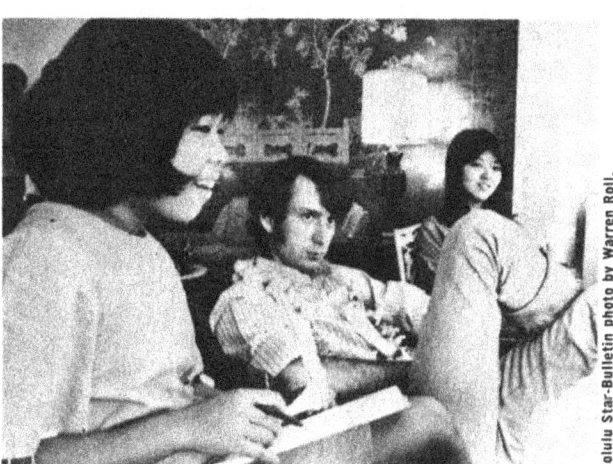
Eileen, Mike and Colleen.

UP-TO-DATE WITH

MONKEES

Talia, Davy & Linda

SAJ

LEN

THE MONKEES' on-again-off-again "break up" is *off again*, it seems. Davy and Micky have *definitely* decided to remain Monkees *forever!* Though both of them *will* pursue separate careers as actors, they will continue to record together and do concerts and live appearances together.

Davy—when he, Linda and their daughter Talia were in London during December and January—was offered his own TV spec in England plus a six-month run in a musical comedy there, and Davy is deciding whether to resume his acting-singing-Monkee career in the states—*now* or a few months hence. Of course, his first move on returning to the States will be to visit his groovy store Zilch at 217 Thompson Street in New York City. He will check up on Zilch's progress and also spend some time with his "New York family"—the Neals and their son Jeff.

While Davy was in England, Micky was busy cutting record "tracks"—which means the music was recorded and Micky's part of the singing was recorded, leaving nothing more to do but have Davy's voice inserted. Just to keep his acting talents sharp, Micky took the leading role in the summer stock presentation of the play *Remains To Be Seen* at the Pheasant Run Playhouse in St. Charles, Illinois. In the play, Micky played an unemployed drummer!

Both Micky and Davy continue to film and record Kool Aid commercials, and Micky has been using his spare time to write a radio serial for eventual syndication. It's a comedy drama with "regulars" —and Micky's will be one of the voices you hear, natch!

MONKEES' NEW TV SHOW?!

But the best news is yet to come! First off, Davy and Micky will be co-hosts on the first of a series of "mini specs" (30-minute specials) which are now under consideration by the major networks. What's more, a special script for a proposed *new* TV series has just been finished by Micky himself—and guess who it will star? The Monkees!! That means Micky and Davy may soon be back on national TV in a regular series!

Micky and Samantha are still grooving on that "good, old married life," doting on their beautiful daughter Ami and doing a whizbang business at their boutique. If you'd like a *free* mail order catalog from Sammy and Micky's boutique, send a large, self-addressed, stamped envelope to One Of A Kind, 12069 Ventura Place, Studio City, California. Be sure to print that you want the One Of A Kind free catalog *clearly* and also write *I Am A 16 Reader* on the outside of your mailing envelope—and you'll get guaranteed prompt service!

Two former Monkees, Mike Nesmith and Peter Tork, are both in the music and record business. Mike is forming his own group, which will be a country and western-hillbilly aggregation. He also has a small part in a motorcycle documentary movie called *Mexican 1000* (starring James Garner and Steve McQueen), so be sure to watch for it when the film comes to your neighborhood movie houses. Peter is quietly pursuing his own singing-composing-recording career. Though he and his group Release still don't have a record contract, they are busy doing lots of bookings in and around Los Angeles—and it's a *for sure* that you'll be hearing more about them soon!

WHAT'S SHAKIN' WITH SAJ?

Swingin' Sajid Khan decided to stay in India awhile longer in hopes of completing a movie there. When Saj moved to America he still owed the Khan Studios a movie, according to his contract with them. Saj was very devoted to the late Mehboob Khan, the man who adopted him when he was two years old—and, of course, he is still very close to Mrs. Khan, whom he affectionately calls Mother. By the time Saj gets back to Hollywood, there'll be several TV deals waiting for him. His one main dream of the moment is to star in a regular television series. Let's all hope that dream comes true!

Let's also hope that when Saj returns he becomes a *more careful driver*. Since Saj got his driver's license about six months ago, he's had five minor "accidents" and one major one. It isn't that he's a careless or speedy driver; it's just that he was brought up in a land where English driving rules prevail. Thus, every so often, he finds himself driving in the *left* instead of the *right* lane! And that can be *super dangerous*, you know!! By the grace of God, Saj is still with us—but learning to drive the American way seems *imperative* for him at this time.

For those of you who would like to keep in touch with Sajid, you can write to him at Suite 204, 324 S. Beverly Drive, Beverly Hills, Calif. 90212.

WHERE'S LEN?!

Last but not least, lovely Len Whiting is hard at work again in London, England. After finishing *Casanova* in Italy, he took a two-month holiday to catch up on things at home and rest a bit. Now he's back in the studio in England working on a film called *Say Hello To Yesterday*. Lovely Jean Simmons is his co-star. The movie is a Cinerama Production and you should be able to see it in your neighborhood theatre sometime this summer.

MONKEES ARCHIVES 1

"WE WERE IN STUDIO A AND THE MONKEES WERE IN STUDIO B AND WE MADE LOTS OF MUSIC TOGETHER!"

BY TOMMY BOYCE & BOBBY HART
TWO OF THE MONKEES' FAVORITE SONGWRITERS AND FRIENDS

Hi, FLIPers.

What a month this has been! We've been working in the studio for the last three months on both the Monkees' next album and our own album.

We really enjoyed cutting our own album. We gave a lot of our material away because certain people needed it then, but we still had some groovy things left for ourselves. Our album's titled "Test Patterns" and our first single is "Out And About." We hope you like it as well as some of the stuff we've done with the Monkees. It was fun recording because we recorded the album at RCA and we were in studio A while the Monkees were in studio B. We'd go back and forth between the two studios and see what they were doing, too.

They recorded three new songs of ours — "Mr. Webster," "I'll Spend My Life With You" and "I Can't Get Her Off My Mind."

"Mr. Webster" is a song we wrote a couple of months ago. It's a caricature of a number of people we've met around Hollywood. It's about this bank detective who stands there in the bank for 20 years making $68. He prevents lots of robberies but never gets a raise.

When he goes to retire they throw a banquet for him and give him a gold watch — after all those years and the robberies he prevented they give him a gold watch! But Mr. Webster doesn't show. In the middle of the banquet they get a telegram saying "I split with all your cash and I'm in Jamaica."

If you want to see the real Mr. Webster, go down to the Bank in Hollywood where we do all our banking and there's this one guy that we see all the time. He just putters around the bank and whenever anyone uses a pen he rushes over and straightens it out. We observed him for about 3 or 4 months and nicknamed him Mr. Webster. Then we wrote this song about him.

The story behind the writing of "I'll Spend My Life With You" isn't quite as interesting. We were in the office one Sunday working on a song called "Music, Music, Music" which wasn't working out. Tommy had the title "I'll Spend My Life With You" and Bobby liked it so he filled in the lyrics and we finished it by the pool later.

What were we doing in the office on Sunday? Well, our job doesn't consist of 9 to 5 Monday through Friday. Sometimes we'll take Tuesday off and go to the beach and then work Saturday or Sunday.

Besides it's quiet in the office on Sunday. Nobody's around and we can think better.

This month both we and the Monkees are going on extensive nationwide tours, so we won't see much of them. But we do cross paths with them several times. We leave after they do, but we just discovered that we'll be in Miami, Fla. on July 9 and so will they, so we'll get to see them there.

We return the first week in August and then leave again the 1st week of August for England. It's our first trip to England and we're really excited about it.

Talk at you next month.

Tommy and Bobby at the airport with The Monkees.

MONKEES ARCHIVES 1

LOOK WHO'S BACK, BETTER THAN EVER!

Dreamy Davy, prankster Micky, shy Tommy and bouncy Bobby—these four guys are the "new" Monkees. And guess what—they're just as dreamy and full of pep as the original Monkees seemed on TV so many years ago! Find out what the future holds for Micky Dolenz, Davy Jones, Tommy Boyce and Bobby Hart—the "new" Monkees!

Hey, Hey, it's the Monkees! Remember them? Many, many years ago, they had a popular (and how!) television show—it was a terrific mix of comedy, music, and the zaniest plots imaginable! Recently, the "powers that be" decided that modern day teens might also enjoy the show and so, re-runs of the old Monkees show are now being broadcast. Now, a whole new generation is laughing along with the original Monkees and their absolutely insane exploits. In fact, the show is so popular that the Monkees, who have long since disbanded, decided to reassemble. Only now they're known as Dolenz, Jones, Boyce and Hart. Micky Dolenz and Davy Jones are actually two of the original Monkees, but Tommy Boyce and Bobby Hart, the Monkees' veteran songwriters from way back when, joined the group in an attempt to replace missing Monkees Mike Nesmith and Peter Tork. (16 is planning an in-depth report on what Mike and Peter have been doing lately—keep posted!)

The "Old" Monkees: (L to R) Peter Tork, Micky Dolenz, Davy Jones, Mike Nesmith.

The "new" Monkees, alias Dolenz, Jones, Boyce and Hart, have been playing to near sell-out crowds wherever they go—they recently played at New York City's ultra-fashionable Riverboat, and even had a successful engagement at 6 Flags, in Arlington, Texas. They're currently planning an extensive tour of the Orient—Japan, Hong Kong, Bangkok, and Manila!

Not only that—their new album, titled *Dolenz, Jones, Boyce and Hart* was slated for release May 10—you should have no trouble finding it by now! Many of the songs on the album (five, to be exact) were written by Tommy and Bobby, but two were written by Micky and Davy, who in all their years in show-biz never thought of themselves as songwriters, only as performers! Can't wait to see what they came up with!

Once you see and hear these guys performing, you'll probably want to write to them. If so, here's the address: Dolenz, Jones, Boyce and Hart, c/o Capitol Records, 1750 North Vine Street, Hollywood, California, 90028.

WHAT'S UP WITH THE MONKEES?

Looks like there's sad news in store for the new Monkees, better known as **Dolenz, Jones, Boyce and Hart**. It seems that they've toured for a year now, made a great album called *Dolenz, Jones, Boyce and Hart*, and although they may or may not record together in the future, they're pretty much going to call it quits as a group. BUT—don't despair, because **Davy Jones**, that super talented fella, and original member of the Monkees, is continuing on his own. Wanna hear a sample of his fabulous voice? Hop down to your local record shop or dial your fave Deejay and ask for "Daydream Believer!" It's by the original Monkees, and **Davy Jones** does the singin'—it's too good to miss!

Not only does Davy have a great voice, but he's a talented actor as well! You can see him on a Walt Disney special sometime this fall, in a TV-movie entitled *The Blue Grass Special*. Davy plays a character called "Davy!" It's super-good, so watch out for it!

If you want to write to **Davy**, here's the address: **Davy Jones**, 1448 N. Sierra Bonita Avenue, Hollywood, California 90046. And if you'd care to write to **Dolenz, Boyce or Hart**, send your letters to Capitol Records, 1750 North Vine Street, Hollywood, California 90028—and tell 'em you read about 'em in 16!

Davy Jones

Come Along With 16 As We Visit DAVY JONES— And Catch Him HORSE-ing Around!

Yep, it's true! Davy's seen and done a lot of things in his life. He's best known as one of those zany, talented Monkees, and more recently as a member of Dolenz, Jones, Boyce and Hart. Now Davy's launching a solo career, but he still misses his days as an apprentice jockey!! Davy's more than just a talented singer—he's quite a horseman, too!

Of course, since he's busy making records and working on TV specials, Davy doesn't get to spend much time riding. But when he does, watch out!

When 16 visited Davy at his friend's ranch in Santa Barbara, California, he was just getting ready to saddle "Lucky," his fave horse, and take her for a ride. First, he led Lucky outside the barn and began brushing her shiny coat to get her ready for saddling. Then he went to the "tack" room ("tack" is the term used to describe all of the horses' accessories) for Lucky's saddle, blanket, and bridle. Soon, Lucky and Davy were ready for their morning workout.

Davy raced Lucky around the corral and jumped hurdles for almost an hour. You'd never know that Davy wasn't born to the saddle—in fact, lots of Davy's closest friends call him "Cowboy."

After the workout, Davy knew it was time to give Lucky a rest, so she grazed in the grass for a while, as Davy put the tack away, and started thinking about his next free morning! It's hard to get out of the studio, and relax with Lucky at the ranch, but Davy always finds time.

Davy's a little nervous about his new solo career. He hopes you'll like him, and he really appreciates every letter he gets. Why not drop him a line at this address: Davy Jones, 1448 North Sierra Bonita Avenue, Hollywood, California 90046.

MONKEES ARCHIVES 1

New Release

Colgems have announced that they will release a new Monkees' single at the end of February in the States. The 'A' side will be "Listen to the Band" which is one of the numbers from their TV Spectacular.

MIKE'S TV SET UP

As the MONKEES MONTHLY reported several months ago, Mike has a close-circuit TV set-up. This has been extended now so that he has cameras covering every gate, door, swimming pool and main room in the house, so that he and Phyllis can see exactly what their two children are getting up to at any time.

Mike is busy working on another L.P. which he hopes to start producing in the New Year. It will be another Mike special, featuring the sort of music that he loves. He has already written many of the songs.

PETER TO LEAVE MONKEES?

It is believed that the TV Spectacular will be the last appearance that Peter Tork will make with the Monkees.

For some time now, he has been wanting to go back to playing his earlier type of music in his own sort of way, and we understand that he will shortly be forming his own group which may well have his girl friend, Reine, as drummer, John Anderson—who has been Assistant Director on many of the Monkees' TV shows and who is currently working on the Flying Nun TV series—as guitarist, and another friend whom we only know as Lowell, also on guitar.

Stand-in Drummer

Peter's girl friend, Reine, who as we told you before is James Stewart's daughter, is a very good drummer. When the boys were filming their Spectacular, Fats Domino's drummer failed to turn up and Reine sat in. She was so good that Fats wanted her to stay on and play with him regularly.

100 HIPPIES

Jack Good wanted an unusual audience for the Monkees first TV Spectacular, which was recorded at the end of November. So, he sent a couple of buses to Sunset Strip and got 100 hippies who agreed, not only to make up the audience for the TV Spectacular, but also to join in with many of the numbers with the artists before the cameras.

BIG BILL

Micky told us that when he returned from their Far Eastern tour he went to the Pet Shop to pick up his and Samantha's pets, which they had boarded there for the four weeks they were away.

They found that his mongrel dog, You, had given birth to six puppies and his cat, Shortie Blackwell, had four new kittens, so the total bill for the four weeks boarding came to $600—how about that! Ever since, he and Samantha have been very busy finding new homes for them all!

 I think Peter must have been telling Davy how much he hated having pies thrust in his face. This picture was taken just before the ones on page 10 of last month's MONKEES MONTHLY

MONKEES ARCHIVES 1

A Box Of Monkees. The original Monkees join Rhino managing director Harold Bronson to announce the release of "The Monkees Deluxe Limited-Edition Box Set" on Rhino Home Video. The 21-volume set is the largest video boxed set ever. It contains all 58 episodes of the show, a 1969 TV special, several Kellogg's commercials and bumpers starring the band, a bonus cassette of the original pilot for the show, and a 48-page color booklet. Shown, from left, are Monkees Peter Tork and Davy Jones, Bronson, and Monkees Mickey Dolenz and Mike Nesmith.

RUMOR: Mike Nesmith's original green wool hat is so dear to him that he's having it cast in bronze to be kept in his new home.

FACT: Mike couldn't stand the nickname "Wool Hat" from the beginning. Though he auditioned in his green hat, and had to wear it from time to time on the TV show, he decided that the best thing to do was to give it to somebody who really wanted it. So, in Cleveland on January 15, Mike tossed his original green hat into the audience, and if you were the lucky girl who caught it — you've got the real thing!

MONKEES ARCHIVES 1

BRAND NEW! EXCLUSIVE!
Available Only From Us...
MONKEES SINGING PIN-UPS

Five Fabulous Posters, Each With Words to a Different Monkees Hit Song!

No self-respecting Monkees fan can afford to miss out on this fantastic, EXCLUSIVE offer! And we're the only ones on earth who can give you these Sensational, Way-out Pin-Ups. For just $1.00 you can own 5 huge kissable — SINGABLE — posters that will make your bed-room walls jump. Complete words to the Monkees' greatest hits are printed right on the pin-up, so you can sing yourself to sleep at night or wake up swinging in the morning. Songs include "Monkees' Theme Song", "I'm A Believer", "Last Train To Clarksville", "A Little Bit Me" and "I'm Not Your Steppin' Stone". What a deal!

ALL 5 FOR JUST $1.00

★ A DIFFERENT SONG ON EACH PIN-UP

★ ALL ARE GIANT 11½" x 16" SIZE

★ FREE POSTAGE AND HANDLING

ORDER YOURS NOW! SUPPLY IS LIMITED!

VICTOR SPECIALTIES, Dept. NG-168
CHARLTON BUILDING, DERBY, Conn.

Enclosed is $.................... Please rush me .... sets of FIVE MONKEES SINGING PIN-UPS at $1.00 per set.

Name .... Age..............

Address ....

City .... State .... Zip ....

(Please print carefully - Include Zip)

MONKEES ARCHIVES 1

AN EXCLUSIVE BEHIND-THE-SCENE-SCOOP!
"HOW WE WRITE A SONG FOR THE MONKEES!"

BY TOMMY BOYCE & BOBBY HART

Tommy and Bobby talking a future Monkees hit over with Micky.

(TWO OF THE MONKEES' FAVORITE SONG WRITERS AND BEST FRIENDS)

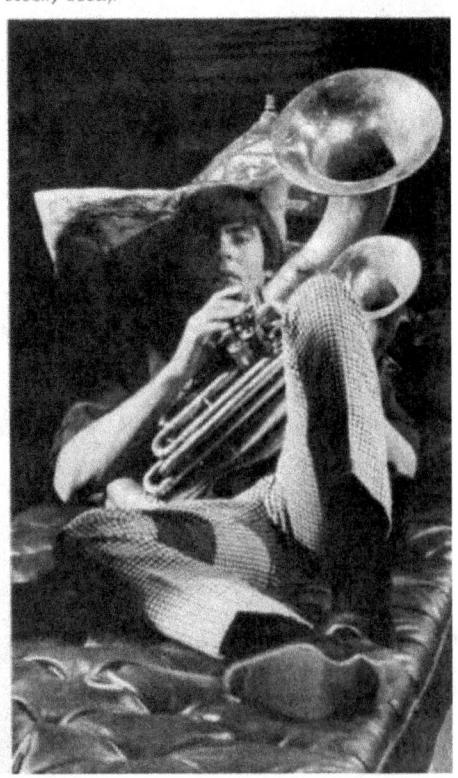

Who knows? Maybe one day Davy will drag this complicated instrument to a Monkees recording session and play it. At a Monkees session, anything happy can happen (and usually does!).

Just as the Monkees enjoyed their first vacation since their formation a year and a half ago, we got our first one this last month. For three weeks we didn't even think about music.

We wanted to last out the whole month, but it didn't work—you just can't not work out an idea for a song when they keep coming at you. So we went back to work on Monkee songs and when they all got together after vacation, we started recording them and you're hearing them right now.

We didn't last out a month without seeing the Monkees either. The minute Micky got back from Europe, there he was on our doorstep, just bursting with news of his travels—you can read all about him in Ric's column.

Then Davy came to our house, full of tales of visiting with his family and the Bahamas and miniskirts. "You can't believe how short they get over there!" (We'd like the chance to try!)

Many of you have asked us how the Monkees decide who's going to sing which song and if there are big fights over who gets which. Well, usually the boys will all listen to the song we've written and it will just sound like it's perfect for Davy or Micky. (Mike likes to do his own songs.)

There have never been any fights, although there have been times when both boys wanted to do the same number. Like with "I Wanna Be Free" Micky just loved the song, but it fitted in with a particular segment of the show which had Davy wandering around all alone, so he sang the song. (By the way, Andy Williams has just recorded it and says it's one of his all-time favorites! Needless to say we and the Monkees were thrilled.)

This month, we're starting a new feature in our column. From now on, each time we'll tell you exactly how we came to write a particular Monkee song. Since "She" is one of the most popular tunes and since the circumstances were pretty weird (even for us!) we'll begin with it.

One morning Tommy took his car to a local garage to have the brakes adjusted. While he was waiting, he noticed that the old library that he used to go to in that area had been torn down and a new one built on the same spot. So he wandered over to check it out. He would up staying there for four hours, just looking through the card files, until he came upon "She," printed on one of the cards. "What a great song title!" he thought. He raced back, picked up his car and by the time he was home he had the song half written. That evening we finished it up and took it to the Monkees' recording session the next day. The boys flipped out over it (which they do frequently, thank goodness for us) and wham, it was a hit.

Even though the boys are trying to record more and more of their own material now, they've asked us to continue writing songs for them and producing the tunes we do, which makes us feel good and will give us more to tell you about our fabulous friends (and yours)—THE MONKEES.

MONKEES ARCHIVES 1

MOVE OVER, MOUSE—HERE COMES "THE MONKEES"!

"The Monkees"—the merriest, madcap series ever made—has always kept audiences glued to the TV. Wholesomeness and family fun made them huge successes on network television. Now in syndication, "The Monkees" is sure to be one of the biggest hits of the new season. Call Columbia Pictures Television to find out how easy a Monkee can move a mouse, or a house, or a market full of households.

"The Monkees." 58 episodes in color distributed exclusively by

COLUMBIA PICTURES TELEVISION
A division of Columbia Pictures Industries, Inc.

Pre-sold in 7 major markets: KBHK-TV San Francisco/WFLD-TV Chicago/WKBS-TV Philadelphia/WKBD-TV Detroit/WLVI-TV Boston/KDNL-TV St. Louis/WDCA-TV Washington, D.C.

MONKEES ARCHIVES 1

MONKEES ARCHIVES 1

AN AFTERNOON WITH DAVY

Davy has friends all over the world and sometimes they get a chance to visit him in Hollywood.

Just recently some of Davy's old mates from England paid him an unexpected visit. They are playing with a professional soccer team, so while they stopped off in Hollywood, Davy got several opportunities to see them. He also got a brief chance to play some soccer with them. This is something Davy has missed very much. He loves all sports, but especially soccer.

MONKEES ARCHIVES 1

HEY, HEY, IT'S DOLENZ, JONES, BOYCE & HART

Rumors had been spreading for months. Whispered comments on Hollywood's grapevine had spun the imagination into high hopes that those luscious loons of the sixties, and TV's top tickling troupers of today, the Monkees, were getting back together. After several cycles of denials and further hints, the word slipped out. The Monkees, or at least the closest thing to the Monkees we would ever again see, were back.

The guys who sang all the Monkees' hits, Micky Dolenz and Davy Jones, had sealed the pact with Tommy Boyce and Bobby Hart, the sensational songwriters who penned most of the Monkees' terrific tunes.

The result? A brand new powerhouse of Monkee memories rekindled along with the fuel for a fine future ready for the firing up.

After innumerable versions of the story about the celebrated reunion made the rounds, we just had to have the real story. So, one day we made a date to have the four come visit our offices and share the whole truth in their own words.

Micky arrived early. Several minutes later Tommy and Bobby strode in. Davy was in the midst of moving and would be late, so we began without him.

Initially, Micky assumed the role of historian, and offered to fill us in on how, after spending years out of the public eye, they were once again playing to record-breaking audiences.

"The original four guys who were in the Monkees met about nine months ago to talk about getting back together," he explained. "Unfortunately, there were a lot of conflicts in what everyone wanted to do. Mike Nesmith said that he would be interested in doing a TV show or movie, but didn't want to go on the road at all or perform, especially the old tunes. Peter Tork voiced just about the same opinion. He didn't want to sing the old songs either. Also, Peter said he would gladly get involved as long as it didn't conflict with his teaching. He's been teaching history, French and music at a school in Venice, California.

"Then a promoter who was friends with Bobby suggested that Bobby and Tommy get together with Davy and I and start a new group," Micky said.

Tommy piped up, "Since Bobby and I love the road and don't teach school, we fit in perfectly."

Micky continued, "Around that time, rumors were already starting about the Monkees getting back together, and we had been getting all kinds of offers. So, this group just fell together."

"We decided to get together just for a week and see how it worked out," added Tommy. "We worked on a few songs and things were going well."

"I think that the four of us have always been closer than the original Monkees in a lot of ways," disclosed Micky. "Davy and I, having done most of the singing, were always working with Tommy and Bobby because they had to teach us the songs. Also, even back then, they were singing the back-up vocals on many of our numbers.

"Once we decided we were going to try and make the new group happen, we had to make the big decision on what kind of show we wanted to do," Micky went on. "Did we want to be a lounge act or a nostalgic rock act that did other people's old hits as well as our own? Did we want to try for the FM and underground market or should we just do the old Monkee hits and take a chance on either bombing or being very successful? We decided to go for broke and start out doing nothing but the things that made us famous in the first place.

"At first we thought about calling the act the New Monkees or Monkees '76 or something like that, but we didn't want to make it just a nostalgic experience and do a couple of live performances, maybe a few TV specials, then disappear again. The idea was to start a new group and have contemporary hits, too. So we decided to call ourselves Dolenz, Jones, Boyce & Hart instead," Micky continued.

"We're using the old Monkees' tunes as a stepping stone in developing a new act. It's obvious that, at least for the present, that's what people want to hear. The act we're touring with is called The Golden Hits of the Monkees' Show–to try and make sure it's clear that we're not the Monkees, but rather a group called Dolenz, Jones, Boyce & Hart that is doing a show of the Monkees' hits," he said.

"In the beginning, I was apprehensive about getting together," commented Tommy. "I didn't know how successful we would be. I didn't know if there was any demand. We were all pretty overwhelmed when we went out and did our first show and broke the house record."

Since then, the four have gone on to draw over-capacity crowds almost everywhere they have played.

"The best venues we play, the most successful, are amusement parks and fairs," said Micky. "Any place where there's a family audience, lots of kids and lots of different age groups."

How is it doing all those fave hits again?

"I had a lot of fun the first few shows and a good time working the show out," replied Micky. "But it's hard work and very difficult to do them over and over again 10 years later. Right now we're trying to work in some interesting visuals with props, costumes and special effects, so we're not just standing there singing.

"The original live Monkees Show used a 40 ft. projection screen, costume changes and make-up; that was 10 years ago, before anybody else did things like that," Micky recalled. "Once again, we're trying to develop a very theatrical, comedy extravaganza."

"We want to do with comedy what Alice Cooper did with horror," proposed Tommy.

Not long after the four joined forces and laid out a plan of action, they went into a studio and cut a record of one of their new songs. Once completed, they took it to Capitol Records. The folks there flipped for it and offered them an excellent recording contract.

Right now the guys are putting the finishing touches on a super-stuff package of musical joy juice which will be ready for release by the end of May.

The energy is so positive around the quartet that it's easy to tell big things are on the verge of happening for them all over again. They're even negotiating with some of the studios and networks on the possibility of a new TV show.

Our conversation was just about exhausted when Davy finally wandered in. Though he had missed out on most of our talk, his presence added the fourth and final component that turned a group of reasonably normal types into a wisecracking, whimsically witty gang of music makers.

And as Dolenz, Jones, Boyce & Hart took off down the hall, faces poked out of every door they passed, wondering what on earth this pack of Monkee types was doing, running and skipping toward the elevator, singing at the top of their lungs. Welcome back.

MONKEES ARCHIVES 1

MONKEES ARCHIVES 1

VOL. 2, NO. 36   SEPTEMBER 16, 1966   SAN BERNARDINO/RIVERSIDE, CALIFORNIA

MARSHALL MEETS MONKEES
(Story on Page 2)

MONKEE CHATTER

By Gary Marshall

Last week in the Tiger Mag we introduced you to the most fabulous bunch of characters to ever hit the silver tube ... THE MONKEES. The Monkees are definitely here, and if you caught their new NBC show last Monday night at 7:30, I know you'll agree that they are also here to stay.

Recently I attended a Hollywood party thrown to introduce The Monkees to disc jockeys, the press and anyone else who was lucky enough to get by the front gate at Columbia Studios. Most of the top radio & television personalities from Southern California were there, half a dozen actors and actresses whose names you were sure you had on the tip of your tongue ... and spent all night trying to remember ... and never did.

It was a very detached group of all kinds of people who appeared only interested in the free food ... until the previews of the series began running in an adjacent building. I waited until later than most to view the shows. But I did realize that as the group left the screening, they had undergone a big change. Suddenly, everyone just had to meet The Monkees ... they had to tell them how absolutely great their show was ... and I soon found out it was much more than that. Not only great ... but original. That's a rare find for television.

I played the whole party scene backwards. I was too nervous to eat any of the free food that the rest were attacking ravenously ... I was concentrating on trying to hear The Monkees who were playing live a few feet away ... and at the first break I elbowed in through Go-Go Girls and press agents to meet them. Before the party I had already decided that these four Monkees were going nowhere but to the top ... and after seeing the series I was certain of it.

The show, called The Monkees, is about four long-haired Beatle-looking-acting-sounding singers who get involved in the funniest, most improbable scrapes. None of it is believeable ... it could never happen ... and that's half the reason it's so hilarious. The rest of the credit goes to the show's production staff. The writers must be kept in padded cells ... they have to be mad to think up such beautiful material. The Director, film editors and special effects people must be the top in the business because their work shines with class. And this series must soon be one of the top not only for these reasons, but also because The Monkees are the most groovy bunch of guys on and off the tube.

Mickey Monkee (Dolenz) told me just before I entered the screening ... "Oh how I hope you like it ... I can't think of a word to discribe how much I hope you like it ... yes I can. I HOPE YOU LIKE IT GOOD!" I did, and so will you. The Monkees are here! The Monkees are good!

CHERISH

As Recorded By The Association
BMI Beechwood Music

Cherish is the word I used to describe all the feelings that I have for you in summer.

You don't know how many times I wished that I have told you

You don't know how many times I wished I could hold you

You don't know how many times I could mold you into someone who could cherish me as much as I cherish you.

Cherish is the word that makes more love grow, more to my heart each time I realize.

Well I'm not going to be the one to share your dreams

Well I'm not going to be the one to share your schemes

I'm not going to be the one to share what seems to be the life that you cherish as much as I do yours

Oh I began to think that man has never found the words that can make you want me.

To write them down with letters, just the right sound that could make you hear, make you see, that you are driving me out of my mind.

Oh I could say I need you, but when you realize that I want you just like a thousand other guys that say they love you for the rest of their lives.

When all they wanted was to touch your face, your hands, and gaze into your eyes. (Chorus). Cherish is the word

Sept. 16, 1966   "KFXM Tiger 59"   p. 3

ED GRrrrrr SEZ...

WELCOME TO THE DAYLITE BILL (Beale) SURREY ... BILL has been hosting the "Tiger Radio 59" ALL-NITER for the past months but now MOVES UP TO the NOON to 3 shift ... CONGRATULATIONS TO ALL of the STASHED CASH WINNERS!!! Lots of you and another example that it DOES PAY TO LISTEN TO KFXM!! A WELCOME TO JOHNNY BISHOP now swingin' on the WEEKENDS ON "Tiger Radio 59." BOB GRIFFIN our REMOTE BROADCASTING KING still swingin' every FRIDAY NITE 9 'til midnight from GOLDFINGER!!! GARY MARSHALL our early AM MC will be RELATING TALES of his days in school ... I heard he might write a couple OF BOOKS on the subject ... TIPS FOR TRUANTS ... AND HOOKEY HINTS might be suitable titles GARY!!! BARRY BOYD MC'ing at GOLDFINGER with the popular MICKEY ROONEY JR. & his group ... really packing them in too ... MICKEY'S MOM and HER HUBBY the WORLD FAMOUS GUITARIST BARNEY KESSELL were FRONT ROW CENTER last Saturday nite ... THE MYSTIC EYE will attempt to continue the WILD WEDNESDAY WORKOUTS with BB & THE WHATT FOUR only the hours will be from 7 'til 10:30 as school is in!!! A STIR in the hearts of our FEMALE STAFFERS at Broadcast City a few days ago WHEN DAVID JANSSEN (The Fugitive) dropped by ... he was filming in the San Bernardino area ... as far as I can find out AL ANTHONY is the only guy who was DISHONORABLY DISCHARGED from the SALVATION ARMY ... They caught him with his hand in THE TAMBOURINE when the rest of the band wasn't playing ... WHOOPS!!!! AL who has been known TO VISIT THE TRACK periodically came up with a little philosophy about it with this statement .. "Did you ever stop to realize that a RACE HORSE is the ONLY ANIMAL that can take THOUSANDS OF PEOPLE for a ride AT THE SAME TIME!!! See ya next week ...

MONKEES ARCHIVES 1

a fave foto feature

THE MONKEES' OUTASITE TOUR

Peter, Mike, Davy and Micky have turned the country upside down this summer with their groovy concert shows. Whether you saw them in person or not, you'll have to agree that this is the most fantastic picture story of the Monkees' great tour!

▲ 1. SENSATIONAL SUNDOWNERS did fantastic job of backing the Monkees and playing their hit "Always You." Here, Bobby Dick pretends to play flute.

▲ 2. A WILD MOB of fans arrived to greet Monkees Mike and Peter appearing on local television show in Dallas, Texas.

▼ 3. EXCITED FANS mobbed Peter's limousine. The boys escaped from the TV studio by climbing over the roof!

▼ 4. "AUNTIE GRIZELDA" was Peter's fave song in the concert because he got to dance all over the stage while he sang.

MONKEES ARCHIVES 1

▲ 5. "HI! BIG D," Mike shouted to the Dallas fans. Since Mike grew up in Dallas and was very poor then, it was a great thrill for him to return so successfully. While he was in Dallas, he visited his old neighborhood.

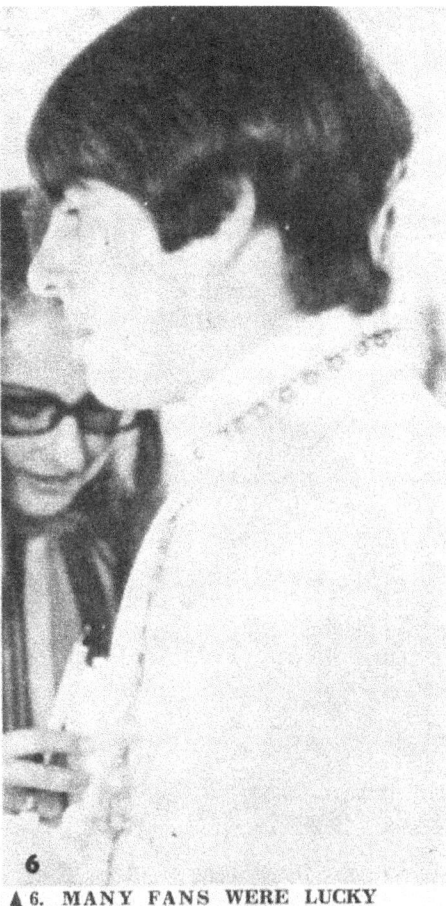

▲ 6. MANY FANS WERE LUCKY enough to meet the Monkees. Shown with Davy is a girl writing interview notes.

▼ 7. ON STAGE THE MONKEES are groovy. They perform longer than any group today. They really give their all!

Cont. on pg. 28

MONKEES ARCHIVES 1

THE MONKEES' OUTASITE TOUR
Cont. from pg. 11

◄ 8. "PETER THE DISC JOCKEY"—is what radio station KVIL in Dallas tagged Peter.

9. THE MONKEES ON TV, but not on "The Monkees" was a different sight. At one stop on the tour they did this pop show and sang "Randy Scouse Git." It fractured the fans! ▼

MONKEES ARCHIVES 1

▲ 10. CONCERTS ARE WHEN the Monkees feel happiest. They adore meeting fans. And, playing to 12,000!

◄ 11. PETER AND DAVY meet the Dallas fan club members. These get-togethers on tour are informal and lotsa fun!

▼ 12. PETER PHONES the radio station in next town Monkees will visit to check out exciting plans in store.

MONKEES ARCHIVES 1

HOW THE MONKEES MADE THEIR NEW ALBUM!

(OR, MICKY DOLENZ AND HIS "ZILCH!")

BY TOMMY BOYCE & BOBBY HART (TWO OF THE MONKEES' FAVORITE SONGWRITERS AND FRIENDS)

Well, fab friends, it's been a fab month for fab us and our fab friends, the fab Monkees.

This month we thought we should tell you a bit about the new Monkees album, "Headquarters." Almost all of the work was done by Micky, Davy, Peter and Mike themselves, along with Chip Douglas and us. It's certainly their most exciting album, we're sure you agree.

Our favorite track is "Shades of Gray." Although it sounds like a lot of extra instruments were used, really there was only one cello and one horn on it.

Peter, who used to play French horn, composed the horn part on this song. He and Davy trade off on the vocal parts. Pete also plays the piano.

Mic's written a song for this album — "No Time." There were so many people visiting them in the studio that night, that the boys just had everyone join in as backing voices!

Micky also sings Peter's composition, "For Pete's Sake." By the way, Peter has a thing for sticking his name into the songs he writes, like, "I'm Torking about You." Davy suggested that he write one called "You Tork Too Much," but so far, he hasn't gotten 'round to it!

When Micky was visiting England (and driving everyone crazy, we understand!), he heard the phrase, "Randy Scouse Git" and worked it into a song. That's a pretty weird title, all right, but our vote for the really way-out one goes to "Zilch." And we thought Bob Dylan had the corner on wild song titles!

Mike's solo is a country-Western influenced number as before: "You Just May Be the One." The Monkees are getting to be such great songwriters themselves, we're beginning to worry! One thing carries us on, though—we've got a lot more time to write, so they'll always need a couple more tunes to round out their albums.

During one of the boys' recording sessions this month (which take place about four nights a week), everyone at RCA Studios got involved in a giant water fight. Why? Well, Micky and Peter had brought along some water guns, handed them round to Mike, Davy and us and you can guess what happened from there! Anyway, by the time the evening was over, there were four wet Monkees, two wet producers, and a lot of wet PEOPLE pouring out of the studios!

MONKEES ARCHIVES 1

MONKEES ARCHIVES 1

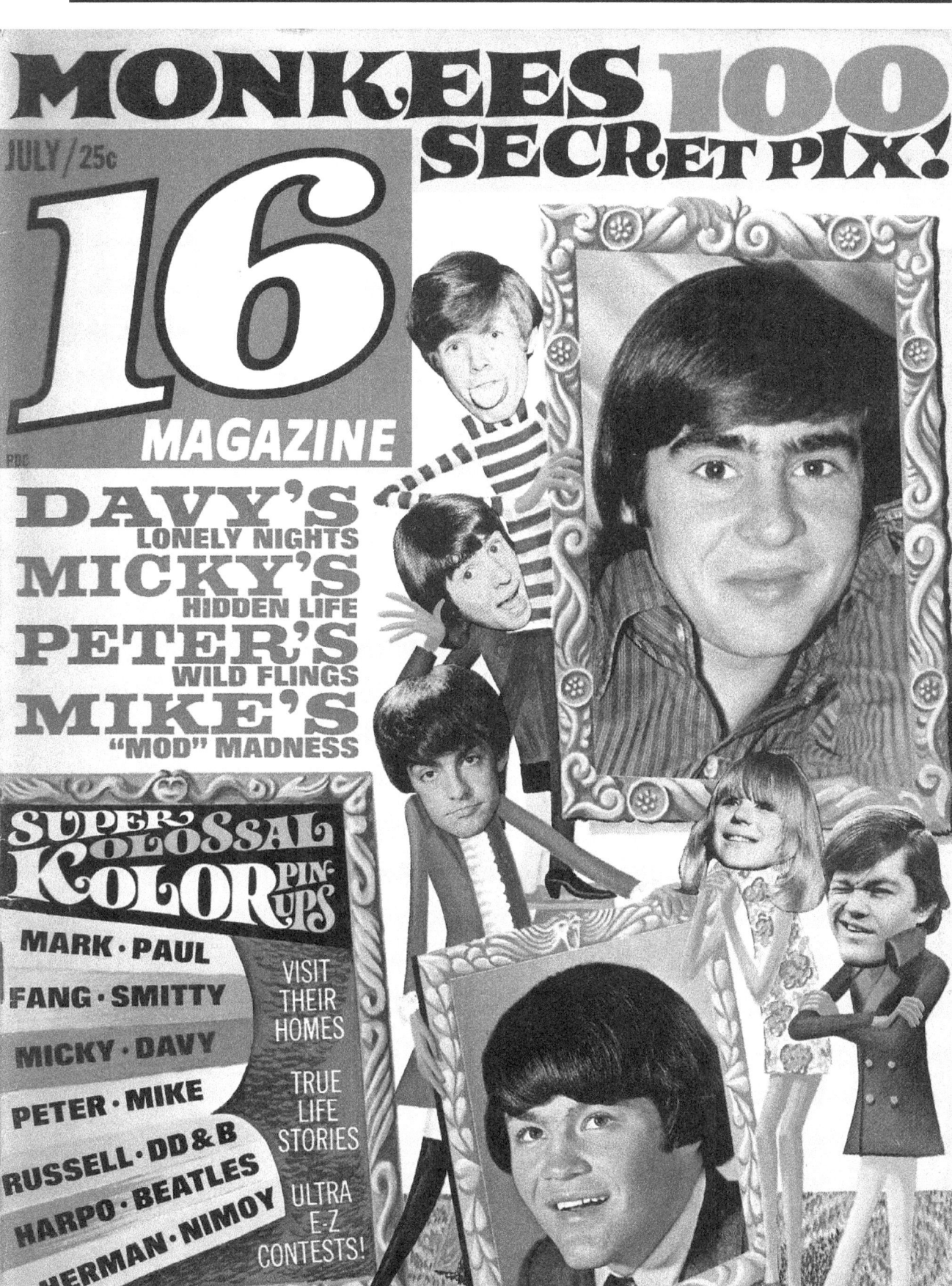

MONKEES ARCHIVES 1

You've Asked For All The Super Scam On Micky's British Girl! Here It Is!

MEET SAMANTHA JUSTE!

"Sam" to some, "Sammy" to others and Samantha Juste to the world at large is a very sweet girl and if that sounds a trifle put-on from me you don't have to take my word. Ask Micky Dolenz for a character reference.

I doubt whether there is one pop star I've met who has not said what a nice person she is after having met her on BBC-TV's "Top of the Pops."

Because viewers only see her once a week they tend to get the impression that Sam is lazing around for the rest of the week but that is not so — she is very busy.

"I'm contracted to the Lucy Clayton Model agency," Samantha told me, "I do a lot of teenage modelling work and when I'm not in demand there (which isn't often) I'm working on songs with my new record producer Mike Leander."

Mike was the arranger the Beatles called in to help on out "She's Leaving Home" track on their last LP and although Sammy's first disc attempt "No One Needs My Love" (Decca) was not a hit Mike is confident that some day soon will see Sam in the charts.

"I can play piano and read music," said Sam, "and I love singing so I'm keeping my fingers crossed. I've got some material from Bob Lind which I'm learning and Mike keeps me rehearsing numbers at least twice a week."

In her long stint on the "Top of the Pops," Sam has met a wide range of top pop people and she has nothing but praise for the American artists on the show. "They all tend to be entertainers rather than just musicians," she says. "Proby was a favourite of mine because he was such a great showman and Sonny and Cher — I love Cher's clothes because she never tries to model herself on anyone and always creates something of her own."

Sam lives in an apartment in London's Westminister overlooking the River Thames which is tastefully furnished with antiques and includes a little coffee table which she says, "is very valuable — it's a George the something. I tour all the little antique dealers picking up things like the chaise lounge and strip off the old paint black to reveal the beautiful carving."

Her most embarassing moment on the show recently when she was late for the first time after getting caught in a traffic jam outside the BBC studios — she arrived halfway through the second half to join Pete Murray.

When Sam shops she generally goes to places like the 21 Shop in Woolens which is Knightsbridge or Sue Locks in the Fulham Road or (when she's got a few extra pounds to spare) Deliss in Beecham Place. Those are all names worth remembering if you should ever shop in London or if you like good young clothes because Sam looks nothing short of sensational in the outfits she buys.

On her visit to America, Sammy spent much time with The Monkees. Here she is aboard their private plane, sitting next to Micky, listening to Davy.

OUTASITE OCTOBER ISSUE OF FLIP! ON SALE AUGUST 10TH! GO ON TOUR WITH THE MONKEES! FIND OUT HOW MUCH YOU REALLY KNOW ABOUT MICKY! LOOK BACK WITH THE ACTION KIDS! LOOK AHEAD WITH THE RAIDERS! GREATEST REAL COLOR PIN-UPS EVER! DAVY JONES' EARLY DAYS AS A STAR! MOBY GRAPE LIFE STORIES! DON AND GOODTIMES! KURT RUSSELL! MARK LINDSAY! SPEC SCOOPS! ALL IN THE OUTASITE OCTOBER FLIP! ON SALE AUGUST 10TH!

MONKEES ARCHIVES 1

FUN TIME WITH THE

BY LYNNE RANDELL

Come along with Lynne on the Monkees' tour of America and share the whole gang's excitements and adventures!

GREETINGS! It's me, Lynne, again — and I've just finished the most fantastic "event" of my life (or anybody else's, for that!). My big event, of course, was being one of the guests on the Monkees' show during their summer tour of America. Because you *all* couldn't be there with me personally, I want to share some of my happy experiences with you through the pages of *16*.

We traveled on a private DC-6 with a huge Monkee emblem painted on the outside of it. We had our own captain and crew, all of whom were thoroughly capable and completely charming. I'd like to take this opportunity to thank them — on behalf of the Monkees, myself and the Sundowners, Jimi Hendrix and all the rest of the gang — for being so wonderful to us.

MICKY — ASSISTANT "HOSTESS"

Lynda, our hostess, got a helping hand from Micky Dolenz, who volunteered to become her assistant. Micky helped to serve food and drinks for every meal — and he did an excellent job. Can you imagine what it's like to look up and see Micky Dolenz leaning over you, asking, "Coffee, tea or milk?"

When we were in Miami Davy, Peter, Mike and Micky gave up all a tremendous surprise. They rented a gorgeous 71-foot cruiser, loaded it with 30 of us "Monkee show people", and we all put out to sea for a whole day of fun and laughter together! It was the Monkees' way of thanking us. Don't you think that was very nice of them?

MONKEE "DREAM BOAT"

Our dream boat was packed with every kind of food imaginable and enough soda pop to float a navy. Of course, everyone tried to get a great tan in *one* day, and among us we used up about a gallon of suntan lotion! Davy spent most of the trip snapping away with his Instamatic. Peter chatted up his various guests. Micky indulged in endless sing-alongs with the Sundowners, and Mike relaxed in the cabin below deck.

In Miami, we stayed at the beautiful Eden Roc Hotel. It's *very* elegant. Micky and Peter went about carrying a tape recorder, which played all their favorite rock 'n' roll hits. Can you imagine how startled some of the older guests were when the elevator door opened and they saw two or three Monkees there doing the shing-aling while the music blasted away?

"THE LOST SUPPER"

Every town we hit was a groove and each was memorable for one reason or another, but Buffalo, N.Y., became unforgettable because of the supper we almost lost. After a strenuous but exciting day of meeting the mayor and doing guest shots on WKBW-Radio, we all congregated in our "Courtesy Suite" at the hotel. We made a great list of sandwiches and drinks, and phoned the list to room service.

"Hey," Davy said about 40 minutes later, "I think some bloke has intercepted our supper!"

Everyone agreed, and my manager, Carol West (who took all the pictures on these two pages, by the way), and I volunteered to go out on a sandwich-and-soda search party. After calling room service, who insisted that our order was "on the way", questioning the elevator operator and roaming around the halls, we decided to look on the stairs. And guess what? On a landing two floors below us was our supper! There were two large serving tables covered with untouched sandwiches and drinks — apparently abandoned by our lost, strayed or stolen waiter!

Carol and I maneuvered the two tables into the elevator and got it up into the "Courtesy Suite" just as the whole gang was about to collapse from starvation. When we walked into the suite Peter, Mike, Davy and Micky led the rest of the troupe in a round of applause. Before Carol and I could take a bow, everyone dived at the food!

I wish I had more space to tell you *all* the funny adventures that came my way on this magical Monkee tour. I'll continue with my story next month. So stay tuned to *16* and I'll see you then. P.S. The December issue of *16* goes on sale October 19.

MONKEES ARCHIVES 1

MONKEES

Mickey & Sundowners Eddie Placidi and Bobby Dick

Davy & Lynne

Jimi Hendrix & Peter

Camera bug Davy

Mike – as photographed by Carol

MONKEES ARCHIVES 1

MICKY IN HYDE PARK

By Jackie Richmond

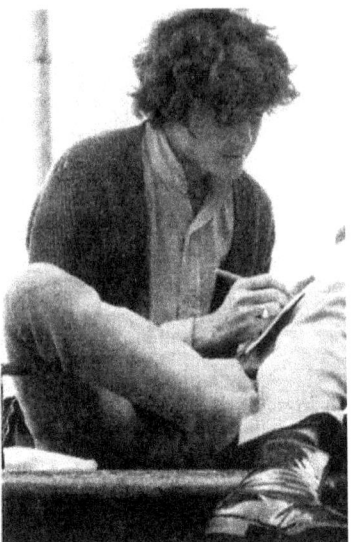

Who is the most incredible, the most unpredictable pop star of 'em all? Well, at the risk of offending supporters of other members of the Monkees, it's Micky Dolenz who currently holds the title. And it's all because he put on the most incredible, most unpredictable pop performance of all time when the boys were in London.

Wanna know more? Well, here's how, when and why it all happened.

ALL-NIGHT VIGIL

Let's set the scene. Daylight is just about managing to creep up over Hyde Park, one of the wide open spaces in London. The Monkees are staying in the Royal Garden Hotel, which overlooks the park. And what's more, the fans KNOW they're staying there, so there is virtually an all-night and all-day vigil kept, either in the parkland itself or out on busy Kensington High Street. Some have camped out all night for a glimpse of the fantastic foursome.

The date is July 4, which also happens to be Independence Day, a highlight for all Americans. After a very late, all-night party, celebrating their successes at the Wembley Pool, the Monkees make their way back to the hotel. They are dead tired, whacked out. All they really want is some sleep, though they own up that they are really too tired to be able to nod off.

They've gone through a hectic spell of sheer hard work, appearing on stage, rehearsing, filming (in Paris), signing pictures, catching up on their shopping.

So in this semi-dazed mood, Micky gets back to the hotel and ponders the question of whether it's worth ordering some solid breakfast—or whether a Coke, or orange juice, would be best.

And as his car speeds up towards the highly-decorative front of the plush hotel, he notices that crowds of Monkee fans are gathered there, hoping to catch sight of at least ONE Monkee. And Micky thinks about this—marvelling at the sheer loyalty of the fans. And he reckons the least he can do is to get out of the car and talk to them.

Now this is a very risky thing

to do... but Micky thrives on doing risky things. There could have been chaos and confusion, but he explained his position to the fans. He pointed out that he was "no different" to them, simply because he was a pop star. That they were all human beings together and there was no reason for him not to talk to them, and answer their questions and tell them about the zany life he leads, twenty-four hours a day.

DON'T RUSH

But he urged the fans not to start rushing him, because that would only cause trouble and panic and he wanted to avoid that. So it happened that around 200 fans followed Micky on a chat and a walk round the park. Micky was, despite his tiredness, in happy mood. He obviously enjoyed this off-beat way of meeting the fans.

Gradually the crowd of fans got bigger and bigger. In the hotel, in safety, members of the Monkees' party were getting a bit worried for Micky, thinking the whole scene could get out of control. Said one: "Well, it's what he wants to do—he loves getting through to people."

Meanwhile, Pied Piper Micky led his "Team" of followers over to a large covered platform right in the middle of the park. He got them all gathered round him, as he clambered up on the boards. Every few minutes, another gang arrived to swell his audience. His "Bodyguard", standing be-

 Micky perched on the bandstand in Hyde Park, from where he gave his hour's-long free performance for all the fans who had gathered outside the Royal Garden Court Hotel on July 4th.

MONKEES ARCHIVES 1

hind the crowd of fans, kept an eye on things, looked dead worried, but let Micky get on with the greatest fan get together of all time.

SANG SONGS

He did his impressions of James Cagney and others. Sang some of his favourite songs, all unaccompanied, but still very well done. He tried to teach the audience an Indian song, which he had learned from Beatle George Harrison at the night before's party. . . .

There were screams, obviously—it would have been difficult to just stand there so near to Micky Monkee and not show SOME reaction. And the crowd grew to around nine hundred, cheering every move by the tireless Mr. Dolenz. Every so often, one of the party in the hotel would go out and see that everything was still all right. But Micky had complete control. He treated the fans like real human beings and they respected him for it—treated him properly out there in the sunshine and the open air of this London Park.

TOO TIRED

Eventually sheer tiredness forced Micky to give up. He asked the fans if they'd enjoyed "our little chat". "Yeah", they yelled. They made way for him as he climbed from the platform and they followed him in a gigantic procession back to the hotel where Micky's plush bed was waiting to lull him into his first "kip" in a long, long time.

He padded in through the foyer, with members of his "Guard" in close attendance. Pressed the button of the lift and got up to the fifth floor and his apartment, his suite of rooms. And even there, as he sank pretty well exhausted on a settee in the hallway, he suddenly had a thought about one of the fans who'd been on his marathon walk and talk-in performance.

He summoned one of the party, Bill Chadwick. Said to him: "I want you to go back downstairs and try and find a girl, about twelve years of age, named Veronica. Bring her up here because I promised her I'd sign a load of autograph books she'd brought along with her. She's waited around for a long time to get to meet one of us Monkees."

SOON FOUND

Off padded Bill, eventually finding Veronica among the crowd still waiting outside the hotel. And you should have heard the comments from those still-waiting fans . . . about how nice Micky was and how you don't get that sort of attention from many pop stars.

And they were still marvelling at the way he'd given up so much of his time, just to walk and talk and hear what the fans were thinking about.

Said one member of the party: "I think the police are on their way to the park now, thinking there MUST be trouble."

NO TROUBLE

And maybe that's part of the trouble that is so often caused. Leave the star to work out his own relationship with the fans, and plead with them to give him "elbow-room" and you don't get the panic.

That apart, however, Micky brought an awful lot of happiness to an awful lot of people. He performed, on that platform, as if he was getting a massive fee for doing so. He didn't think about his own tired self, only that the fans were enjoying themselves and that it was his way of repaying them for their long vigils outside the hotel.

I've written this because it's something that should be known by all the fans. Being there was an unforgettable experience. It's only right that this new chapter of Monkee history should be shared with ALL of you, not just the lucky few who happened to be in the right spot at the right time.

And I'll say again that Micky stays right there where I said he was: the chart-topping most incredible and unpredictable pop star of them all.

THE END

" All the poor guy said was, 'Where's Texas?' "

MONKEES ARCHIVES 1

Above: Mike took time off during their last American tour to try his hand at rifle shooting.
Below: Davy, Peter and Micky pictured during the press conference at the Royal Garden Hotel on Thursday, June 29th.

MONKEES ARCHIVES 1

POW! MONKEE MEETS BEATLE!

MONKEES ARCHIVES 1

THE MONKEES MEET THE BEATLES — & TAKE ENGLAND BY STORM!

COME ALONG WITH MICKY, MIKE & DAVY AS THEY TAKE OVER THE MERRIE OLDE ISLAND LIKE SHE'S NEVER BEEN GRABBED BEFORE!

THE FIRST real live Monkee (not counting Davy Jones, of course — cos he came from there in the first place) to hit England was madness' own Micky Dolenz. He arrived at London's Heathrow Airport on February 6 to an unexpected (because his arrival had been kept "secret") crowd of over 300 super-enthusiastic female fans. Because the security police were caught off guard, Micky had quite a time — losing a few buttons and a piece of his hair — getting through the crowd to his waiting limousine. After a frantic but glorious battle (thoroughly enjoyed by everyone — press, fans and Monkee — except the under-staffed guards), Micky and his retinue made it to their hotel. Let's join them there and go along with Micky — and, eventually, with Mike, Phyllis and Davy — as they take over merrie olde England like she's never been grabbed before!

Photos World Copyright By *16* Magazine

Micky gets swamped while astounded airport officials seek to rescue him.

Whew — that was exciting! Well, what shall we do next, luvs? How's about a shopping spree on Carnaby Street?

First stop: Lord John's soopa chic boutique. I like this sweater — and I love that jacket over there!

Ah-ha — a perfect fit. So Micky decided next to look at a suit.

Single-breasted tweed with diagonal pockets — well, what do you think?

MONKEES ARCHIVES 1

Micky, old chap — what do you think of England?

Wow! It's crazy, man — cray-zee!!

The greatest moment of all comes for Micky — he meets Paul McCartney at a London disco and Beatle Paul invites Monkee Micky to his home in St. John's Wood.

What's more, Micky gets a royal introduction to "Martha", Paulie's groovy English sheepdog — talk about **long hair**. (For the greatest Dolenz-McCartney **ever**, turn to Page 19.)

Even **more**? Yep — the next day, at **Disc-Music Echo's** "Valentine's Day Award," Micky met Beatle chieftain Brian Epstein.

MORE 👉

MONKEES ARCHIVES 1

Helen Shapiro cops Jimmy Savile's cap for Micky —

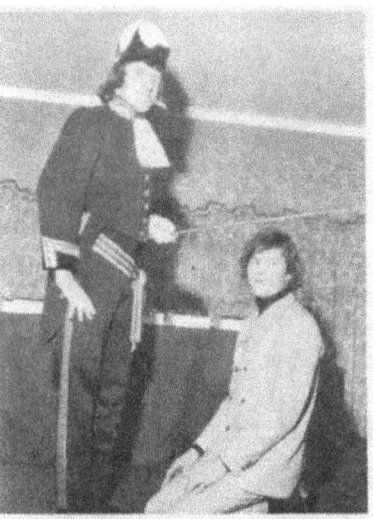

— But Micky returns it and Jimmy, the forgiving kind, promptly "knights" Sir George Michael Dolenz, Jr.!

Just before going to **Pop Inn**, BBC's top radio show, Micky ran into two old buddies of his.

Inside, he met two **new** buddies — Tom Jones and Herman (Peter Noone).

Micky poses with pop newcomer Cat Stevens, pop regular Cliff Richard and model Samantha Juste (he later dated "Sam" — but don't cry, t'weren't nothin' **serious**).

MONKEES ARCHIVES 1

CONTINUED FROM PAGE 16

"Do the Monkees **really** make their own recordings?"

Aww — you're not going to ask that tired old question again, are you?

Tell you what — see that gentleman in the white jacket carrying a tray of sandwiches? Well, he's the one who cuts all our records!

Next night Micky meets Spencer Davies (second from left) Group at the Marquee Club. They are his second favorite English group — the Beatles come first!

The quietest Monkee arrival in England was made by Mike and Phyllis Nesmith, who sneaked into London in the wee hours of dawn.

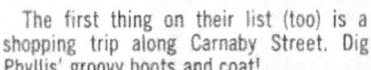
The first thing on their list (too) is a shopping trip along Carnaby Street. Dig Phyllis' groovy boots and coat!

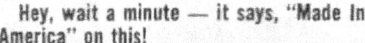
Hey, wait a minute — it says, "Made In America" on this!

Can you tell me in American dollars how much this pipe is — sir?

MONKEES ARCHIVES 1

CONTINUED FROM PAGE 18

At Lady Jane's, Phyllis looks at a wig, but decides that she'd rather have a dress instead.

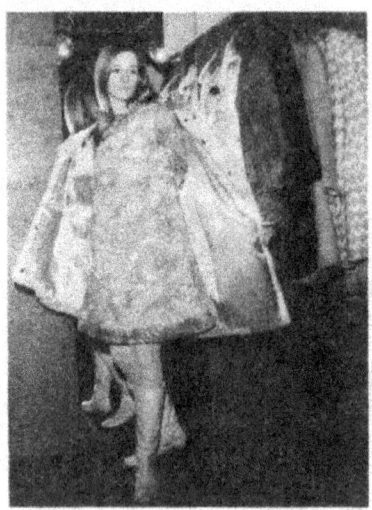
She finally chooses a pale paisley shift and a fuzzy coat.

What does hubby think? Well, just take a look at the expression on Mike's face and figure it out for yourself.

Later that day, Mike visits four of his faves, the Kinks, at their recording session. But the biggest thrill is yet to come —

The scene is a Beatle record session that is being filmed for a British TV spec. That's Mick Jagger sitting at Paul's feet.

Wearing a butcher's apron and a '30's tie — Paul conducts a 41-piece orchestra —

MONKEES ARCHIVES 1

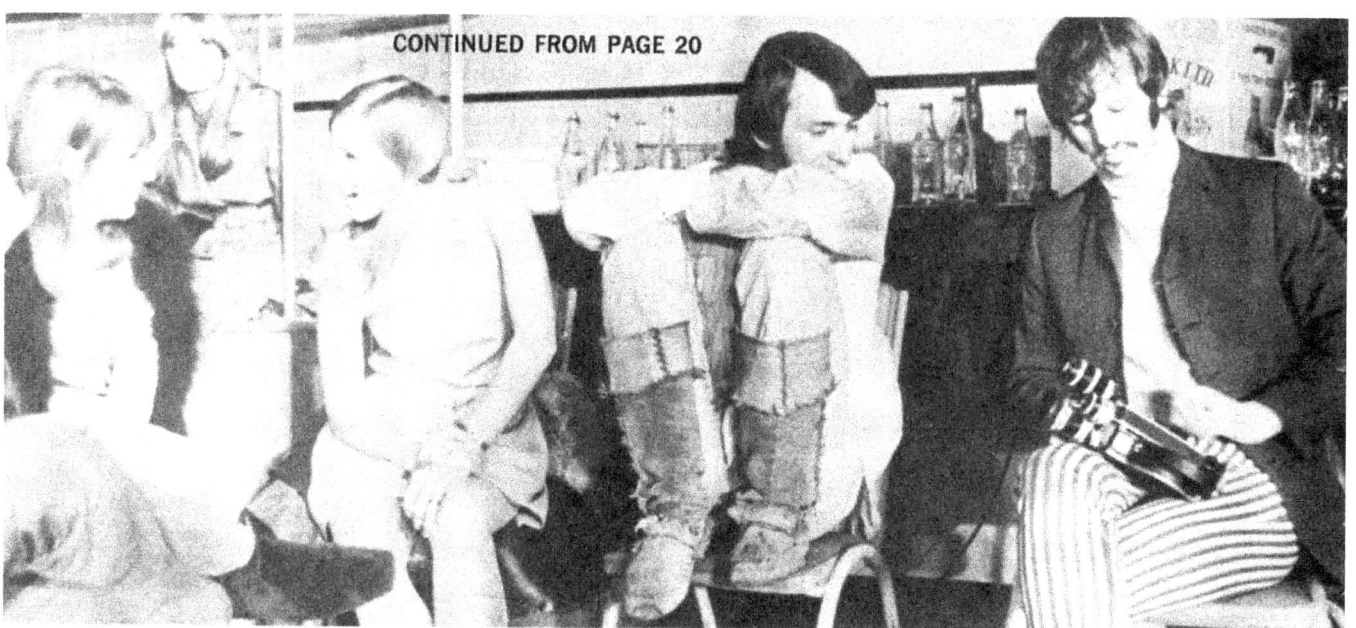

CONTINUED FROM PAGE 20

— while a "happening" audience — Cyn Lennon, Astrid Kirschner (Beatle-buddy from Hamburg, Germany), Phyllis Nesmith, Mike Nesmith and Ringo Starr — groove among themselves!

The next day, on behalf of the Monkees, Mike received a Gold Disc for **I'm A Believer** — then he and Phyllis went off to Surrey to spend the weekend with their new friends, Mr. and Mrs. John Lennon!

The next Monkee to hit London was native Mancunian David Jones — who was met (along with his buddy, David Pearl) by 700 stampeding fans!

Just before the **deluge,** Davy innocently stops and gives an airport attendant his autograph. Seconds later he was immersed in screaming English teeny-boppers!

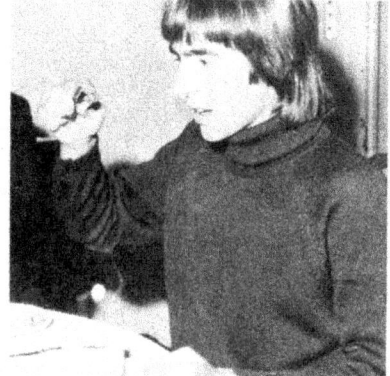

Locked in his suite in a London hotel for two days — literally to avoid causing mob scenes in the streets — Davy whiles away the hours "bombing" his tea cup with sugar cubes —

— and rolling about on the floor!

MONKEES ARCHIVES 1

Before he is "smuggled" out of town, Davy gets to meet and greet his former TV "Grandma" of **Coronation Street**, Ena Sharples.

Safely "hid out" in Middleham, Yorkshire — Davy teaches David Pearl how to "pull a pint" in the local pub.

He reminds the "resident experts" that he's still got a good hand for throwing darts, too!

Peace and freedom at last! Davy rides English racing champ "Candid Picture" across the deserted moors.

Don't worry, me luvvies — I'm coming back. See ya' Monday night — same time, same station!

MONKEE BUSINESS FANZINE

An all-Monkee magazine since 1977.

Subscription rates per year:

U.S., CANADA & MEXICO	$5.00
ALL OVERSEAS	$10.00

Monkee news from around the world

Questions and Answers

Trivia

Photos

Special between-issue advance notice of Monkees events in your area!!!

Special coverage of Monkees concerts and conventions

Record, TV, and Book Reviews

Collectors' info

Pen Pals

Classified ads

Special club items for sale

MONKEE BUSINESS FANZINE comes to you four times a year, in March, June, September, and December at the rates listed above. Each issue is over 20 pages of the best possible mixture of informative and entertaining features! MONKEE BUSINESS is currently celebrating its 9th anniversary in print———if you've missed the first 9 years, join now to be in on all the news and info!!!

MONKEE BUSINESS is registered with the National Association of Fan Clubs.

RR686

YES, PLEASE SEND ME THE NEXT FOUR ISSUES OF
MONKEE BUSINESS FANZINE. I'VE ENCLOSED $____.

NAME_____ AGE_____
ADDRESS_____
CITY_____ STATE_____ ZIP_____
PHONE (___)_____ FAVE MONKEE_____

All checks or money orders payable to:

Maggie McManus
2770 South Broad Street
Trenton, New Jersey 08610

MONKEES ARCHIVES 1

CHIP DOUGLAS INTERVIEW

CHIP DOUGLAS TALKS ABOUT THE MAKING OF PISCES, AQUARIUS, CAPRICORN AND JONES, LTD.

CHIP

Chip Douglas, at just 25, is one of today's brightest producers and has produced both the Monkees' albums, Headquarters and Pisces, Aquarius Capricorn and Jones, Ltd.

Chip was born in San Francisco, California and moved to Hawaii with his family when he was three years old. His father was a doctor on a sugar plantation on the north shore of Oahu.

When Chip was older he came to Los Angeles and joined the MFQ. He later played bass for the Turtles and last year was asked by the Monkees to do their record producing. Many hours went into their latest and greatest album on Colgems; and Chip recounts the interesting details below.

How long did you and the Monkees work on the new album?
Well, really it's been on and off since we finished the last one.

Were there any big plans made before you started actual work on it?
No, there's never any chance to plan *exactly* what you want to do, you just do what has to be done. Recording comes third on the list as far as the Monkees go. First it's shooting the TV show, then touring, and finally we squeeze in a little recording time.

Was it hard recording the album in different cities?
It took a while to get used to each studio, maybe a couple of hours more than usual. For the most part they were on tour and doing a lot of singing, so the vocals came off pretty good. We only recorded vocals on the road and they came out a lot better because the boys were doing a lot of singing and their voices were used to it, so they could hit a lot higher notes.

Why did you decide to leave in the talking before the songs start?
We probably shouldn't have left it on "Daydream Believer." The disc jockeys don't like the talking at the beginning, because it's hard to cue up. I just mixed everything down for an album. I wasn't thinking about singles. Then, they decided to put "Daydream Believer" out as a single. I completely forgot about the talking intro on that, but it's just as well anyway.

We try to leave as much of the talking bits on as possible, because it's a little something extra for the listener. I think the Monkees should do a lot more of that sort of thing. I think it would be groovy if they had about six numbers where they weren't even singing—just talking and doing bits. Hank, our engineer and I went over some of the left over tapes the other day and there's a lot of funny stuff left. They'll probably go on the next album for sure.

How did you come to use a Moog synthesizer on the album?
Micky found it. He heard of it somehow and he went over to some guy's house who had one. Micky has been interested in electronic music for some time. The guy who had the Moog did the score for "Forbidden Planet" some years ago and he was showing

MONKEES ARCHIVES 1

it to Micky. The Moog synthesizer is an electronic thing which duplicates any kind of sound. So Micky bought one. He played it on one tune, and we all dug it. Then we thought it would be kinda neat to have a jazz solo on this other tune, so we got Paul Beaver, the guy who built it, to come down and play it. He does some work around Los Angeles with his Moog, like he did the news breaks for KHJ radio and the sounds at the end of Screen Gems' films are done with the Moog synthesizer. It's just breaking into pop music.

Did the Monkees have fun experimenting with it?

Micky was having a ball on this tune "Dayly, Nightly", so we let him go four times on it, and just kept overdubbing stuff all over the place. Then later we sorted it out on the tape and I just brought up the best parts on the final track.

Who chose the name for the album?

I don't remember who it was exactly. It seems that one of the Monkees was on the phone and Lester Sill, who publishes their music, and I were discussing what we were going to call the album. Someone had thought of the idea "Monkees 4 U." But then one of the Monkees came up with "Pisces, Aquarius, Capricorn and Capricorn, Ltd." For some reason, I don't know how it started, the name just popped up from nowhere in the office and someone said, "How about Pisces, Aquarius, Capricorn and Jones, Ltd."? I laughed, and I thought, "That's great!" All the Monkees thought it sounded groovy, so that's what they called it.

Can you recall any funny incidents while recording this album?

There was the time that Ann Moses and her friend came in and clapped on "Daydream Believer" and that was pretty funny, because we had to do it several times because you have to clap a special way.

We had many, many hilarious hours riding to and from the studio in New York. The scene with the girls following the limousines was incredible. They'd follow us all the way into downtown New York.

Once a little girl got in the limousine with Davy and she didn't even know what to do. She just sort of jumped in and there she was face to face with David Jones for the first time! And Davy had one of those shocked looks on his face. She didn't know what to do, so finally she grabbed him and locked her arms around him and wouldn't let go. Finally we let her out a little ways away from the crowds. I'll never forget that!

Also, there's a whole bit that's not on this album that Micky did ad lib. Micky does this whole comedy thing where he starts talking about the Walls of Jericho and he does a whole thing on that. I've got it on tape and we edited it and put it together and it's really funny. Then Davy's trying to play a French horn in the background and it's very funny.

How did you come to include pieces like Peter's tongue-twister, which aren't really songs at all?

Peter has a bunch of those things he does every once in a while. One is called "Alvin," that his brother wrote. "Alvin" didn't get on this album, but it's very funny. Peter did that "Peter's Percival..." thing for me one day and I cracked up and I thought, "How great, we'll stick it on the album!" I wish we could have more of them, but we didn't have the time.

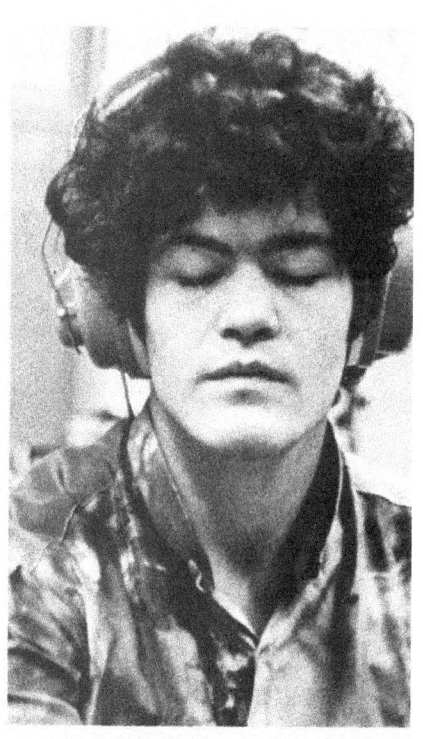

How did you get Mike's voice to sound so different on "Don't Call On Me"?

That's just another side of Mike Nesmith. He just sings that way. He had been saying for some time, "You ought to let me sing a ballad." And everybody would say, "Okay, great." So finally he came up with this ballad and everyone said, "Hey, great song, let's do it!" So we cut the track on it.

Did you use a special effect to make his voice sound different?

No! It's just him, one take, no doubling, no nothing. He's just singing really soft and close to the microphone.

MONKEES ARCHIVES 1

CHIP DOUGLAS INTERVIEW
CONT. FROM PG. 49

Whose voice is the most difficult to record?
Mike's is the hardest to record when he sings out. It's a lot better since he's had his tonsils out. His voice is very hard to get crisp. It sounds kind of fuzzy all the time, but that's the way it is. Only when he gets into a certain register does it start popping through and he has to really sing hard and intense in order to get the words across. So his, sound-wise, is the hardest.

Some people still question the Monkees' ability to play their own instruments. Did they play on this album?
Sure. Sometimes we may use strings and things like that, and they can't do those things. But the basic tracks they do themselves. There's at least a couple of them there on the tracks all the time. Maybe not all four of them exactly, only on every little thing, but they do their own backing tracks.

Why do you record mostly at night?
Well, first of all, they work during the day. Also, their voices get warmed up at night. They don't really like to record during the day. Micky doesn't. He doesn't like to come in before six in the evening and then he likes to work until about two a.m. Everyone is different. I like to record during the day. I believe you can get the most done because you're freshest in the early part of the day, as far as tracks go, and then get into vocals in the evening time.

How much time would you say goes into one album track from start to finish?
I'd say maybe 18 or 20 hours for each tune. It can be as much as 24 or 25 hours. Sometimes it's four hours, but usually because we can't record every day when we come in we have to start from scratch. We have to go through all the sounds on the instruments, get the arrangement down and things like that. The Monkees don't like to practice outside the studio. They like to rehearse right in the studio.

Do you see the boys much outside the recording studio?
Sure, as much as possible. I go over to their houses and talk about the songs first and then it's always a good idea to plan out what we want to do. We're doing that more and more now—getting together and talking about the songs. It works out a lot better.

Have your impressions of the Monkees changed after working with them for over a year now?
No. I hold the same high opinion of each of them that I always have.

Who are some of the other artists you are working with?
I'm producing a group called the Dillards, whose single should be out around the first of the year. Their sounds are like an updated bluegrass-rock; and I think the record we're working on now is going to be a gigantic success.

I'm also working with a group whose name isn't quite set yet because they may be adding another member. John Stewart and Buffey Ford is what they call themselves at the moment. John wrote "Daydream Believer."

You have redone several of the Monkees early tunes, do you think you'll re-record "Valerie"?
It's quite possible.

There was talk of putting out a Monkee album recorded live at one of their concerts. Do you see this in the near future?
We recorded them live at three of their concerts with the act they did for the summer tour. Some things came out good and some things didn't come out so good. Mainly the big appeal in a live album is in-between the numbers all the clowning around. The excitement with all the kids screaming is groovy, but it's not that great sound-wise. Live rock and roll things are very difficult to record, but it's really groovy. There're no immediate plans and no release dates, but we will quite possibly put some of it on the next album.

MONKEES ARCHIVES 1

IS MIKE NESMITH ANOTHER JOHN LENNON?

BELOW, MIKE SIPS TEA IN LONDON WHILE PHYLLIS LOOKS ON.

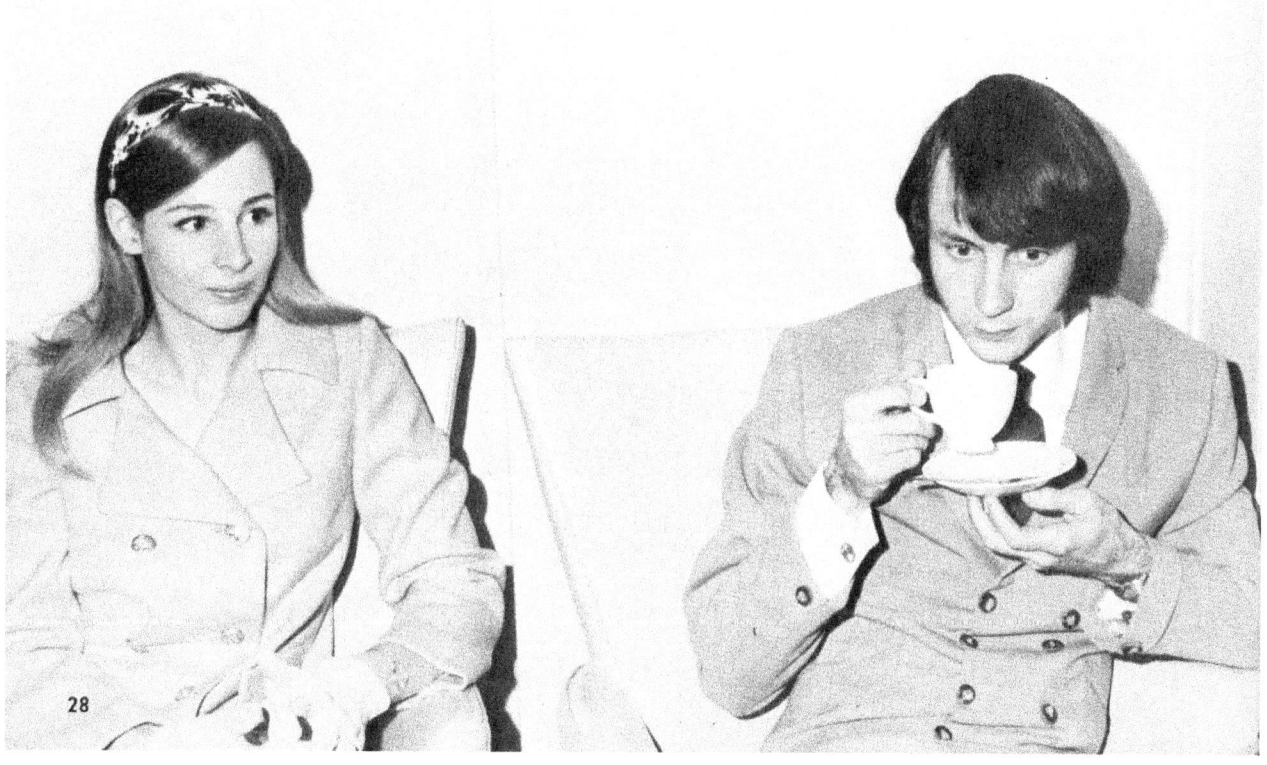

MONKEES ARCHIVES 1

If you were to see John Lennon and Mike Nesmith standing together on a street corner, talking and waiting for the light to change, you'd wonder what the two of them could possibly have in common. True, they'd have the bond of music to discuss, but aside from that—tall, lanky Mike and the shorter, stable looking John seem as different as the sun and moon and as far apart in their past lives and thoughts as Houston is from Liverpool.

Are They Different?

Are they really so different though? Let's stop and take a deeper look at these two brown haired, brown eyed, slouching young men. John and Mike though different in many ways, have more in common than their fame and love for music. Each is the second oldest member of his group and both had things in common when they were children.

John grew up in Liverpool where he lived with his Aunt Mimi in some comfort. There were times when things were a little tight, but mostly it wasn't terribly bad for them. Of course, John's school story is something else. He attended high school and later visited the Liverpool College of Art. John was an inattentive child, who just didn't apply himself to his work. School held no interest for him, because there were too many things he wanted to know that just weren't taught in school. As a result he cut classes several times and did miserably in his grades. He was a bright, quick boy who just refused to work.

Mike's Difficult Life!

Mike Nesmith was the kind of child who wanted to know why water dripped down instead of up and why dead chickens couldn't lay eggs. His life wasn't easy as a child and he once said that a meal was like Christmas. He lived with his mother in Dallas and was thought of as weird by the other kids in school. Mike cut classes at every opportunity, got really bad grades and never finished high school. He got into college in San Antonio after completing an entrance exam. School still did not interest Mike.

Meanwhile, back in school in Liverpool, John had picked up the guitar and his love for music occupied his mind almost completely. After teaching himself how to play he joined Paul McCartney and, eventually, the other Beatles in the long fight for recognition. They played clubs on the Liverpool - Hamburg circuit and John's music eventually became so much his life that he never finished college.

A quick switch back to Texas where Mike got hold of a guitar at 19 and taught himself a few chords. He didn't know any songs, so he wrote one. He became so engrossed in music that he played clubs in San Antonio and Hollywood in his battle to become a well known singer. He too, dropped college for the glory of the music field.

Marriage

One very important thing happened to both of them during the time they attended college — they both met their wives. John married slim, blonde, blue-eyed Cynthia and Mike married blonde, slim, blue-eyed Phyllis. (Both wives, incidentally, have seven letters in their first names.) Both weddings were small and quiet and this was not due to a need for secrecy because of great fame, for both of them were married before fame hit them over the head. Though people knew about both weddings, it was in John's case at least, a secret for approximately two months after the Beatles smashed the charts. In Mike's case, it was printed in the official biography, but the public was not really conscious of a marriage until almost two months after the Monkees crashed the scene.

Both men freely admitted that they were married and each had one son, but they refused to let the public in on a great deal of their private lives because both of them believe that their private lives should be kept private and that their families have a right to be protected from the limelight as much as possible. They like the fans who respect the privacy they have asked for, the nice, polite fans — not the noisy, rowdy ones. Both John and Mike are touched by certain letters and gifts that people send them.

Sensitive People

They are both sensitive people, but quick with a sharp verbal comeback when people are rude or stupid just for the sake of being nasty and deliberately dumb. John is very aware of everything that goes on around him and Mike is very sharp and has great insight. John and Mike can both get right to the heart of what's going on and neither one is fooled by the appearance of the situation. They look directly at the facts. They are both witty, intelligent and impulsive. They are stimulating people to be with, because they are both individuals. They value their freedom to be themselves before anything else and neither will totally subject himself to discipline of any kind. The courage to say and do what they wish is another common bond Mike and John share.

Ambition rules both of them. Mike is coolly ambitious and John admits to being lazy about everything, but he gets what he wants when he wants it. They always feel that things will somehow come out right for them. Mike can find a joke in anything he sees and John's ability to find a laugh in any situation is well known throughout the world.

(Continued on next page)

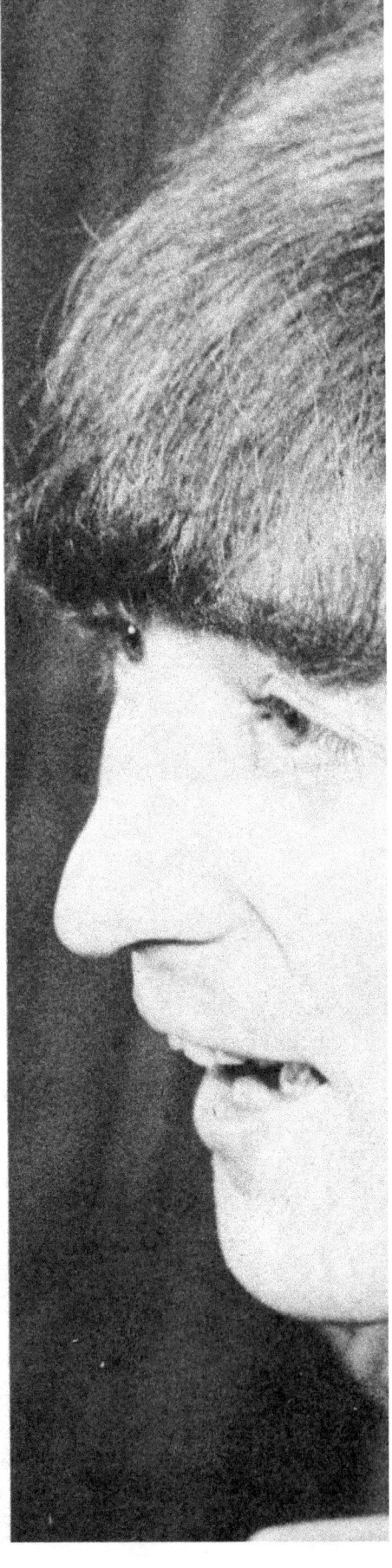

MONKEES ARCHIVES 1

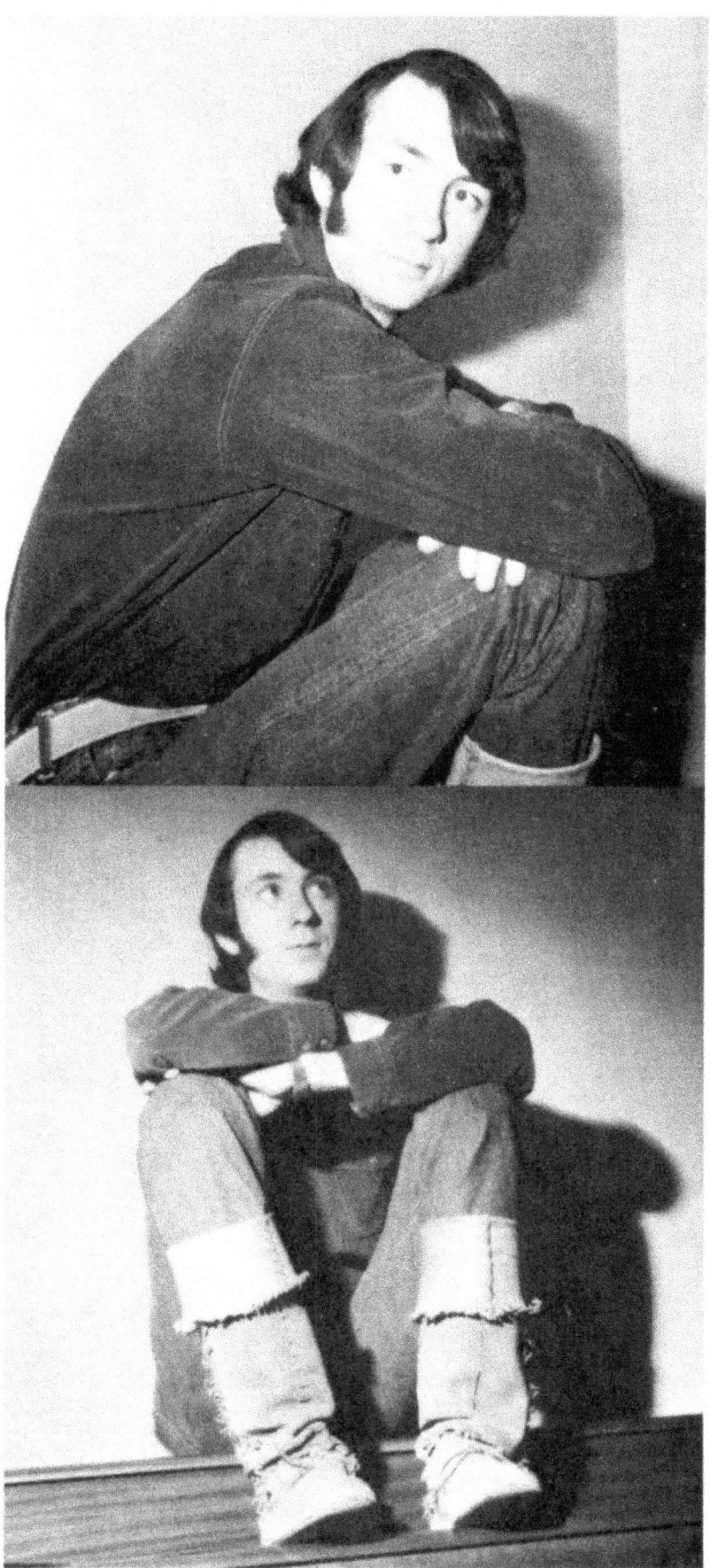

(Continued)

Though both Mike and John have a quiet way about them, they are apt to pull some really crazy stunts on those around them. They are both eccentric guys and their eccentricity shows up in a number of different ways. John's clothes' combinations are unbelievable and Mike's clothes run a close second. John loves putting T-shirts with striped blazers and sandals and things and on him it looks really groovy.

Mike grew up in Texas and that has a lot to do with the knee high moccasins, mod boots, and western type clothes he wears. Of course, if he wore anything else, he wouldn't be Mike Nesmith.

Their Houses

They both live in older houses. Mike's is a sparsely furnished Spanish and John's is a partially painted Tudor with red and green blinking light boxes (that don't blink anymore) sitting in a corner of the house. He bought them as Christmas jollies for his mates and then forgot to deliver them to everybody. Perhaps you think that there is no common bond uniting Mike and John and blinking lights. Well, all you really have to do is step inside Mike's dressing room, full of safety pins, letters from fans and —red and white tubular lights that blink on and off at one second intervals. In fact both their houses are full of so many different weird objects that they've collected, that I'm sure you'll find that they have more in common than the blinking bulbs.

Since they have become stars, they've both had to be careful about new friends. Neither likes to be taken by people close to them and for this reason John and Mike have

MONKEES ARCHIVES 1

IS MIKE NESMITH ANOTHER JOHN LENNON?

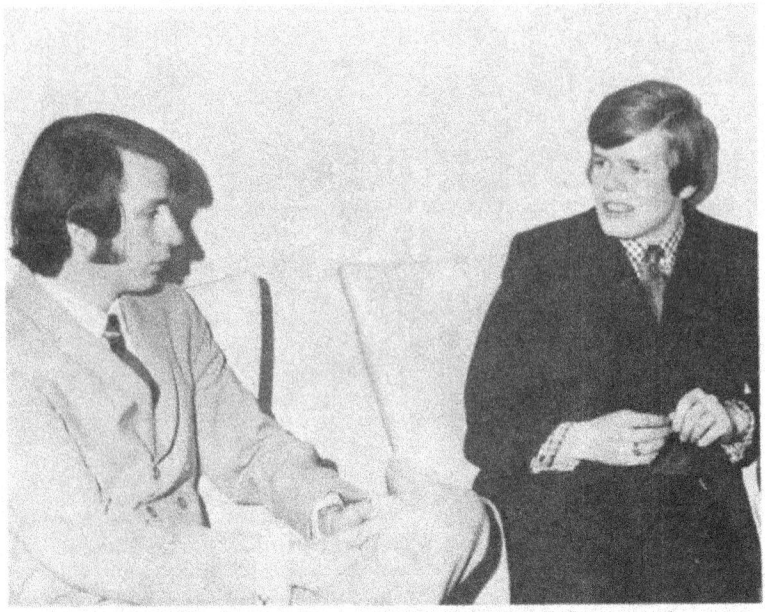

MIKE AND HERMAN met and talked in England. He found Herman to be a very bright fellow and Herman was surprised at how much Mike knew about music. Wherever Mike went in England, he was well received and the impression he created was one that demanded respect from other English artists. This helped the Monkees' popularity in England.

very small groups of friends whom they can trust. Most of these people have been friends for years — you know, the people who grew up with them and the people who have no reason to use them or their talents so that it would hurt them.

Talents In Common

Both Mike and John have an amazing number of talents in common. Though music is their main interest and both of them play at least two instruments, they are also very good actors, song writers and excellent mimics. Mike can imitate anybody around with alarming accuracy and John's different accents are fantastically exact. They both write songs on inspiration and John is always rearranging words and sentences in his mind, which makes it a bit hard for him to carry on casual conversations without getting all muddled. Mike doesn't go about rearranging words—he rearranges situations in his mind. He tends to get very involved in his daydreams.

They are both very good at weaving stories out of nothing. John puts his stories down in books or tells them to friends. Mike usually tells his tales to anyone who happens to be around when the inspiration hits him. These stories are always funny bits in a weird sort of way because that's the way Mike and John are. They are different in the way they express things, but not in what they are really trying to say to us.

So there they are, standing on a street corner together, talking, and now the light has changed and you can see that they do have more in common than just the musical world that surrounds the lives of John Lennon and Mike Nesmith.

MONKEES ARCHIVES 1

Mike's Made It!

NOT ONLY IS MIKE NESMITH A SUCCESSFUL MONKEE, HE'S ALSO RATED AS A TOP FLIGHT RECORD PRODUCER. WHEN MIKE PRODUCED HIS SPECIAL ALBUM "WICHITA TRAIN WHISTLE," MONKEE SPEC CAMERAS WERE THERE TO CATCH THE ACTION. YOU CAN TELL BY HIS EXPRESSIONS THAT THERE ARE DEFINITELY TWO SIDES TO MIKE, THAT OF THE CAREFREE MONKEE AND THAT OF THE SERIOUS RECORDING PRODUCER.

MIKE PACES the recording studio where the more than 75 musicians he hired do their stuff. He personally paid them all and at the end of the session, they gave him a great tribute by acknowledging his fine professionalism.

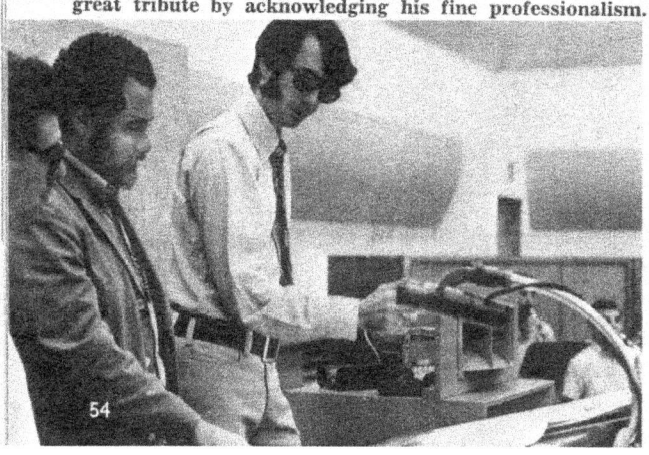

This is the last issue of Monkee Spectacular but you can keep reading about Mike in TiGER BEAT and FaVE each month!

MONKEES ARCHIVES 1

MIKE the REC

The cheers are yet to come, but they'll be here when Monkee Mike becomes a full-fledged record producer. This is something Mike's wanted for a very long time, so when he conducted his first session, our cameras were along to catch some of Mike's moods.

For any of you who've heard that the Monkees aren't musicians, this photo spread should be proof that these statements have been false. As you can see, Mike is not only a singer, but a talented musician. In fact, Mike believes it takes a lot more musical know-how to be behind the scenes on a record than in front of the mike. Above you see him conducting a special musical effect along with the regular conductor.

MONKEES ARCHIVES 1

RD PRODUCER

Photo below shows Mike listening to the playback in the control booth. He is intent on making this recording as perfect as possible. Above right shows Mike at the end of the session. For a Monkee who seldom smiles, Mike looks pretty pleased with the night's work!

MONKEES ARCHIVES 1

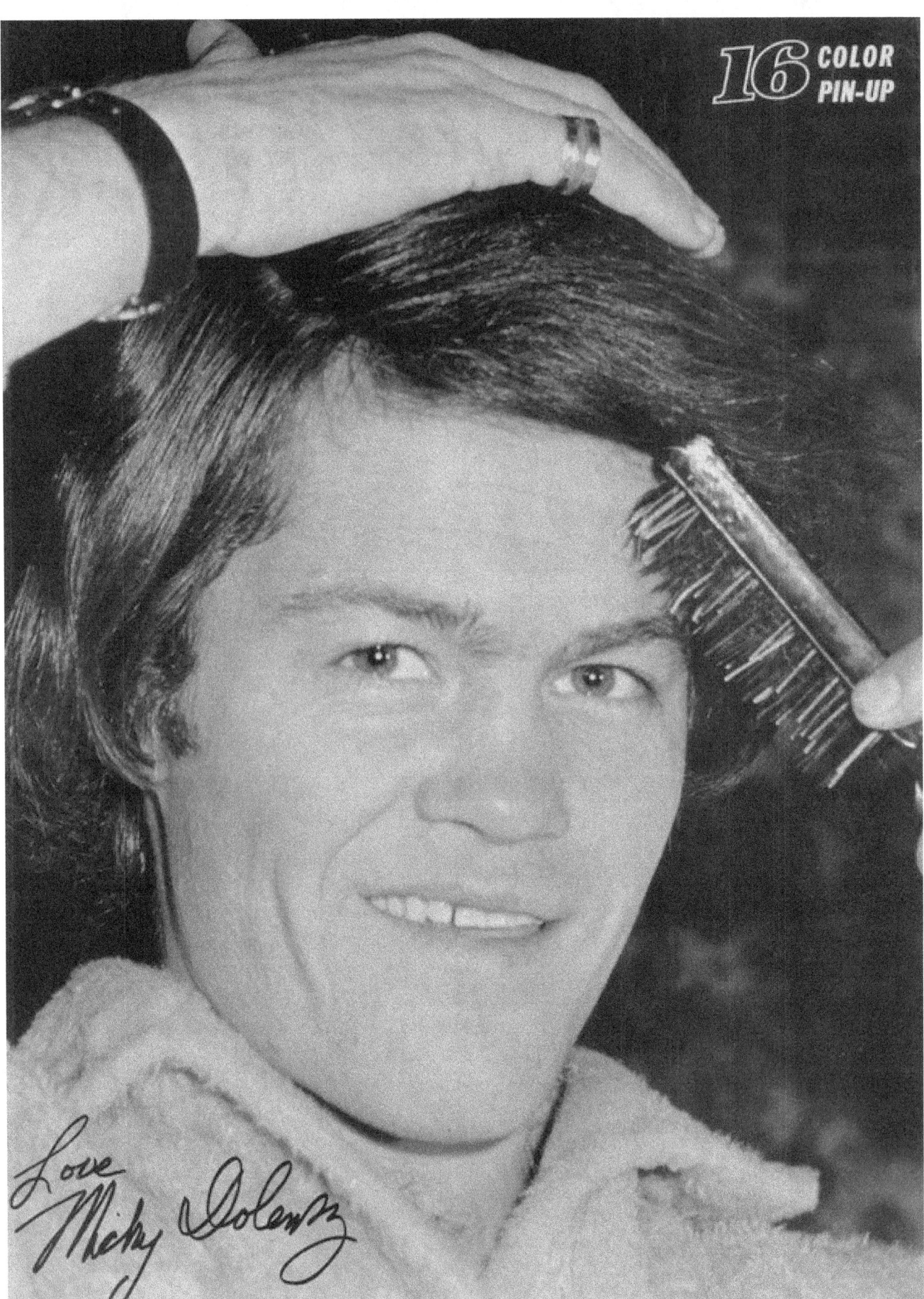

MONKEES ARCHIVES 1

Micky's all time favorite place to buy his hobby materials—Kit Kraft has EVERYTHING! Micky travels across the hills separating Hollywood from the San Fernando Valley to shop here.

Both Peter and Mike have played here and all the Monkees still come to see the show. Peter still plays on "hoot nights" when anyone in the audience can get up and do their act. ▼

Right across the street from Lenny's, just a few doors from Screen Gems where the Monkees film, this is the place you usually find the Monkees eating lunch on filming days.

Another favorite Monkee place-to-go. The Whiskee A Go Go is in the heart of the famous Sunset Strip and carries many of the top acts in the business. All the Monkees come here to see the show. ▼

MONKEES ARCHIVES 1

THE MONKEES

SAMANTHA, DAVY, AND MICKY WERE VERY EXCITED ABOUT THIS TRIP!

The Monkees are flipped out over Indians . . . East Indians . . . American Indians . . . you name them. The Monkees love them!

When they had three days off during their summer tour, Peter flew a group of 30 up to Wisconsin to visit an authentic Indian Village. Mike was the only Monkee who didn't go. The Buffalo Springfield were along to add to the fun and Henry Diltz took the groovy photos you see on these pages.

As Micky says, "The Indians had the right idea. They built everything in a circle so nobody would be left out . . . no corners." The Monkees are trying to live their lives this way so all their fans and their loved ones can be very much included in their exciting lives!

MONKEES ARCHIVES 1

PETER WORE BEADS and was quite impressed by the beauty of the Wisconsin countryside. He spent a lot of time talking to fans who recognized him on this side tour.

DAVY WALKS FAST and the rest of the group had a hard time keeping up with him. He wanted to see everything and not miss anything. Once you've walked with Davy, you don't forget it, because he moves quickly.

MICKY WENT BAREFOOT and brought his camera along to catch the action. A bus was hired to bring the Monkees' party into the village. Some fans spotted the bus along the road and followed it to the village.

GO INDIAN!

FLOWERS FOR PETER from a fan. Peter loves to get flowers as a gift and he carried these with him as he toured the village. Peter is very thoughtful and treasures the things given him.

DAVY'S SUEDE INDIAN jacket looked appropriate for this tour. His beads also looked just right. After the Monkees toured the village they spent that night on a Pullman Train car which was parked outside of the village.

MONKEES ARCHIVES 1

Now you can cash in on the meteoric success of the MONKEES, the hottest group in show business, by owning a MONKEES SOFT DRINK NITECLUB

YOU CAN BE FILLING THE ENTERTAINMENT GAP AND YOUR POCKETS OPERATING YOUR OWN MONKEES "STAGE TO STARDOM" SOFT-DRINK NIGHTCLUB. REQUIRES NO EXPERIENCE, CAN BE RUN ON A PART-TIME BASIS AND ONLY NEEDS A $15,000. INVESTMENT.

The biggest, growingest, spendingest market in the country today has no place to go. We're talking about the Youth Market. The 30 million teenagers who watch the MONKEES on TV each week. The same kids who spend 30 billion dollars each year. The same kids who are neglected by big business and left to make do for themselves. They've got a need, they are a major market and we've got something that's just for them.

THE NEED, THE NAME, THE MARKET

Who needs a MONKEES SOFT-DRINK NIGHTCLUB? Ask any teenager. Ask them what do they do for fun. The movies?... "a drag." The luncheonette?... "a big bore." The pizza parlor?... "nowhere." Here's where the MONKEES "Stage to Stardom" nightclub fills the gap. The teenage response has been wildly enthusiastic. This is what they get... an evening's live entertainment in an atmosphere that is "groovey"... one where they feel "in," "together," "with it." It's a place where they're treated right, enjoy kooky soft-drink and ice cream concoctions. All at a price that's right for them and for you. They love it. You'll love it. Because you'll be really making it. Making it to the tune of $............ (we're not allowed by the publication to mention specific amounts but we'll show you operating statements and clubs in operation which are enjoying more MONKEE business than they can handle.)

Who are these MONKEES? Ask any teenager. Just the most popular singing/acting group in the country today. A group that in only five months has captured the youth market completely. A group that America's young people identify with... body and soul. We'll tell you all about them later.

In the youth market you've got to be a teenager to sell a teenager.

The MONKEES themselves are your salesmen. They have won the love and respect and have completely captivated the hypersensitive teen market. Just one more reason why your MONKEES STAGE TO STARDOM must succeed.

MONKEE BUSINESS MEANS MONEE BUSINESS

The success story of the MONKEES has been told and retold in the nation's press and magazines. Bert Schneider and Bob Raphaelson, at Raybert Productions, came up with the idea of creating a TV series with a new group that would capture the imagination of America's youth. And on the show they would introduce the MONKEES new records. The show was produced in association with SCREEN GEMS and opened on the NBC TV network to rave reviews. The MONKEES first record album has already sold 3 million plus, an all-time record. And their single record of "I'm A Believer" has sold more than 2 million copies in just six weeks.

YOU WILL ENJOY THE ADVANTAGES OF MILLIONS OF DOLLARS WORTH OF PUBLICITY AND PRODUCT PROMOTIONS

Look, Parade, Time, Business Week and other national publications have all featured articles on the MONKEES. Soon... a feature film! Each week... the network TV show! Plus personal appearances! The MONKEEMOBILE! Stories have already appeared in many major news magazines about the MONKEES meteoric rise to success. Dozens of MONKEE products (slacks, belts, bicycles, bubblegum, to name a few) are sold, advertised and promoted throughout the country.

And in hundreds of daily newspapers across the country — rave reviews by TV critics plus hundreds of feature stories and items. Literally millions of dollars worth of publicity. All this plus the amazing number of times MONKEES records are played on radio (just tune in your local rock 'n roll station and see if you don't hear a MONKEES record at least every half hour), all helping promote your own MONKEES STAGE TO STARDOM. And this is only the beginning.

THE MONKEES STAGE IS THE SPRINGBOARD TO STARDOM

The MONKEES STAGE TO STARDOM is more than just a soft drink nightclub for teenagers. You, as operator of your club will be an impresario, discovering youthful talent, developing them to stardom. In much the same way that the MONKEES themselves have become SUPERSTARS. And this concept... a nightclub where many of the entertainers are teenagers themselves, will build your following, will win you the devotion of the teenage market in your community. The MONKEES STAGE TO STARDOM clubs will be operated on the highest standards and the possibilities for your growth as star-builder and successful nightclub operator are tremendous.

The COLGEMS management will have its scouts out discovering new talent at the MONKEES STAGES TO STARDOM. (COLGEMS is the Company which launched the incredibly successful MONKEES records.)

REMEMBER NO EXPERIENCE IN SHOW BUSINESS REQUIRED... ALL YOU NEED IS A MINIMUM $15,000 INVESTMENT AND YOUR SPARE TIME ON WEEKENDS

The MONKEES STAGE TO STARDOM is practically a turn-key operation. No fuss, no muss, no bother. We provide you with everything you'll need to get going... everything from complete theatrical lighting systems to bookkeeping methods. And we train you, too. In every aspect of your new business. Especially on how to handle big crowds. Because that's what you're going to get. Big crowds and big money.

CALL TODAY FOR IMMEDIATE INTERVIEWS
(Be prepared to give all references, please)
NATIONAL MARKETING DIRECTOR

**N.J. (201) 676-6000 or
N.Y.C. (212) 267-1600**

The MONKEES "Stage to Stardom"

Entertainment International
Subsidiary of Spectrum, Ltd.
725 Park Avenue, East Orange, N.J. 07017

Gentlemen:
I want to be a MONKEES UNCLE. Please send me all information necessary for me to make up my mind and arrange for a personal interview. I am sure that I can qualify as a licensee for the MONKEES STAGE TO STARDOM.

Name ....
Address ....
City .... State .... Zone ....
Phone ....

MONKEES ARCHIVES 1

MONKEES DO SHOWS FASTER

Not puppet!

FIRSTLY, we dealt with the subject which most people appear to be ducking — the resentment felt very strongly in some show business quarters that the Monkees are really non-playing puppets and have no right to their success as a pop group. (Before I get swamped with letters, may I say that the Monkees in my opinion are 'what's next' and I go happily around with the wheel.)

"I can only speak for myself," said Davy. "I am an actor and I have never pretended to be anything else—the public have made me into a rock'n'roll singer. No one is trying to fool anyone!

"People have tried to put us down by saying we copy the Beatles. So all right, maybe 'The Monkees' is a half-hour 'Hard Days Night!' But now we read that the Who are working on a TV series around a group. Now who's copying who?

"In our show we all play ourselves with the exception of Peter Tork, who plays a 'thick' and he's not. Pete doesn't really dig the teenyboppers scene. Some fans wrote to him that they were watching his house through high-powered binoculars and now he has the curtains drawn all day!

"There are 32 Monkee programmes now completed and in about two programmes' time you should notice about 180 per cent improvement. We really began to get on top of it—ad libbing and taking the script from the top.

"Originally the show took five days to film. Now we've got it down to two-and-a-half. But people still have no idea how hard we work or they'd never put us down."

There has also been considerable speculation over how much the Monkees are masters of their own destinies. How much say does the group have? Or are they completely controlled by management? Davy side-stepped this one and, bearing in mind our company, it was forgiveable.

"Look," he went on, "we're just out to make people happy and enjoy ourselves at the same time!"

NEXT WEEK — Davy talks about the big subject — BEATLES v. MONKEES! Don't miss it!

Last week: A big hug for DAVY JONES from Mrs. Sharples (VIOLET CARSON).

DAVY & Mrs. SHARPLES

IT was a sentimental journey for Davy Jones when he visited the set of Granada's "Coronation Street" in Manchester recently. Waiting to greet him was his "grandmother," Ena Sharples, actress Violet Carson.

In March, 1961, soon after the TV series started, Davy was brought into the programme to play 11-year-old Colin Lomax, Ena Sharples' grandson.

Davy was in Manchester to visit his relatives, and his father went with him to the studio, where Davy introduced him to the "Coronation Street" cast.

Little Lucille Hewitt—actress Jennifer Moss—renewed her acquaintance with Davy.

"You've grown," she cracked.

"Grown?" said Davy. "Why, even you used to be taller than me."

In the bar of the Rover's Return, the street's fictitious pub, grandma Sharples told Davy: "You've done very well for yourself.

"But make the most of it while it lasts. The public can be very fickle."

MONKEES ARCHIVES 1

DAVY JONES looks pleased with life during his interview with Keith Altham in London recently. The interview continues next week when Davy talks about the Beatles, religion and many other things. And more pics, too!!

In 1961; when **DAVY JONES** acted in "Coronation Street" with **VIOLET CARSON**, as Mrs. Sharples.

MONKEES ARCHIVES 1

MONKEES ARCHIVES 1

The Monkees clown for the photographer. They are (from left): Mickey Dolenz, Davy Jones, Mike Nesmith and Peter Tork.

Monkees' Antics Are A Screaming Success

By TOM STITES
Of the Post-Dispatch Staff

WHEN THE MUSIC ENDED at the Monkees show Saturday night and the squeals and screams died away, imaginary whistles sounded and bells rang in the ears of several thousand St. Louis teenagers.

Mike Nesmith, eldest of the four singers, knows the roar of delirious fans and is acquainted with the bells and whistles the roar causes.

"I wear earplugs," Nesmith said at a lunch the day before the concert. "You know what happens when a gun goes off right beside your ear? You can't hear for a little while.

"Well, my doctor says that every time we give a concert, it's the same as a gun going off, only it lasts for an hour. I've lost 12 per cent of my hearing."

The Monkees have four 200-watt amplifiers and 18 large speakers, but the fans at Kiel Auditorium Convention Hall outyell the amplifiers 50 to 1. It's not the sound system that does the damage, it's the screams.

"It's frightening," Nesmith said. "You step out there sometimes and wish you could go back. It's really enough to shake you. We can barely hear ourselves."

After the Monkees get accustomed to the noise, they have to contend with flashbulbs. Hundreds of bulbs went off almost continuously, creating an impromptu psychedelic light show. When Davy Jones, the handsomest Monkee, was singing a solo, he had to turn away and shut his eyes.

Then there's physical assault. Eighteen ushers deployed across the front of the stage were not enough to prevent a few girls from lunging onto part of the stage.

Someone is always bugging the Monkees. For example, some industrious fans penetrated the security that surrounded the group and learned

TURN TO PAGE 3

MONKEES ARCHIVES 1

MONKEES ARCHIVES 1

HANG ON to your hair-ribbons, sweeties, cos it's Monkees' travel-time again—and now the destination is Birmingham, Alabama! The on-the-go trio went down South recently, making two appearances for radio station WSGN in Birmingham—one musical and one conversational! Davy, Mike and Micky were asked to be the special guests at a giant youth rally held at the Alabama State Fairgrounds. Davy was unable to get to Birmingham until late at night and until he got there Mike and Micky "rallied" to the occasion and kept the talk going in their usual madcap fashion! The Monkees' second day in Birmingham was devoted to making music—deejay-wise at the WSGN studios and live at City Auditorium. Davy, Mike and Micky captivated thousands of Birmingham teeners who came to see and sigh over their adorable favs. Now—let's go and spend some time with the Monkees in Birmingham!

The fun-filled two days began when Micky and Mike arrived at Birmingham's airport and were greeted by WSGN Program Director Walt Williams and thousands of Monkee-lovers.

Davy arrived later with (left) Colgems Records' executive Danny Davis. Throngs of fans were on hand to welcome Davy with love beads, flowers and warm smiles.

WSGN deejay Dave Roddy seems amused while Mike takes another of Micky's jokes in stride! The zany pair made a special talk appearance at the youth rally—and they were super!

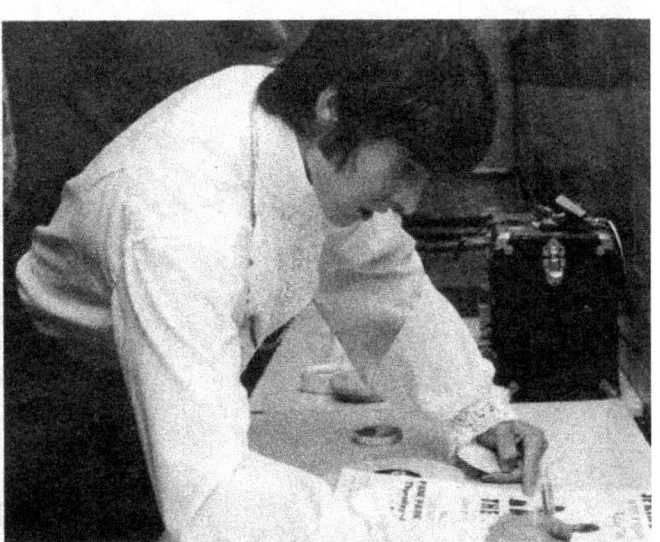

When Davy wasn't signing posters, he was Monkeeing it up with Mike and Micky—and mesmerizing audiences (radio and live) with the magic of Mommy and Daddy and Good Clean Fun—just great!

MONKEES ARCHIVES 1

During their New York City press conference, when a reporter asked Micky Dolenz what he wanted to do if and when The Monkees decided to stop being The Monkees, he didn't even have to think about his answer!

"A disc jockey," he said, kind of cheerfully, looking kind of happy when he pictured himself in the role of a raving DJ!

What kind of a DJ would Micky or any of the other Monkees make? Porbably the greatest!

So, it wasn't surprising that when The Monkees visited radio station KRUX when they appeared in Phoenix, Arizona, they took over the studios!

FLIP was there the day The Monkees turned the turntables!

Here, Micky, Davy and Mike check over the equipment. All the guys dig electronic equipment.

Micky, as a matter of fact, has just bought a machine to help him work out electronic music at home.

the monkees turn the {turn} tables!

MICKY, DAVY, MIKE & PETER FIND OUT WHAT IT'S LIKE TO BE ON THE FLIP SIDE!

As Micky checks out the engineer's panel, Mike tries to help him discover what each of the switches can do. Somehow, Micky always managed to pull the right switch and press the right button!

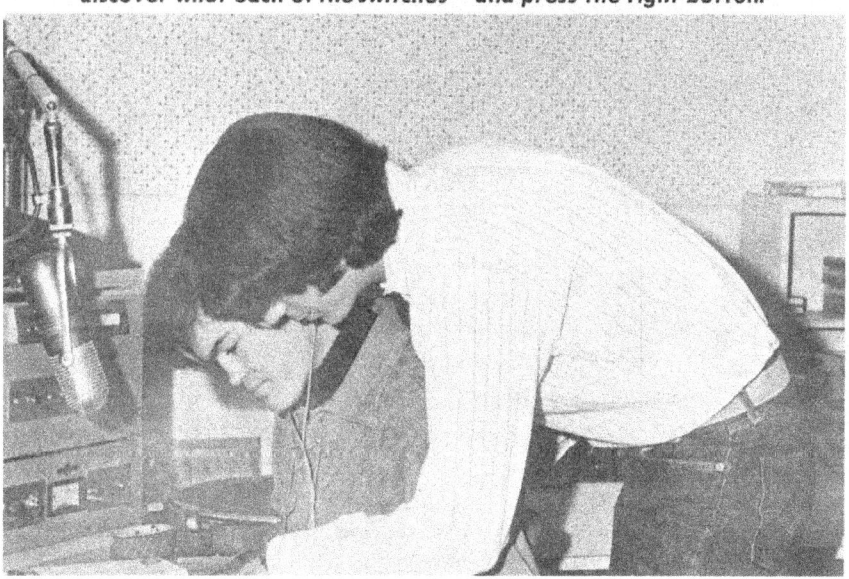

Now, Micky's on his own! Headset snapped on, one of their super-hit albums ready to play, microphone in place, Micky is ready to go on the air!

MONKEES ARCHIVES 1

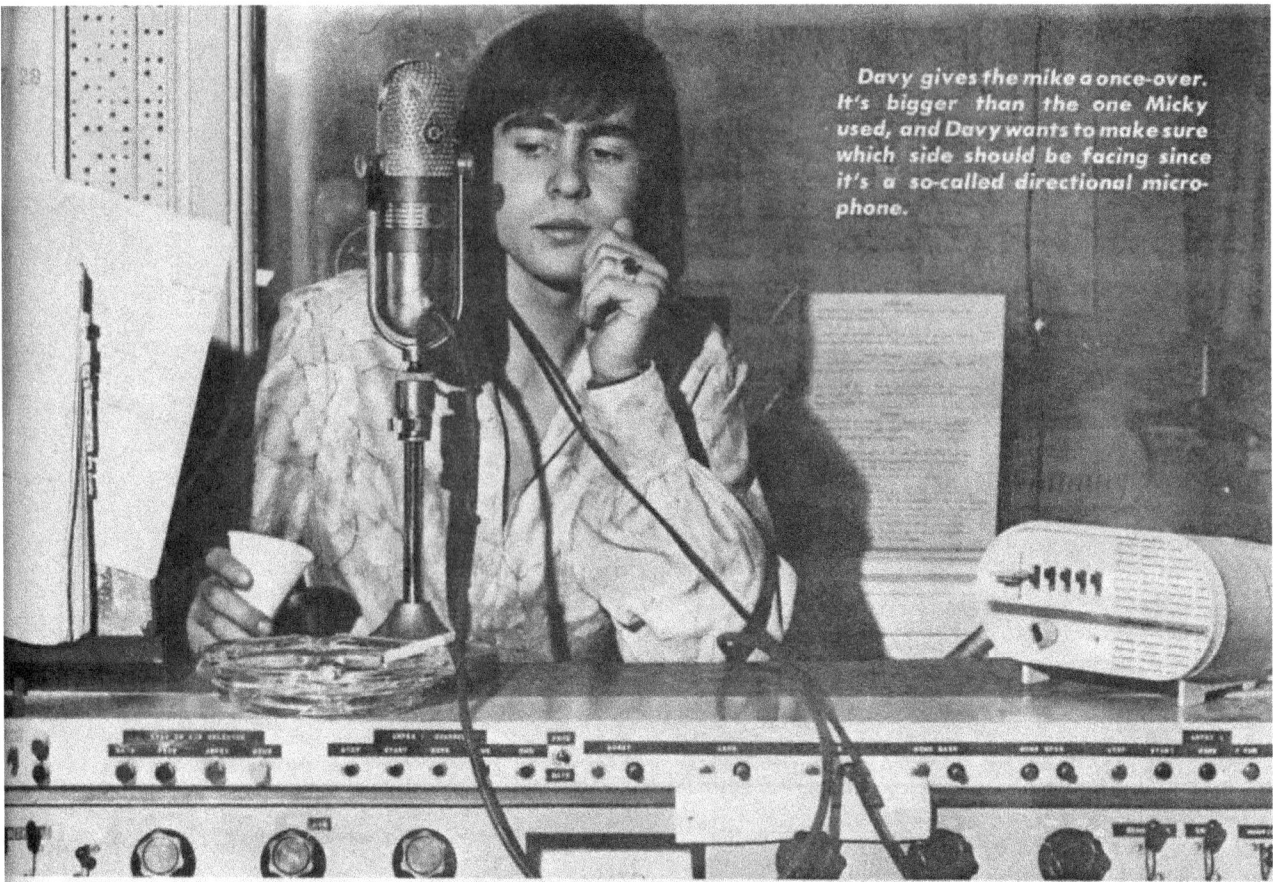

Davy gives the mike a once-over. It's bigger than the one Micky used, and Davy wants to make sure which side should be facing since it's a so-called directional microphone.

Quickly, Davy sizes it up and, cup of water in hand, is ready to rave on over KRUX. Davy makes a perfect DJ although, unlike Micky, he's never really thought of becoming a disc jockey. (At one press conference this summer a reporter asked Davy, "I understand that you were a disc jockey before you became a Monkee. Are you ever thinking of going back to it?" As everyone laughed, Davy gently answered, "No . . . I was a horse jockey!")

Mike's on the firing line here, and like the others, he enjoyed his day as a DJ—the day The Monkees turned the tables, playing their records instead of recording them!

MONKEES ARCHIVES 1

TIGER BEAT'S OFFICIAL
MONKEE
SPECTACULAR #2

Wild Color! 75 Super Monkee Scoops
Coco tells on MICKY ★ ★ Inside DAVY

REPRINT OF ORIGINAL SPECIAL FIRST PUBLISHED NOVEMBER 1967 PLUS UPDATED INFORMATION ON THE MONKEES TODAY!

MONKEES ARCHIVES 1

TIGER BEAT'S OFFICIAL MONKEE SPECTACULAR #3

$3.95 / $4.75 IN CANADA

MONKEE SONGS: Who Writes Them? Who Sings Them?
RUMORS ANSWERED: Davy's In Love... Micky's Married
FIND OUT HOW YOU CAN GET A JOB WITH THE MONKEES!

REPRINT OF ORIGINAL SPECIAL FIRST PUBLISHED FEBRUARY 1968 PLUS UPDATED INFORMATION ON THE MONKEES TODAY!

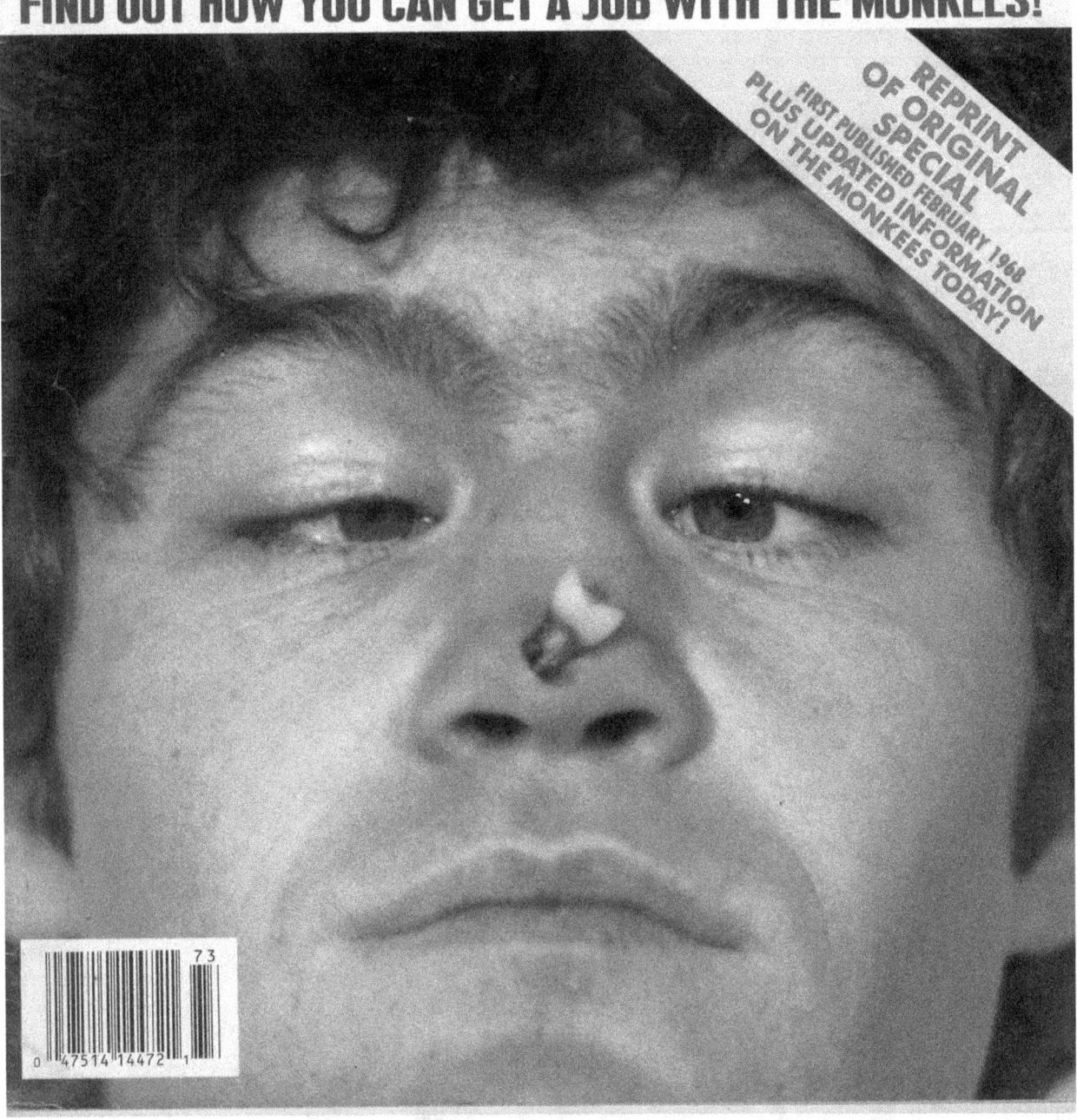

MONKEES ARCHIVES 1

Ad No. 307—396 Lines—3 Cols. x 9⅜ Inches

Ad No. 220—126 Lines—2 Cols. x 4½ Inches

Ad No. 228—100 Lines—2 Cols. x 3⅝ Inches

MONKEES ARCHIVES 1

'HEAD' AD CAMPAIGN 'A'
FOR THE 'TURNED ON' GENERATION

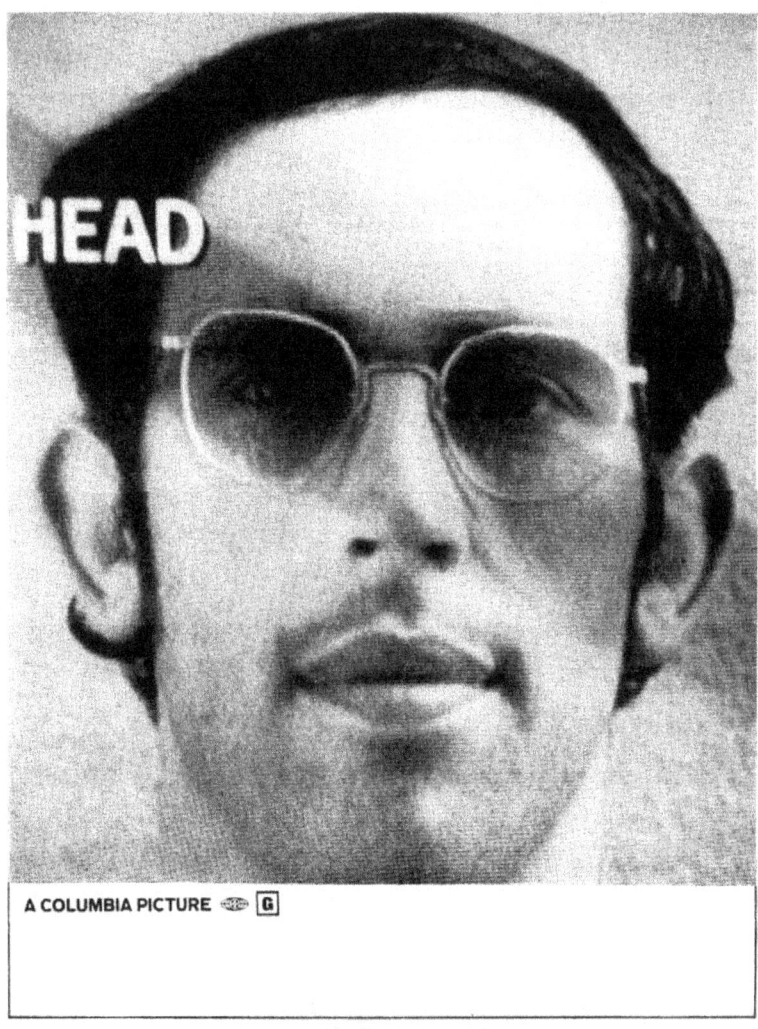

A COLUMBIA PICTURE G

Ad No. 406—536 Lines—4 Cols. x 9⅝ Inches
Also Available as Comparable Ad No. 301—366 Lines—3 Cols. x 8⅞ Inches

MONKEES ARCHIVES 1

"In terms of sheer cinema, there is a mountain of creativity adding up to mod impressionism! **HEAD** is refreshingly up to date, as if '8½' had been made by a flower child!"

—William Wolf, Cue Magazine

G Suggested for GENERAL audiences. Original sound track album on Colgems Records.

COLUMBIA PICTURES Presents THE MONKEES in "HEAD"
Written and Produced by BOB RAFELSON and JACK NICHOLSON Executive Producer BERT SCHNEIDER
Directed by BOB RAFELSON TECHNICOLOR C

Ad No. 311—303 Lines (including imprint space)—3 Cols. x 7⅛ Inches

REVIEW 1-SHEET 'C'

Also Available
as comparable
Ad No. 310—483 Lines
3 Cols. x 11½ Inches

"America is making great and meaningful movies— 'HEAD' is one of them!"
—Elvera Herbstman, N.Y. Daily Column

Ad No. 213—100 Lines—2 Cols. x 3½ Inches

"'HEAD' is memorable! A fun-movie that encompasses every other movie form!"
—Joseph Gelmis, Newsday

Ad No. 215—70 Lines—2 Cols. x 2½ Inches

"'HEAD' is a mountain of creativity, as if '8½' had been made by a flower child!"
—William Wolf, CUE MAGAZINE

Ad No. 212—62 Lines—2 Cols. x 2¼ Inches

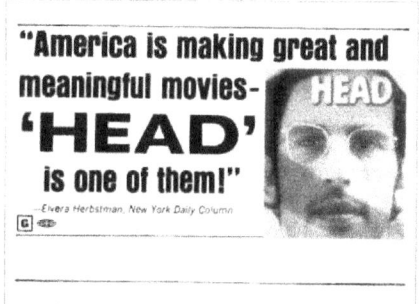

"America is making great and meaningful movies— 'HEAD' is one of them!"
—Elvera Herbstman, New York Daily Column

Ad No. 216—70 Lines—2 Cols. x 2½ Inches

MONKEES ARCHIVES 1

TWO UNIQUE 'HEAD' CAMPAIGNS REACH AUDIENCES AT EVERY LEVEL

A —For the "Modern" Film Audience!

CAMPAIGN 'A' POSTER!

Use Campaign "A" One-Sheet and ads first as teasers and, later, with credits wherever "Hip" crowds gather: local discotheques, women's mod fashion shops, avant gard stores, restaurants, Carnaby Street clothing departments, libraries, high school and college spas and newspapers, stores selling art posters and books, etc. . . . Staple two posters, back to back, around telephone and light poles in town . . . send pretty girls, wearing posters front and back sandwich-board style, to news offices, radio/TV stations, etc.

FOR 'HEAD'-LINES!

Put a psychedelic light show into your lobby, well in advance of playdate; if nothing else, then a color-wheel and flasher light aimed at a Campaign "A" poster! . . . Girls compete for best "Head" styles: unusual coiffures or make-up; a beauty shop specialist might do a job in the lobby, teaching cosmetic usage to volunteers. . . . Promote a used car, paint it with psychedelic designs, add Campaign "A" posters, and send it around town . . . follow-through, after opening, with the Review One-Sheet "C", shown on page 8.

GO GURU-ISH FOR 'HEAD'!

Abraham Sofaer as a guru, an East Indian religious teacher, wears long hair and a beard and a long, flowing robe for his role in "Head." Use Still No. 30 (left) as a guide in costuming a local bally as a Guru, to walk through town with a sign on his back: "The Guru Says Go-Go, See 'Head' State Theatre!" At other times, your guru can sit on a pillow near the entrance or sell tickets.

B —For The Monkees' Fans!

USE THE TITLE

For a week before playdate, take photos of pedestrians around town, circle one head in each picture and post on a lobby board; guest tickets to those identifying themselves at the theatre . . . A deejay's representative can stop passersby and ask them whose head appears on a 5, 10, 20, 50, 100, 1,000 or 5,000 dollar bill; those correctly naming Lincoln, Hamilton, Jackson, Grant, Franklin, Cleveland and Madison respectively, win guest tickets to "Head" . . . Get local barbers to tie-in with posters in windows: "Your 'Head' is Our Business! See 'Head', etc." Hat stores can cooperate similarly.

TIE-UP STILLS

Plant the following "Head" tie-in stills in appropriate store windows.

- Men's Fashions—Still No. 13, Mike Nesmith in Mod costume; Still No. 35, The Monkees in Mod costumes.
- Music—Still No. 12, Mike Nesmith with guitar; Still No. 41, Peter Tork and Micky Dolenz with guitars.
- Sports—Still No. 22, Victor Mature, golf; Still No. 26, Sonny Liston.

Remember, please, there can be no real or implied endorsements.

ULTRA-MINI GIRL IN 'HEAD'!

Miss I. J. Jefferson, lovely new starlet in "Head," models an ultra-mini she wears in the film. An unusual stunt would be to invite all mini-skirted girls to see "Head" as guests of the theatre when accompanied by boys paying admission. As part of the stunt, award prizes for shortest, most unusual, most colorful mini-skirts and to girls with the best mini-skirted legs. Still No. 28, shows Miss Jefferson at right.

AUDIO-VISUAL AIDS
For Both Campaigns

TELEVISION TRAILERS
One 60-, one 20-, one 10-second trailer that sell the exciting showmanship of the Monkees!

RADIO SPOTS
One 60-, one 30-, one 10-second spot keyed to The Monkees and their unique motion picture debut in "Head" and one 60-, one 30- and one 10-second spot high-lighting the rave reviews accorded the film!

THEATRE TRAILER
A showmanship first! Exciting multi-image theatrical trailer that works with both of the newspaper advertising and exploitation campaigns!

ACCESSORIES
For Both Campaigns

- SIX SHEET (B)
- THREE SHEET (B)
- ONE SHEET (B)
- REGULAR TRAILER
- INSERT CARD
- 22 x 28
- EIGHT 11 x 14's
- TEASER TRAILER
- UTILITY MAT
- WINDOW CARD
- 40 x 60, 24 x 60, 24 x 82, 30 x 40
- TITLE DISPLAY
- HI-RISE STANDEE
- STILL SETS (Color and B W — Color, for lobby and store displays; B W still for newspaper planting)

In addition to the Accessories listed above, there are:

- ONE SHEET (A)
- REVIEW 1-SHEET (C)

These are to be used only with the 'A' newspaper advertising campaign.

Order From National Screen

Monkees Make Movie Bow in Hectic New Comedy, 'Head'

The Monkees—Micky Dolenz, Davy Jones, Mike Nesmith and Peter Tork — currently make their motion picture bow, collectively and individually, in "Head," new Columbia Pictures comedy with music at the ..... Theatre in Technicolor.

Television, recording and concert stars, The Monkees as a team easily are America's greatest entertainment group.

Formed in 1966, they burst on the musical scene with a single, "Last Train to Clarksville," which immediately sold 500,000 copies and since has climbed considerably higher. Their television show won the attention of millions. Now, The Monkees' singles and albums never sell less than a million copies, and their concert appearances in major American cities and in London attract thousands of adults and teen-agers.

"Head" reportedly is an exuberant comedy with music in keeping with The Monkees' record of successful entertainment innovation. On location for the film or in Columbia studio sets, The Monkees sought the new and unusual, including a hectic sequence filmed in a Los Angeles sewage disposal plant!

The sound stages at Columbia housed some of the "wildest" sets ever seen at the studio. One room, The Monkees' "pad," was furnished with such unlikely items as a barber's chair, a glass rocking chair, an old poster of Teddy Roosevelt, a gold encrusted ancient piano, a glass pillar sitting in the middle of the floor, hanging cardboard cutouts of a man's anatomy, some cola signs, etc., etc.

Cinematographer Michel Hugo has dubbed the picture his "most exacting assignment," based on the fact that director Bob Rafelson wanted so many quick cuts, wipes, dissolves, etc. Hugo had some ideas of his own, filming scenes with the camera tilted, or upside down, or side-ways.

"Head" is a "different" kind of movie and, as such, Hugo gave more attention to angles and new usage of the camera than he did to whether the lighting was just right or the boys' makeup was as it should be. On one occasion, for the filming of a comedy scene where a girl leaps from a four-story roof top, Hugo used a wheelchair and a hand-held camera, thus being able to bring his camera into the middle of a crowd and shoot the girl from their viewpoint.

In a day and age when Hollywood is testing new approaches, filming new story lines, trying for the different and unusual, The Monkees and "Head" executive producer Bert Schneider and director Rob Rafelson are in the forefront of that effort. Their uniqueness is obviously not just a fad. It is, rather, a broadening of the scope of picture-making. The audience reaction to "Head" augurs well for The Monkees and their behind-the-camera experts.

Featured in "Head" are Victor Mature, former heavyweight champion Sonny Liston, Annette Funicello and Green Bay Packers star Ray Nitschke. Rafelson wrote the script wih Jack Nicholson, and the two men also produced the film.

(Mat 2C; Still No. 33) The Monkees—from left to right, Peter Tork, Micky Dolenz, Davy Jones and Mike Nesmith—make their big-screen bow in "Head," exuberant new comedy in Technicolor released by Columbia Pictures. Victor Mature, Sonny Liston, Annette Funicello and Ray Nitschke also are in the zany new feature film.

(Mat 1A; Still No. 45) Davy Jones and lovely screen newcomer I. J. Jefferson are shown in a scene from "Head," new Columbia Pictures release in Technicolor. Starred with Davy Jones in "Head" are the other members of The Monkees; Micky Dolenz, Mike Nesmith and Peter Tork.

Micky Dolenz

Unlike his three colleagues in that exuberant foursome known as The Monkees — Davy Jones, Mike Nesmith and Peter Tork — Micky Dolenz came to show business with an entertainment background; his father, the late George Dolenz, had been a screen and stage player. Micky, who currently makes his motion picture debut, along with the other Monkees, at the .... Theatre in "Head," also enjoyed something of a headstart on stardom. He had played the title role in the successful television series, "Circus Boy."

"Head," the swift-paced comedy with music released by Columbia Pictures at the .... Theatre in Technicolor, features Victor Mature, former heavyweight champion Sonny Liston, Annette Funicello and Green Bay Packers star Ray Nitschke.

Dolenz returned to school after his three-year stint as "Circus Boy," completing his junior and senior high school studies and then taking up the study of architectural drafting at Los Angeles Trade and Technical College. A realist, he also kept a foot in the television door, making appearances on various shows like "Playhouse 90," "Mr. Novak" and "Peyton Place."

"I know this business well enough," he says of the entertainment world, "to know that if you're smart you don't put all your eggs in one basket." Hence, the architectural drafting studies, even as he developed his abilities as an entertainer.

Bob Rafelson, who directed "Head," wrote the script with Jack Nicholson and the two of them also produced the film.

Davy Jones

Davy Jones is a young British singer-dancer who is a vital element in that distinctly American entertainment group known as The Monkees. He also is a former racing jockey.

Davy, along wih his fellow-Monkees—Micky Dolenz, Mike Nesmith and Peter Tork—makes his motion picture debut in "Head," the Columbia Pictures comedy with music now at the .... Theatre in Technicolor. Reportedly as delightful as their spectacular television series, "Head" surrounds The Monkees with such featured players as Victor Mature, former heavyweight champion Sonny Liston, Annette Funicello and Green Bay Packers star Ray Nitschke. Young Davy, who is five feet three, provides a sharp contrast to Mature and the athletes; on the other hand, he is the Monkee who becomes involved, in "Head," with Annette.

A native of Manchester, England, Davy was 14 when he left home with his family's blessings and a yen to be a jockey. After serving his apprenticeship, and achieving some success as a jockey, Davy began frequenting the haunts of England's younger set, to hear and to enjoy the great new musical sounds of the day. He met show business people and, in time, found himself playing a juvenile delinquent in a radio drama. This, in turn, led him into a steady job on a daytime program. But Davy continued at the track until he won a role in Lionel Bart's musical, "Oliver!"; as The Artful Dodger, he starred on both the London and Broadway stage. Later, he appeared in "Pickwick."

Mike Nesmith

Mike Nesmith was a country-and-western singer-guitarist before he became one of The Monkees, that fast-moving quartet which brought the New Sound to records, television and concerts.

Now, at the .... Theatre in "Head," a zany and original screen comedy with music, Nesmith and his Monkees' associates—Micky Dolenz, Davy Jones and Peter Tork—make their motion picture debut. A Columbia Pictures release in Technicolor, "Head" features Victor Mature, former heavyweight champion Sonny Liston, Annette Funicello and Green Bay Packers star Ray Nitschke.

Nesmith is a native of Houston, Texas, who taught himself to play the guitar and then found himself in the embarrassing position of being unable to read music and, therefore, of being unable to play the music around him. He resolved the problem by creating his own songs. One "Head" song, "Circle Sky," is Nesmith's.

While at San Antonio College in Texas, he moved from the country-western genre to the New Sound which was beginning to sweep the country and, in Los Angeles after college, he developed a considerable following while singing and playing his own material. Guitar-playing lead singer of The Monkees, Nesmith is gratefully aware of the reception his music is getting today.

Bob Rafelson and Jack Nicholson wrote and produced "Head," which Rafelson directed. Bert Schneider served as executive producer.

Peter Tork

A gifted musician tuned in to what is known as the New Sound, Peter Tork has achieved a considerable fame as one of The Monkees, that irrepressible, fast-moving group of young zanies who made entertainment history with their records, their concert appearances and their television show. Currently, Tork and his fellow-Monkees—Micky Dolenz, Davy Jones and Mike Nesmith — make their motion picture debut in "Head," an original comedy with music presented by Columbia Pictures in Technicolor at the ..... Theatre.

Featured in "Head" are Victor Mature, former heavyweight champion Sonny Liston, Annette Funicello and Green Bay Packers star Ray Nitschke.

The son of an associate professor of economics at Connecticut University, Tork is an expert with guitar, ukelele, five-string banjo, bass, piano and French horn, among other instruments. He planned to be a teacher, but quit Carleton College in Minnesota after three years, to devote himself to music.

He became a singer-musician in New York's Greenwich Village, performing in various pass-the-hat hideaways, and later toured as an accompanist for The Phoenix Singers. While on the West Coast, where he was appearing in various clubs and coffee houses, Tork auditioned for, and became a member of, The Monkees. Two "Head" songs "Can You Dig It," and "Long Title, Do I Have to Do It All Over Again," were written by Tork.

Bob Rafelson and Jack Nicholson wrote the "Head" script.

Monkees' First

Television, recording and concert stars, The Monkees—Mickey Dolenz, Davy Jones, Mike Nesmith and Peter Tork — make their first feature film appearance in "Head," the Columbia Pictures release in Technicolor at the .... Theatre.

All, of course, have been on television; The Monkees' show was one of the most eagerly-watched in network history. Jones was on the London and Broadway stage as The Artful Dodger in the Lionel Bart musical, "Oliver!" Nesmith and Tork appeared in coffee houses and night clubs as singers and musicians. Dolenz began his theatrical career in the title role of television's "Circus Boy," and also has played dramatic roles on other shows.

"Head" is The Monkees' first motion picture, individually or collectively.

Victor Mature

Victor Mature, who has played in motion pictures just about everybody from Samson, the Biblical strong man, to Doc Holliday, one of the West's more famous gambler-gunmen, plays an actor named Victor Mature—himself!—in Columbia Pictures' ebullient new comedy, "Head," The Monkees' debut film at the .... Theatre in Technicolor.

Also in "Head," in addition to Mature and The Monkees — Micky Dolenz, Davy Jones, Mike Nesmith and Peter Tork—are former heavyweight champion Sonny Liston, Annette Funicello and Green Bay Packers star Ray Nitschke.

Playing himself, according to Mature, is "quite a compliment. Hollywood's made scores of pictures about actors, but there has only been one, Audie Murphy's 'To Hell and Back,' in which the star played himself." Mature is gratified for another reason by the fact that he plays himself. "After all," he grins, "that's my favorite subject."

Bob Rafelson directed "Head," based on a script he wrote with Jack Nicholson.

The Music

The Monkees, that spectacular entertainment quartet making their motion picture bow in "Head," new Columbia Pictures release at the .... Theatre in Technicolor, sing six songs in the course of the hectic new comedy. They are "Porpoise Song," "Circle Sky," "Can You Dig It," "As We Go Along," "Daddy's Song" and "Long Title: Do I Have to Do This All Over Again."

(Mat 2B; Still No. 106) A zany sequence from "Head," new Columbia release in Technicolor, has Davy Jones telling Annette Funicello he would rather fight than fiddle, while Mickey Dolenz is a U. S. Cavalryman from "another picture" entirely! Mike Nesmith and Peter Tork are other Monkees starred in "Head."

(Mat 1B; Still No. 68) Peter Tork of The Monkees has his hands full in "Head," new Columbia release in Technicolor. Also starred are the other Monkees: Micky Dolenz, Davy Jones and Mike Nesmith. The girl here is June Fairchild.

MONKEES ARCHIVES 1

Hey, hey, it's the Monkees

HEAD opens at the Forum cinema tomorrow for a two-week season.

Instead of a cast of thousands, it has Davey Jones, Mike Nesmith, Peter Tork, Micky Dolenz, Victor Mature and Sonny Liston.

The first four of those names belong to the pop group, The Monkees.

Head their first big movie, is in color—headache color.

The Monkees' TV series has just wound up, so if you are one of those who miss them, this should be your chance for a good long yell-and-scream session.

The Monkees were gathered together in America to compete against the Beatles for popularity and money.

Head has 14 songs.

It has a giant vacuum cleaner, Indians, surrendering Italian troops, a Coca Cola vending machine that gets its just deserts in the desert, some war, a boxing match, a female impersonator, belly dancers, kissing, a toilet with a difference.

It's enough to give your granny nightmares.

"I would like a glass of cold gravy with a hair in it", is the line which sticks in my throat most after watching the preview.

If religion is the opium of the masses, this kind of film—with all its psychedelia — is their LSD.

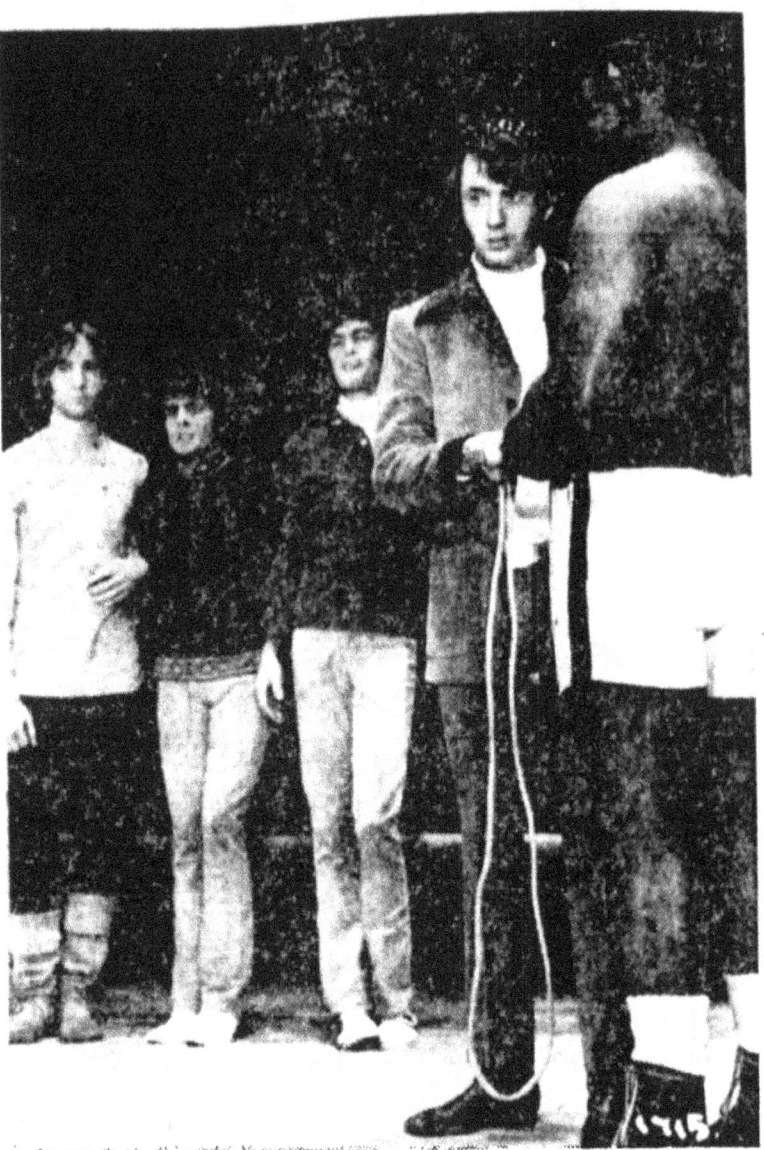

Monkee Mike Nesmith is Sonny Liston's second in Head. His third, fourth and fifth are Mickey Dolenz, Davey Jones and Peter Tork. Head opens at the Forum tomorrow.

MONKEES ARCHIVES 1

BOSS HIT BOUNDS

ALL I SEE IS YOU	
Dusty Springfield	Philips
GET OUT OF MY LIFE WOMAN	
The Leaves	Mira
DON'T START CRYING NOW	
Them	Parrot

RIDE WITH THE BOSS JOCKS AND THE MONKEES ON "THE LAST TRAIN TO CLARKSVILLE!" SEND A POSTCARD WITH YOUR NAME AND ADDRESS TO: MONKEE TRIP, BOX 38-130, HOLLYWOOD. GO ALONG FOR THE RIDE... AND WIN ONE OF _FOUR_ COLOR T.V. SETS FROM...

93/KHJ
BOSS RADIO
IN LOS ANGELES

BOSS 30 FROM 93/KHJ

THE MONKEES IS COMING TO 93/KHJ!

BOSS HIT BOUNDS

REACH OUT I'LL BE THERE	
The Four Tops	Motown
SEE SEE RIDER	
The Animals	MGM
WHAT A PARTY	
Tom Jones	Parrot

MEET THE MONKEES!

LISTEN FOR DETAILS ON...

93/KHJ
BOSS RADIO
IN LOS ANGELES

BOSS 30 FROM 93/KHJ

THE MONKEES IS COMING TO 93/KHJ!

MONKEES ARCHIVES 1

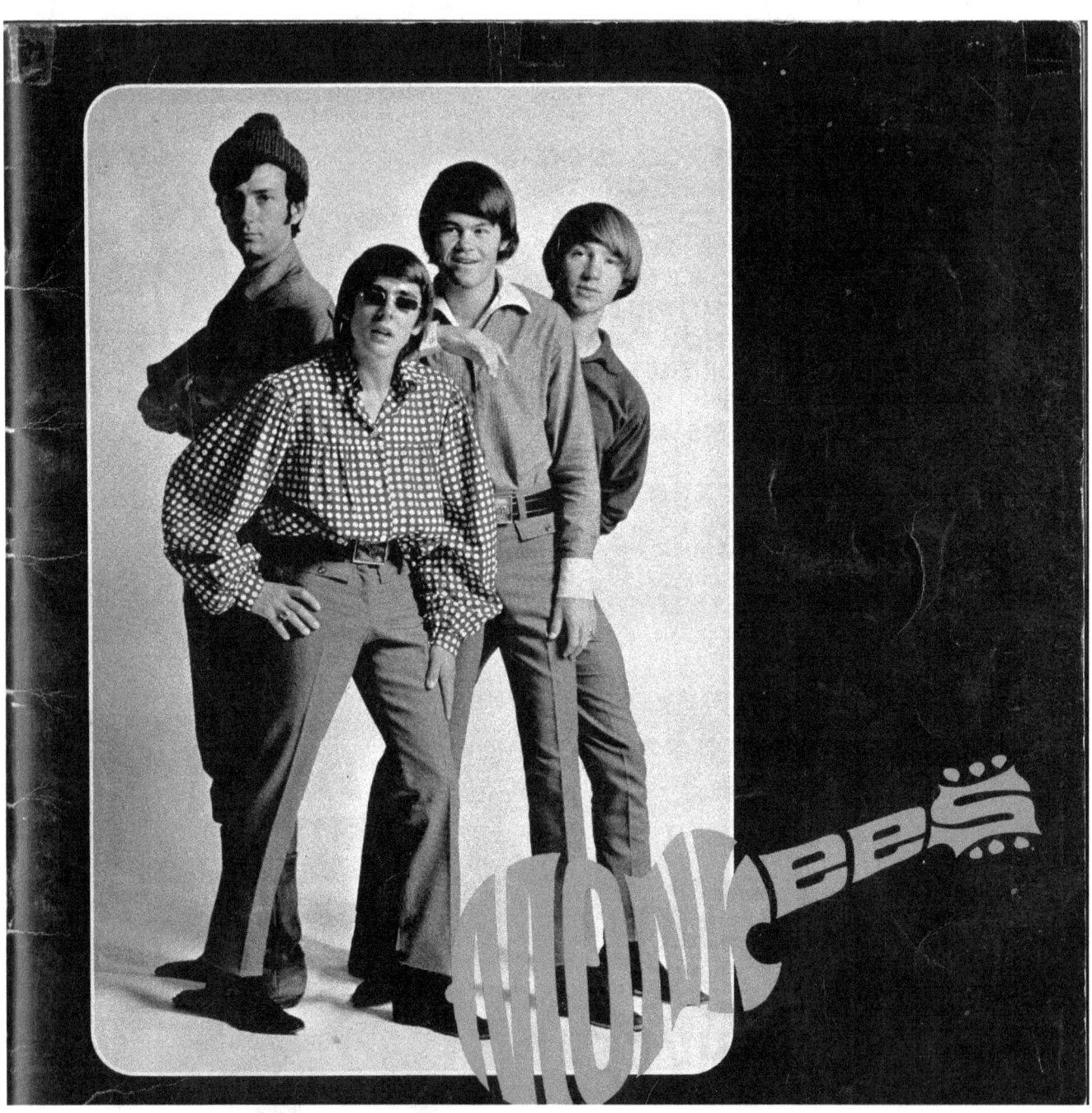

Members of the national **MONKEE CLUB** receive a membership kit filled with pictures of Micky, Davy, Mike and Peter, fact-filled biographies of each boy, a membership card, Monkee button and lots more exciting items. Members also receive private newsletters about **THE MONKEES'** activities, a chance to win a personal telephone call from your favorite Monkee, and invitations to meet **THE MONKEES** when they visit your city.

If you would like to be a member of the only official national **MONKEE CLUB,** clearly print your name, address and zip code number and send it with one dollar to:

Monkee Club
Box 9
Los Angeles, California 90051

© 1966 Raybert Productions, Inc.
Trademark of Screen Gems, Inc.

MONKEES ARCHIVES 1

MONKEES ARCHIVES 1

MONKEES ARCHIVES 1

MONKEES ARCHIVES 1

MONKEES ARCHIVES 1

MONKEES ARCHIVES 1

MONKEES ARCHIVES 1

MONKEES ARCHIVES 1

MONKEES ARCHIVES 1

MONKEES ARCHIVES 1

MONKEES ARCHIVES 1

MONKEES ARCHIVES 1

MONKEES ARCHIVES 1

MIKE NESMITH

Solemn-faced Mike Nesmith taught himself to play guitar when he was about 19 years old. He didn't know any songs and he couldn't read notes, so he composed his own material.

As a student at San Antonio College, he began making appearances, first as a country-and-Western singer-guitarist and eventually as performer of other varieties of today's "sound."

After college, he moved to Los Angeles and he teamed with bass player John Lundgren with whom he toured Southern California. Adding a drummer, they formed a promising trio which was eventually broken up by the local draft board.

Mike's next stop was Ledbetter's, an L. A. folk club. There he developed his first major following, singing and playing his own material. A year ago, his friends had to urge him to interview for an acting-performing role in a TV pilot, supposedly envisioned as a symbol of the young generation. Dressed in Levis and wearing a green knitted hat, he finally went over to the Screen Gems lot to see what it was all about. Mike was quickly recognized as a born "monkee" and that was that.

Nesmith was born in Dallas, Texas on December 30. He is six-feet one-inch in height, weighs 155 pounds, has dark brown hair and eyes. He lives on a hill in West Hollywood.

MONKEES ARCHIVES 1

Micky Dolenz, drummer-singer-comic and all-around noisemaker, left a Los Angeles technical trade school to become lead singer in a pop-rock group called The Missing Links.

Between appearances with The Links, he acted in television series, including "Peyton Place" and "Mr. Novak." And when singing or acting jobs were scarce, he worked as a mechanic.

Micky was born in Los Angeles on March 8, 1945 the son of an actor — the late George Dolenz. At ten, he began a three year run as star of a TV series, "Circus Boy," following which he returned to public schools in the San Fernando Valley. After graduating from Grant High he entered Valley College. He transferred in his second semester to L. A. Tech-Trade. Then he made his first serious move toward music.

Like Davy Jones, Mike Nesmith and Peter Tork, Micky responded to an ad in Daily Variety a year ago calling for "insane boys" to audition for roles in a comedy series for today's young people. And like the others, he was tested and signed because he was indeed a pre-ordained "Monkee," whether he knew it or not.

Micky is six-feet tall, lean, athletic and restless. His hair and eyes are brown. He shares a pad with David Jones in West Los Angeles and drives a motorcycle.

MONKEES ARCHIVES 1

MONKEES ARCHIVES 1

MONKEES ARCHIVES 1

MONKEES ARCHIVES 1

MONKEES ARCHIVES 1

DAVID JONES

David Jones left his home in Manchester, England to "become something," when he was fourteen and a half. But he left with the full blessing of his dad, a railway fitter.

Davy was born December 30, 1946 with a great will to succeed. His dad knew it then and he knows it now. The tough, compact lad headed for England's Newmarket Racetrack as a jockey trainee. Of course, he became a very good jockey. Between riding jobs, he discovered life among England's young set and explored places from which the great new musical sounds were coming. Eventually, he was part of the scene at The Celler, launching pad for today's greatest groups.

His first acting job resulted from an audition at the BBC where he played a juvenile delinquent in a radio drama. This lead to a steady job on a daytime series called "Morning Story." And with all this, he continued at the racetrack. Through his riding, he met London theatrical executives who helped him land a leading role in the musical hit, "Oliver" in which Davy played the Artful Dodger. His next show was "Pickwick," in which he won special acclaim from American critics. He has lived in the United States for nearly four years now, but returns frequently to England for visits with his father and sisters. His mother died six yars ago.

Now starring in "The Monkees," David shares a small rented house in West Los Angeles with co-star Micky Dolenz.

MONKEES ARCHIVES 1

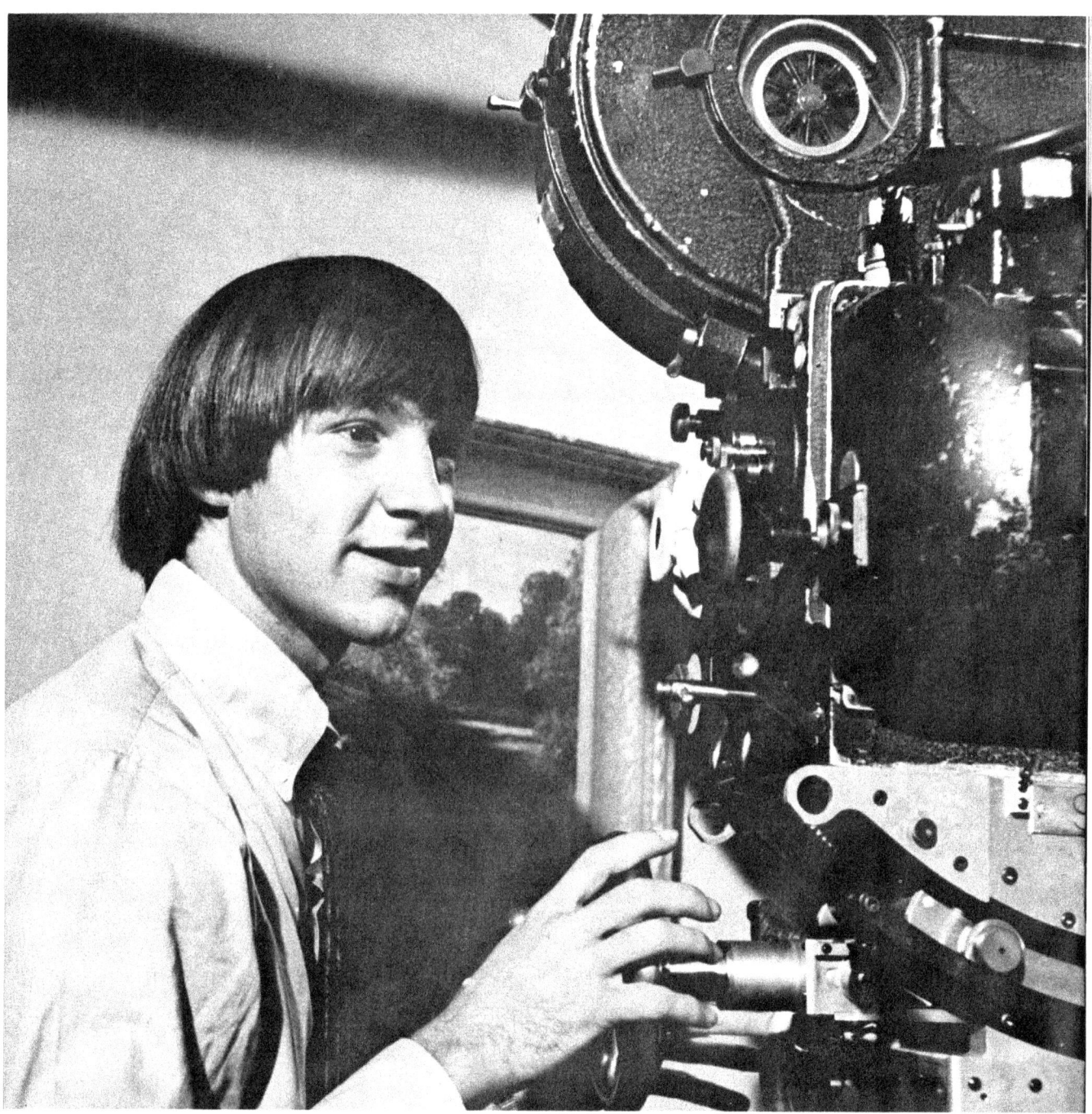

MONKEES ARCHIVES 1

PETER TORK

Peter Tork was playing guitar, ukelele, five-string banjo and bass before his voice changed. Later he picked up piano, French horn and others, all of which he learned well.

He began his musical career in New York City's Greenwich Village, performing as singer-musician in various pass-the-hat hide-aways where the music was always new. When money became something of a necessity, he toured with the Phoenix Singers as accompanyist, but The Village was his "scene" until a little over a year ago when he hit Los Angeles.

There he appeared alone and with others in various clubs and music houses, including the Troubadour in West Hollywood. He had been on the Coast only two-months when an audition at Screen Gems landed him a starring role in "The Monkees" — a Raybert Production.

Born in Washington, D. C., February 13, 1944, Peter was raised in Connecticut. His father, H. J. Torkelson, is Associate Professor of Economics at the University of Connecticut. Pete attended Carleton College in Minnesota for three years before dropping plans for a teaching career. From there, he moved to New York and The Village.

Pete is 5-feet 11-inches tall, weighs 152 pounds, has reddish-brown hair and brown eyes.

MONKEES ARCHIVES 1

MONKEES ARCHIVES 1

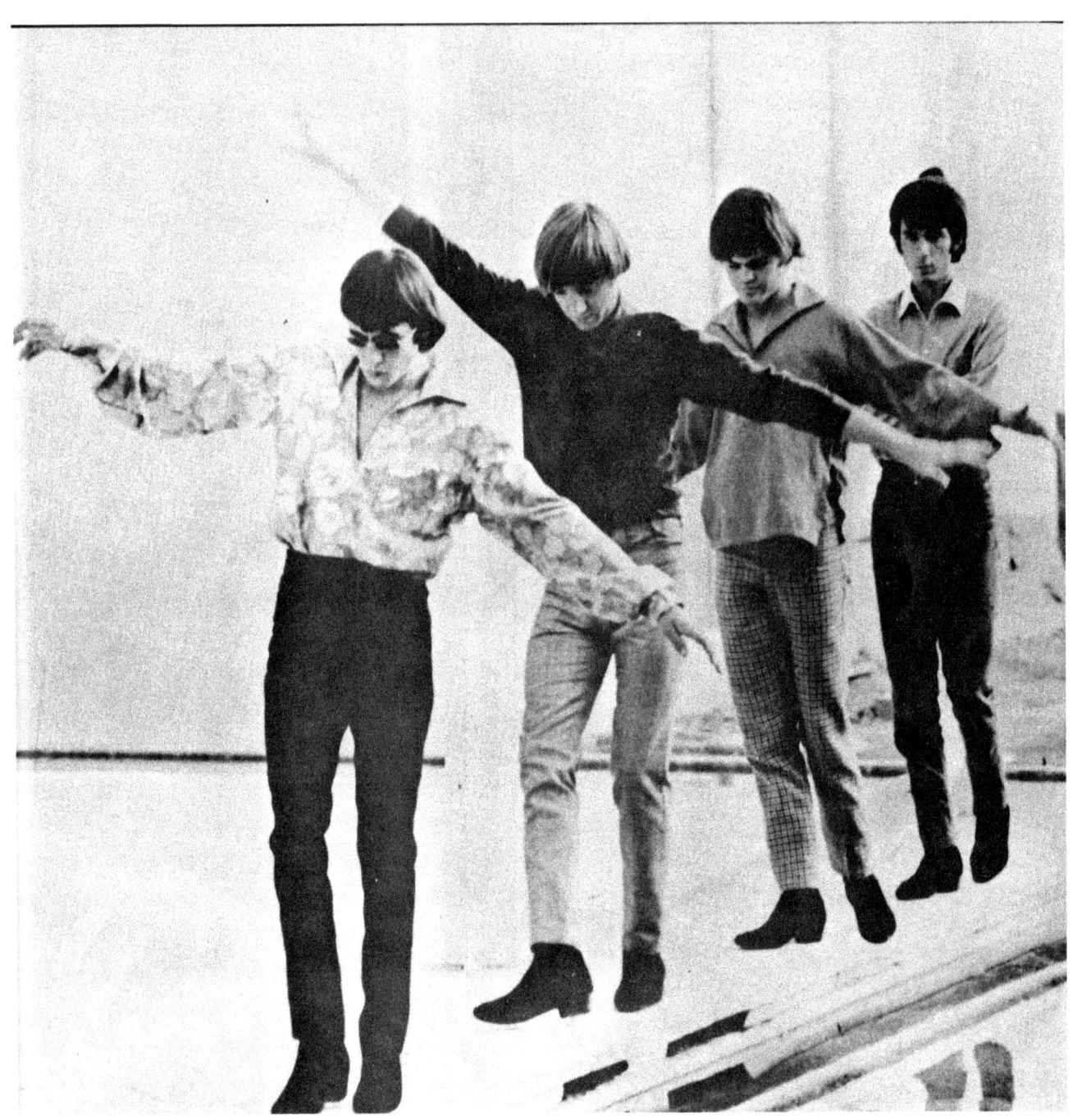

MONKEES ARCHIVES 1

MONKEES ARCHIVES 1

MONKEES ARCHIVES 1

MONKEES ARCHIVES 1

MONKEES ARCHIVES 1

MONKEES ARCHIVES 1